# Praise for *Help for the Helper*

"This book should be very useful to practicing psychotherapists, social workers, nurses, psychiatrists, and especially those in training for these fields. The
variety of skill-building exercises offers help for many issues that arise during
training and practice."
—Bulletin of the Menninger Clinic

"Written with a lot of common sense, it is easy to read and will be helpful to
all therapists, whether they work with trauma and disaster victims or not."
—International Review of Psychiatry

"[A] valuable contribution to the field of body psychotherapy."
—British Journal of Biodynamic Massage

"The book is written from a pragmatic, non-spiritual perspective and is a
great reminder of the fact that we do need to look after ourselves, as well as
giving us a variety of useful strategies to help survive the ups and downs of
therapeutic life."
—The Fulcrum

"[T]his concise, well-organized book is full of useful ideas and practices for
almost anyone who is struggling to take care of a human being in need."
—Greater Good

T0339371

# HELP FOR THE HELPER

# HELP
## FOR THE *HELPER*

### PREVENTING COMPASSION FATIGUE

### AND VICARIOUS TRAUMA IN AN

### EVER-CHANGING WORLD

UPDATED + EXPANDED

## BABETTE ROTHSCHILD

**Norton Professional Books**

*An Imprint of W. W. Norton & Company*
*Celebrating a Century of Independent Publishing*

This book is intended as a general information resource for professionals practicing in the field of psychotherapy and mental health, as well as practitioners in other helping professions, including doctors, nurses, emergency workers, first responders, and massage therapists and other body work practitioners. It is not a substitute for appropriate training or clinical supervision. Standards of clinical practice and protocol change over time. No technique or recommendation is guaranteed to be safe or effective in all circumstances, and neither the publisher nor the author can guarantee the complete accuracy, efficacy, or appropriateness of any particular recommendation in every respect. Individuals with balance problems of any kind are advised not to try the balance exercises.

Most of the patients described in this book, and all session transcripts, are composites. Any URLs displayed in this book link or refer to websites that existed as of press time. The publisher is not responsible for, and should not be deemed to endorse or recommend, any website, app, or other content that it did not create. The author, also, is not responsible for any third-party material.

Find Babette Rothschild online at www.trauma.cc

For information about permission to reproduce selections from this book, write to Permissions, W. W. Norton & Company, Inc., 500 Fifth Avenue, New York, NY 10110

For information about special discounts for bulk purchases, please contact W. W. Norton Special Sales at specialsales@wwnorton.com or 800-233-4830

Manufacturing by Lakeside Book Company
Production manager: Gwen Cullen

ISBN: 978-1-324-03049-2

W. W. Norton & Company, Inc., 500 Fifth Avenue, New York, NY 10110
www.wwnorton.com

W. W. Norton & Company Ltd., 15 Carlisle Street, London W1D 3BS

1  2  3  4  5  6  7  8  9  0

*This book is dedicated to all of you helpers, especially those of you on the front lines of crises around the world, who are raising up yourselves as well as your families, clients, communities, and countries.*

# Contents

# Introduction to the Revised Edition

## The World Has Changed

Since the publication of the first edition of *Help for the Helper* in 2006, the world has changed. Significantly. Due to existing and growing threats of war, increasing areas of civil unrest, the COVID-19 pandemic, financial collapse, natural disasters, and more, therapists and other helping professionals now often find themselves in a particularly tricky position: They are struggling to personally cope with the same kind of traumas and massive stresses as the clients and others they serve. To address the unique challenges involved, added to the aims of the original version, the goals of this revised edition now also include further helping therapists to carry on helping their clients while also maintaining their own safety and sanity in crisis situations,[1] as well as managing the usual stresses and challenges during normal times that the first edition focused on.

During the best of times, we—I count myself among you[2]—tend toward

---

[1] I imagine there will be a good number of readers from among other helping professions (doctors, nurses, emergency workers, first responders, massage and other body therapists, supervisors, administrators, and so on) as well as lay persons. Please feel free to translate the examples and exercises into your own language and realm of professional or personal experience. You are welcome to try out and share any of the information and exercises in this book with your own supervisees, colleagues, and students.

[2] I rarely reference "we" and "us" in my books, preferring to write to my reader's situation. However, to be honest, as a helping professional myself, I need the help of this book as much as any of you. So I will include myself in the mix wherever I fit in.

aspiring (or feeling bound) to be superheroes for everyone, including our clients, colleagues, family members, and friends. We expect of ourselves and are expected by others to rise above the fray, putting everyone else first, and *fix it* (whatever *it* is). On the rare occasions when there is an ounce of precious time or energy to spare, we come last. It is always a challenge to make time for us. And though we do not like to talk about it, we, as a profession, do suffer from both the joys and burdens of helping others. In the last few decades our professional risks have become more noticed, and we have even gained our own set of diagnostic categories: *vicarious trauma* and *compassion fatigue* (both discussed in Chapter 1). However, recently our challenges and obligations have multiplied exponentially as the world has become more and more chaotic. As if the usual did not offer up enough challenges and pressure, events of 2020 and beyond have added significantly to the weights on our shoulders. In the "new normal" that began in the spring of 2020, we all faced unprecedented additional challenges that have further complicated our lives and continue to do so.

Depending on your area of service, and the location where you serve, you might be able to look back longingly on the past where, even though you might have struggled from time to time, you often had the luxury of standing outside of the major issues that were impacting those whom you were helping. However, now it is more likely that you are reeling from many of the same events as the people you support. As a result, you have been hit hard with additional stresses, traumas, challenges, and burdens. It may even be the case that you are just as, or sometimes even more, rattled as the ones you are meant to, and want to, help.

It is important to note here that some of you reading this new edition have been experiencing extreme stress for many years or even decades while living and working in parts of the world where violence, poverty, war, systemic racism, and such have an unrelenting hold. For you, this idea of shared experience with clients will not be new in the way it is for readers for whom the 2020 pandemic was their first major community crisis. Nonetheless, your challenges and stress have also been increased and further complicated by the pandemic and other factors that have destabilized families, communities, and countries throughout the world.

Before I get much further into this book, as I indicated above, I want to acknowledge that I have also been affected by local, national, and world events. My own situation definitely gave me pause before I agreed to write this revision. In many ways, my dilemma is parallel to the one many of you have: How can I help you when I am similarly rattled? That challenges me in my personal and professional life, and on every page I write. Nonetheless, after much consideration, I realized that perhaps my own situation could further illuminate my point of view: To a large extent, I can relate to what you are dealing with from the inside. At the same time, I (like many, if not all, of you) also stand to benefit from being able to help others in these tough times (e.g., hopefully by writing this book)—is that not why we become psychotherapists in the first place, because it rewards and nourishes us to be able to help others?

Though I have never thought of myself as an expert (experts are supposed to know everything, and I know very well that I do not), I do take pride in being a specialist in the theory and treatment of trauma and post-traumatic stress disorder (PTSD) as well as self-care for therapists and other helping professionals. I have published several well-regarded books on these topics (see under my name in the reference section). As such, I am often one of those looked to for advice in these times, just as your clients and others look to you. Similar to you, I need to figure out how to manage my own energy and emotions and establish balance so that my needs do not get completely lost in the mix while I am engaged in helping my colleagues, supervisees, and students. And, as I suspect you might relate to: I do not always find that particularly easy to do. So, when I speak of "we" as being impacted and challenged by world events, I am consciously and honestly intending to include myself.

Every one of us (both reading and writing this book) can be distressed in multiple ways. At the same time, we carry on because others look to us for support even when we may need support ourselves. We are also human. We are also vulnerable. And whether those we are helping are on the front lines (soldiers, first responders, medical personnel, organizers, and so on) or simply endeavoring to manage their daily lives, we all hope to be able to help without succumbing, ourselves, to extreme stress. I hope this revised edition will further assist you toward finding the balance necessary for you to maintain your physical, emotional, and mental equilibrium as you aid others to do the same.

### Contact and Support

As always, good contact and support are major combatants against the effects of stress and the development of PTSD. I imagine (and hope) that most, if not all, of you are telling your clients and patients the same thing. However, this also applies to you. Contact and support are just as necessary for the helper as for the helped. And I am not talking only about your personal therapy and professional supervision here. You, just like everyone else in the world, also need time with your family and friends, even when some or much of that is (at some points in time) necessarily online. Throughout history, connection with others has been the main factor that has ensured survival of our species during times of strife and crisis. In fact, long before there were psychotherapists, social workers, or psychiatrists, reaching out and gathering in support of one another has been the primary way that humankind has conquered trauma and PTSD.

In that vein, certainly, you could read and make use of this book on your own. However, consider whether it might multiply its usefulness if you were to invite one or more colleagues to read and process this book together with you. That could serve as one of your, and their, steps toward self-care by increasing good contact with others. In addition, reaching out to colleagues would be a gesture of your support of them—a win-win.

### What Is Your Boat Like?

A few weeks into the COVID-19 pandemic, I read and heard multiple discussions online and through various media about our being "all in the same boat." It is an apt metaphor for shared experiences during abnormal times, including societal upheaval such as war, hurricanes, earthquakes, pandemics, and other human-made or natural disasters. However, it is important to remember that although a situation might be global, each person, family, and community is rocked in their own way. Perhaps a more accurate analogy is that we are in different boats while traversing similar storms;

for some a single storm, for others a rash of storms. For you it could be a Category 1, but for your neighbor a Category 4, and so on. While discussing this topic, my UK colleague, Michael Gavin, who is also an avid sailor, reminded me of something important: He said that when out in a storm, no matter how big or small, the most important thing for safety is to keep one hand on the tiller (in a small boat) or ship's helm (in a large boat). That is, make sure to be in control of the steering mechanism. His point is apt for this metaphor: Each of us absolutely needs to keep control of the direction of our own boat throughout any and all storms. And that is the aim of this revision: to make sure you have the knowledge and tools you need to be able to steer your life, no matter how severe your storm.

Right now, before you read further, might be a good time to take a few minutes to illustrate or write your sense of the waters currently around you and your boat. Remember that your clients, friends, family, and neighbors may all be experiencing the same or similar waters, but each of your boats is likely unique. If you are drawing, feel free to use whatever medium you wish (pencils, paints, sculpture, collage) and also any colors (or lack of them) that feel right to you. If you are writing, it might be a narrative, an outline, a song, a rap, or even a poem. Make sure to include a reference to the steering mechanism of your boat in your illustration or among your words.

I am much more adept at writing than drawing, so my boat-and-waters descriptions will be in words. The description below is a reflection from winter 2021 in the midst of the COVID-19 pandemic:

*The waters I am in are stirred up by a storm. The force of it shifts often. There are calm sunny times and others with dark, heavy clouds and roiling seas. However, gratefully, I feel my boat surfing the waves without too much water seeping over the edges, even though I might feel seasick at times. Central for me, much of the time it feels that my boat is balanced and guided by the support of my families, friends, angels, and spirits who help me steer and keep it steady. And, admittedly, one of the tools that is helping me through this rash of storms is the writing of this book. Of course there are times that I feel adrift and flounder, but usually those come in spurts and do not last too long. I notice that what most endangers my boat is when I become frightened that I might not be able to steer it through the next wave or storm surge. It is my fear of not being able to cope that threatens me the most. What helps me is to look around and identify features of the present storm accurately without trying to foresee the next one. Perhaps it will sound trite, even to myself, but when I can stay in my boat and just focus on the current wave or period of calm, my boat stays steadier and feels more secure. And in general, I do notice that my boat feels most secure and easy to steer during the day. That is because sometimes at night, in the dark, the waves can feel nearly overwhelming. A confession: I also envy my friends who tell me that they are able to have "fun" and find "joy" as they sail roiling seas. Though I manage fairly well and usually feel more steady than I would have expected, I find little actual fun or joy during storms of strong magnitudes and always look forward to the return of those pleasures once the storms clear.*

As you write about or artistically conceive your own boat, remember that it is your experience, and it is up to you whether you want to share what you create with anyone else. Nonetheless, you are welcome to share or discuss this exercise (and any of the other exercises in this book) with colleagues, friends, or family, as you feel appropriate and useful. For example, if you live with others, perhaps it could be fun, or at least useful, for each person, young or old, to participate in discussing their individual boats and perceptions of the storms. That could stir a rich interchange and increase compassion among you. It is certainly an exercise you can offer your clients, though I might not recommend that you share your own boat with them.

### Author Disclosure

Speaking of disclosure, per the exercise above, along the way, I intend to be candid with various experiences of my own. I may be sharing more than I have in previous books, though I aim to prevent this volume from regressing into memoir. I want to make sure that I do not give a false impression that I have risen above it all. I cannot predict whether my disclosures will be helpful, or even interesting, to you. So, if you would rather not get to know me to that degree, please feel free to skip those sections.

I will also be discussing some of the strategies I have found helpful as well as those that I may not have tried but have identified as useful to others. Please note that in no way am I suggesting that you should do what I do. On the contrary, I have and will continue to encourage you to create and stock your own unique tool kit with tools and resources that are tailored to your needs and no one else's. Everybody's experience is different. Likewise, what helps or hurts is completely individual.

## What Is New in the Revised Edition?

- Addition of a Skill Building section to Chapter 1 that features discussion and application of mindfulness to professional self-care, including its documented role in reducing risk for compassion fatigue and vicarious trauma.
- Supplemental to the empathy theory and tools in Chapter 2 is an introduction to the concept of a personally controllable empathy dial that allows you to monitor and regulate your own degree of empathy, which will help you to prevent vicarious trauma and compassion fatigue.
- Addition to Chapter 3, Keeping Calm, that features description and application of my full-color, six-column autonomic nervous system (ANS) table that was first published in *Revolutionizing Trauma Treatment* (Rothschild, 2017, 2021). In the Skill Building section, tools for maintaining balance and strength as well as for shifting arousal levels are included.
- A new penultimate chapter devoted to the unique challenges of shared crises, those that therapists face when experiencing the same world, national, or community stresses and traumas as their clients. This chapter also includes pointers for those therapists who had not chosen a specialty in trauma treatment, but, because of increased world and community stressors, now find themselves working with more traumatized clients than ever.
- Additional theory, tools, and permissions woven throughout toward the goal of increasing your ability to care for yourself while caring for others.
- Editing the content and tone throughout with relevant updates and to be more conversational and less academic than the first edition.

## *Disclaimer*

As with all of my books, lectures, and training programs, I want to state clearly the limitations of the content of these pages. In general, probably every tool works for at least somebody, but no tool works for everybody. The theory I share here is just that, theory. There are no hard facts in this book, as actually in the areas of trauma, stress, PTSD, compassion fatigue, psychotherapy, and so on, there are no hard facts—in science and medicine there are few. Knowledge develops and changes all the time, as it should. Do not be alarmed if you disagree with some of my views. It is healthy and necessary for there to be disagreement within a profession; without differences of opinion, knowledge and skill do not evolve. Much of what I write about I have come to via some measure of disagreement with the views of others. What I have to offer here are opinions, not facts. My favorite slogan for my self is, "I get paid for my opinion; I do not get paid to be right." (I often lament that the world might be a better place if those in power realized that same limitation: All any of us has to offer are opinions.) Never forget that you are the best expert on you. It is up to you to decide what best helps or hampers you for self-care or, for that matter, anything else.

# Using Common Sense

In the introduction to *The Body Remembers Casebook* (Rothschild, 2003), I discussed the importance of applying common sense to work with trauma. Generally, I find both the skill and trend sorely missing in the practice of psychotherapy. That is why I speak about common sense regularly in lectures and training programs. It continues to amaze me that many, many therapists approach me during breaks to say how "important" or "refreshing" it is to "finally" hear someone talk about using common sense. When I take an informal poll of how many in my audience were taught or encouraged to use their own innate common sense during their education or professional training, somewhere between 10% and 33% raise their hands. I have never seen as much as half the audience with their hands up. Though I am proud to contribute to filling this very neglected gap, I am appalled that it is necessary. Every training program in psychotherapy (university, organization, agency, or institution alike) should be teaching, promoting, and supporting the use of common sense alongside the other theory and tools that are being taught. The success of both the clients' psychotherapy and the self-care of psychotherapists is greatly enhanced by the liberal application of common sense. With regard to the topic of this book, *Help for the Helper*, applying common sense could save heaps of professional pain and suffering. Moreover, it could also probably save institutions, agencies, and HMOs plenty of actual dollars.

Temple Grandin, author of *Thinking in Pictures* and *Animals in Translation*, is the well-known animal behaviorist who also is challenged with high-functioning autism. Her brilliance in designing systems for handling livestock (which she has done over much of the United States and Canada) is not only rooted in her talent for visualization but is also largely the product of common sense. Her cornerstone is a simple assumption: If animals are scared, then something is scaring them. For her, it is that simple. As a result, she counsels, for example, that no matter how much or how carefully you use an electric prod, the animals will still be afraid to cooperate and will balk at what you want them to do. The more you prod, the more afraid they will be. Grandin demonstrates time and again that simply identifying and changing or removing the source of fear—the trigger, as we would say (often something as simple as covering a reflective piece of metal)—removes the need for electric prods. Once the source is identified and remedied, the animals naturally become calmly cooperative.

The same principle applies to us. If we are suffering under the weight of our work or from interactions with particular clients, then identifying and changing the triggering circumstances should give us much-needed relief. Of course, sometimes making such changes is easier said than done. But the principle is the same: Use your common sense to identify your work stressors (no matter how obvious or obscure) and then develop and experiment with strategies to intervene. Here is one example.

During a recent consultation, a fairly experienced therapist complained of severe stress due to feelings of failure and guilt. He had been struggling with one of his clients and felt unable to help. Probing, I discovered that he actually did not have the knowledge base necessary to work with that type of client. From the perspective of common sense, I saw two basic options: (1) refer the client to someone who did have the skills and knowledge that were needed, or (2) hire a supervisor or consultant who could coach him through or teach him what was needed along the way. Either choice would go a long way to assuaging both guilt and failure feelings, and the client would actually be helped. I further advised that the therapist make peace with this reality: No single therapist can, or should, treat all clients. That is also common sense.

Amid the theory and exercises in this book, you will find (what I hope are) generous helpings of common sense. I expect, and welcome, that some readers will finish this book and say, "Yes, how simple!" in reaction to portions of the theory and skills presented. Much of it really is simple. Becoming adept at self-care does not require long training programs (though I do love to give workshops on these topics). Mostly, you just need to use your common sense.

# Introduction to the First Edition, 2006

*Toward the end of the Haunted Mansion ride at Disneyland, the black coach I'm riding in turns to face a mirror. I can clearly see the reflections of myself and the friends I am riding with. There is also the faded reflection of one or more ghosts who appear to be riding along with us, sitting on our laps. They are smiling and carrying suitcases, intent on hitching a ride home with us. Of course, at the end of the ride, there are not really any ghosts hanging on to us, nor are they in the car when we get home.*

With our clients, however, that is not always the case. Sometimes it seems as though some of them are more successful than the Haunted Mansion ghosts: In essence, they hitch a ride home with us or, more accurately, inside of us. Often we are not aware that we have brought home an unwelcome visitor unless we notice that we are agitated rather than calm, have trouble sleeping, or pick a useless fight with our partner and make the connection. When this happens rarely, the consequences are usually minimal. But for practitioners who consistently bring their clients home—consciously or unconsciously—the impact over time can be severe. This book's mission is to prevent just that, and to promote the stance that we need not bring our clients home with us to qualify as compassionate or competent practitioners. In fact, the opposite may actually be the case: The better we take care of ourselves and maintain an appropriate professional separation from our clients, the more we will be in a position to be truly empathetic, compassionate, and useful to them.

It is my hope that this book will radically change the ways in which psychotherapists conceptualize, as well as act on, the risks of their profession, including compassion fatigue and vicarious traumatization. Additionally, I hope to influence current thinking about ways in which therapists are affected by their clients. Along the way, I will discuss the science of these phenomena and offer practical strategies that will aid the therapist in taking charge of these potential hazards rather than feeling at their mercy.

Of course, psychotherapists are not the only helping professionals who are affected by these and other phenomena discussed in this volume. However, since therapists constitute the vast majority of potential readers, vocabulary and examples are aimed at them. As happens with all of my books, I expect that a good number of readers will be members of associated helping professions (doctors, nurses, emergency workers, first responders, massage and other body therapists, administrators, etc.) and others will be home caregivers and other laypersons. Please feel free to translate the examples and exercises into your own language and realm of professional or personal experience. You are welcome to try out and share any of the exercises in this book with your own supervisees, colleagues, students, and family. In addition, if you have any questions or if you have particularly positive or negative results from using the skill-building sections, please let me know (my contact information is on the copyright page following the title page—email is easiest).

## Overview

Negative consequences of therapeutic work are often unconscious. All too many therapists career toward burnout without noticing it. Therefore, the major goal of this book is to equip practitioners with tools that will increase their awareness and reduce their vulnerability to the factors that could lead to compassion fatigue, vicarious trauma, and burnout. Some of the case examples involve therapists who work with traumatized individuals, because the impact of client trauma poses an additional risk to the therapist. However, this book is written for all psychotherapists—also those not working with traumatized clients. Any of us can be adversely affected by our work.

Therapist self-care requires the proper functioning of at least three neuropsychological systems. All three are necessary for therapists to be fully in control of their own well-being even in the most distressing of situations. The first involves the brain mechanisms that operate in interpersonal empathy. The second depends on balance in the autonomic nervous system (ANS) and arousal regulation. The third requires clear thinking that relies, in part, on the balanced functioning of all brain structures. In short, for therapists to minimize risks to their emotional and physical well-being, they need to be able to find ways to balance their empathetic engagement, regulate ANS arousal, and maintain their ability to think clearly.

Theories already exist about the cognitive mechanisms and psychological impact of therapeutic risks. However, for the most part, the neuropsychological and somatic aspects have yet to be studied in depth. This volume introduces solid research from neurobiological, experimental, social, and folk psychology that will explain the origins of the risks therapists encounter in their work with clients. Scientific findings then form the foundation for the design and support of new skills therapists can use to improve their own situations.

Though neuroscience is daunting for some, I would urge you to take the time to understand it; I will do my best to make it as accessible to you as possible. The risks to therapist well-being that are addressed here are all intimately linked to the body and brain. Knowing how you are affected by your clients will enhance your control over those effects.

Of course, not all of the many interventions and skill-building exercises offered in each chapter will suit everyone. Understanding your own psychophysiology will put you in a good position to choose skills and tailor additional interventions to your own individual needs. Moreover, comprehending these processes will give you the potential to create and develop skills that are particularly suited to you.

## On Assessment

Your best tool for evaluating your own personal situation will be mindful self-awareness, body awareness, and your own common sense. Throughout this volume in theory and skill sections as well as case examples, various difficulties that can arise in psychotherapeutic work are described alongside suggestions for intervention. As a whole, this book will provide you with a basis for identifying when you might be having difficulty or moving in that direction. However, there is no way to cover everything. Remember, when in doubt, fall back on your common sense and knowledge about yourself.

## A Word About Burnout

Burnout is a term commonly used in many professions, not just the helping professions, to describe the consequences of varying forms of extreme job stress. In the vernacular, it can mean anything from the need for an extra day off to becoming totally dysfunctional or decompensated. Many factors can lead to burnout, some of which are covered in this volume. Beyond the scope of these pages, however, are stressors that stem from workplace structural or administrative issues, and from personal (nonprofessional) relationships and circumstances.

## Why All Those Pages on Psychology?

Knowledge is power. The more you understand how you are affected by your clients, the more you will have the choice to maximize those effects when beneficial, and minimize them when they pose increased risks to your—or your client's—well-being.

Thankfully, in recent years, neuroscience and other branches of scientific study have turned their attention to interpersonal relationships. That literature has produced a wealth of information that can be used and adapted in the therapeutic setting.

Many of my therapist colleagues shy away from scientific theory because they are bewildered by it or have no clue how to apply it. They complain to me that seminars only teach theory, which is easy to forget in a few weeks. Practical application and practice are often missing from professional training experiences. For that reason, this book includes many case examples as well as exercises in an effort to bridge the gap between theory and application.

## Organization[3]

Throughout the book, several concepts and techniques are illustrated with transcripts that are composites of professional consultation sessions. Most of those sessions focus on the psychological and somatic experience of the practitioner and ways to mediate risk factors. Such body-oriented professional guidance will not be new to many somatic or body psychotherapists, though some specific interventions may be. In general, it is my hope that supervisors and consultants in mainstream and alternative realms of psychology will be encouraged to pay more attention to what is happening in their own bodies and in the bodies of the therapists they are assisting.

Chapter 1 introduces the basic concepts that are explored throughout the book. Chapters 2 through 4 each discuss theory and skill building in their respective topics. The theoretical sections include discussion of the most relevant research, past and present. Each skill-building section is linked to the theory of that chapter, so that each management strategy fits within the context of the science being discussed. This maximizes the likelihood that individuals will be equipped to further develop their own strategies and build skills that are not already in their repertoire. Case examples illustrate common therapist dilemmas. Exercises follow to enable the learning of new skills and strategies for improved coping. Chapter 6 ties together both the theory and skills discussed throughout the book. One appendix appears at the end and reviews three ongoing[4] research projects on topics related to this book.

---

[3] This section refers to the structure of the first edition. I have endeavored to maintain the same structure in this revised edition with a few exceptions as noted in the *Introduction to this Revised Edition*.

[4] At the time the first edition was published.

It is suggested that the reader approach each skill-building section as an experiment. Try the skill out before you commit yourself to adding it to your repertoire. The skills proposed here are intended to increase your options for self-care, to add more choices to your toolbox, not to decrease them. Please do not abandon any tools you already find useful.

This book is about therapist self-care, including reducing vulnerability with clients and paying attention to optimal separation and boundaries. It is important, however, to keep in mind that being open and vulnerable with clients can also be of use—sometimes just the right thing. It is not my aim to radically change your way of working, but merely to help you recognize your areas of vulnerability and give you more choices in managing them.

There is a wealth of literature on most of the topics discussed among these pages, some of it overlapping. I have reviewed much of it, but have surely missed some. Where possible, I have endeavored to identify the originators of terms and concepts and to cite ideas accurately. If, however, I have erred in giving appropriate credit to any publication or individual, I would appreciate being notified of my oversight. On the page following the title page you will find author and publisher contact information.

## Disclaimer

Disclaimers appear in the introductions to all of my books. I carry on that tradition here with another, pertinent to this subject matter.

The pages of this volume are filled with both historical—tried-and-true—and cutting-edge theories. Please keep in mind that a theory is just that; it is not fact. In science, facts are few. They are even scarcer in the branch of science called psychology. Among these pages, I express my own considered opinions, based on the considered opinions of others. Readers are encouraged to formulate their own opinions and to not regard mine as the last word.

No one expresses this sentiment better than Antonio Damasio: "I am skeptical of science's presumption of objectivity and definitiveness. I have a difficult time seeing scientific results, especially in neurobiology, as anything but provisional approximations, to be enjoyed for a while and discarded as soon as better accounts become available" (1994, p. xviii). What follows are the best approximations (mine and others') available at the time the final manuscript went to press.

# HELP FOR THE HELPER

# CHAPTER 1

# Psychotherapists at Risk

*We are born with the capacity . . . to experience what others
experience and participate in their experience by virtue of the way
we are grabbed by their nervous system. One of the real questions
is not, "How in the world does this happen?" We're beginning to
have a really good idea. The real question is "How do we stop it
from happening so that we are not the prisoner of someone else's
nervous system all the time." There have got to be a lot of brakes
in the system, and probably that will be a very interesting area of
research which has not been addressed, so far.*

—Daniel N. Stern, "Attachment: From Early
Childhood Through the Lifespan"

All emotions are contagious—the ones that are pleasant and the ones that
are unpleasant. The entertainment industry capitalizes on this feature of
emotion, using it to tug at our feelings with strong affects as portrayed by
actors, and infecting us with the raw emotions of participants in reality programs. The popularity of makeover shows is a great example. Typically, at
the end of these shows an individual or family is presented with something
near and dear that has been incredibly transformed (bodies, cars, homes,
etc.). The joy and excitement that is always expressed by the recipients is
so contagious that it is impossible not to feel happy with them as well as for
them. These shows take advantage of emotional contagion to manipulate
our feelings. As helping professionals, our emotions are also vulnerable to

provocation through becoming infected by our clients' feelings. Sometimes this is an advantage, helping us to feel inside their worlds, walk in their shoes, so to speak. At other times, it is not at all advantageous to be infected by a client's state.

# Theory

### Therapist Strengths and Hazards

The capacity that Stern alludes to in the quote above is empathy. As psychotherapists, empathy is our major, greatest, and most reliable tool. Often it is our capacity for empathy that brings us to the helping professions in the first place. As Stern said, we have "the capacity to experience what others experience." Empathy allows us to relate to those in our care, to have a sense of what they are feeling. It also helps us put their experiences into perspective, understanding how they are being affected by the incidents that we are trying to mediate. When we have an insight, an accurate hunch, or seem to read the client's mind, that may also be a result of empathy. Without it, we could not be the effective therapists that we are. Empathy is an integral, necessary tool of our work.

That is one of the benefits of empathy. At the same time, it has detriments. If empathy is such a central and beneficial tool of psychotherapy, why do so many of our dedicated and experienced colleagues reel from working with distressed clients? Is it possible that empathy is actually a double-edged sword, wielding both help and harm? Does the same tool that facilitates our understanding of our clients also threaten our well-being at times? The short answer is yes. It is my hypothesis (and observation) that many therapists suffer in their work as a result of unconscious empathy— that is, empathy processes that are outside of the therapist's awareness and therefore also outside of his control. Many of the common therapist pitfalls have roots in, or at least a relationship to, unconscious empathy gone awry, including the phenomena defined later in this chapter: unmanageable countertransference, projective identification, compassion fatigue, vicarious traumatization, and burnout.

Why are therapists suffering as a result of their jobs? Certainly, general problems of the workplace can contribute to burnout. When long hours, client loads, insufficient compensation, colleague and administrative conflicts, bullying, and so on are inadequately managed, any employee on any job can suffer. As ubiquitous as such problems are in most types of workplaces, they are beyond the scope of this book. Here the focus must be on the consequences that are due to the unique relationship that develops between the therapist and the client. When and why can the act of helping actually hurt the therapist? Could it be that some psychotherapists are just ill-suited for their line of work? Or is it more likely, as Stern implied, that a therapist can become "the prisoner of someone else's nervous system"—the nervous system of a client?

Some of the clues to answering these questions are to be found in the branch of psychotherapy that specializes in treatment of traumatized individuals. Since the diagnosis of post-traumatic stress disorder (PTSD) entered the American Psychiatric Association's *Diagnostic and Statistical Manual of Mental Disorders* (DSM) in 1980, work with traumatized individuals and groups has become popular. Over the ensuing years, it has also become commonplace for psychotherapists, as well as their consultants and supervisors, to observe negative effects from working with traumatized clients. One might think this is a problem for the individual; however, the consequences extend beyond the impact on the psychotherapists who suffer. Their workplaces can lose out because of lost work hours due to sick days and personal leave, worker's compensation claims, and the expense of early retirement. Also, of course, relationships with family and friends can be hurt when the stress of client work is allowed to intrude into a therapist's personal life. As a matter of fact, I became interested in this topic because of therapist complaints during my various training programs. I was stymied by the intensity of distress being expressed. Some of my students even considered quitting their jobs as psychotherapists and trauma specialists to find new work or revert to previous work such as accounting or manual labor.

It is not new for therapists to suffer negative consequences from working with traumatized individuals. However, it is new for the professional community to pay attention to it in an organized manner. The first books to recognize such risks were published in the mid-1990s and focused on those working with trauma: Wilson and Lindy's (1994) *Countertransference in the Treatment of PTSD*, Figley's (1995) *Compassion Fatigue*, Stamm's (1995) *Secondary Traumatic Stress*, and Pearlman and Saakvitne's (1995) *Trauma and the Therapist*. Each of these books has contributed to the field with relevant theories. They all include recommendations for therapists to pay more attention to their personal and professional needs, including obtaining regular consultation. However, none of them have looked at what is going on inside the therapist who succumbs to the impact of a client's trauma—what is happening in the therapist's brain and body. And none has looked beyond behavioral interventions. In the coming pages, readers will learn how client distress affects the therapist's brain and body and will receive training in somatic and cognitive skills to both increase awareness and mediate the effects.

The next section reviews the current terminology that applies to the various risks therapists face. Under typical therapy conditions, the risks discussed below are ever present, just by the fact of indirectly bearing witness to terrible traumas, as therapists listen to their clients' accounts and the resulting difficulties in their daily lives. In addition, therapists can likewise be impacted (as is discussed in Chapter 2) merely by being in the presence (in-person or online) of a traumatized client. The power of empathy (for better and for worse) works its spell even, and often, in the absence of words.

Much of the time therapists are helping clients who are experiencing (or have experienced) highly stressful and traumatic incidents that are outside of the professional's current daily experience, even though, from time to time, most of us have had our own trauma memories provoked by the situation or memories of a particular client. However, what of therapists living in areas of the world where therapy conditions are never, or are no longer, normal? That includes those working in locations impacted by civil or international war, political or racial unrest, famine, natural disasters, and, since early 2020, pandemic or the threat of pandemic, and so on. Such extreme complications mean that a large proportion of therapists are also, simultaneously, experiencing—and trying to self-manage—many of the same types of stresses as their clients. Of course, such situations present additional challenges to helping the helpers to take care of themselves while they are also helping others.

The discussion of terminology below, from the first edition of this book, accounts for a wider range of challenges and risks therapists face also in the light of extreme world and community circumstances.

### Identifying Terminology

Four terms have become popular to describe the negative risks therapists face: compassion fatigue, vicarious traumatization, secondary traumatization, and burnout (these terms are individually discussed and cited below). From a search on the PsycINFO database, it appears that burnout is the oldest of these concepts, first mentioned in relationship to mental health workers in Pines and Maslach (1978). I will first give an overview of the concepts and their history, followed by a closer look at each, including a perspective on how they have become more relevant, as caring for ourselves as we care for others has become all the more challenging.

### OVERVIEW

The term *vicarious traumatization* first appeared in 1985 in a journal article on the vulnerability of children to the trauma of others (Terr, 1985). It then entered the therapist vocabulary as a descriptor of negative effects on psychotherapists with the publication of McCann and Pearlman's *Vicarious Traumatization: A Framework for Understanding the Psychological Effects of Working With Victims* in 1990. They applied the term *vicarious* in recognition that therapists may vicariously experience aspects or effects of a client's trauma as if it had happened to themselves.

*Secondary traumatization* seems to have first appeared in an article by Rosenheck and Nathan (1985). For many years, *secondary trauma* was used to describe the effect of traumatic contagion—how trauma symptoms can seemingly be caught just like a cold or the flu—between family members (Benjamin & Benjamin, 1994; Solomon et al., 1992; Waysman et al., 1993). However, in 1995, secondary trauma took on a new meaning with the publication of Stamm's *Secondary Traumatic Stress*, an edited anthology on self-care for clinicians. She applied the term similarly to vicarious traumatization. That same year, Figley (1995) published another edited book on the same topic, coining a new term with his title, *Compassion Fatigue*. Figley's term has caught on as a readily understandable concept and catchphrase. Since Figley's initial publication, multiple books and numerous articles have been published applying the concept to all ranges of compassionate work. Most psychotherapists, as well as those in other helping professions, recognize that their compassionate work can lead to exhaustion.

Also in 1995, Pearlman and Saakvitne published *Trauma and the Therapist*, expressing their own views on countertransference and vicarious traumatization in psychotherapists working with the special population of incest survivors. They were the first to spotlight what may be happening to a therapist during a psychotherapy session.

Since the publication of those three pioneering books, there has been some professional confusion about how, exactly, to use and distinguish the four terms: burnout, secondary traumatization, vicarious traumatization, and compassion fatigue. They are often used rather interchangeably in professional and self-help literature and discussions. Some attempt was made by Pearlman and Saakvitne (1995) to circumscribe the concepts. A further stab at clarification of my own follows.

These terms are used throughout this text with the meanings as specified below. I have made an effort to strike a compromise between conflicting definitions as they exist throughout the professional literature. These definitions are certainly still open to debate—as is vocabulary in any field (as per my disclaimers, above). At the least, my interpretations should help make the content of this book clearer.

*Compassion fatigue* (Figley, 1995) is a general term applied to anyone who suffers as a result of serving in a helping capacity, whether professional or lay, including family members caring for ill or disabled loved ones. Bonnita Wirth (see Chapter 3) gives a good description of unconscious compassion fatigue resulting from the stresses of psychotherapy practice.

*Burnout* is reserved for an extreme circumstance. It describes anyone whose health is suffering or whose outlook on life has turned negative because of the impact or overload of their work. Anyone in any profession can be at risk for burnout, including shopkeepers, lawyers, firefighters, police, businesspersons, teachers, medical personnel, and so on.

*Primary traumatization* is understood as the impact of a traumatic incident on the obvious victim or firsthand witness of that incident as defined in the *DSM* (American Psychiatric Association, 2013). This includes survivors of all types of traumatic events, including those who are rescued from disaster sites, mental health clients, and medical patients injured by trauma such as a house fire. This category also includes everyone, including psychotherapists, who have been directly affected by a traumatic incident through being injured or assaulted, losing a relative or close friend, and so on. Moreover, all categories of disaster first responders (including police, firefighters, EMTs, emergency room personnel, and so on) are vulnerable to primary traumatization, as they are often firsthand witnesses to violence and violent deaths.

*Secondary traumatization* has two categories. The first involves family members and close associates who may suffer from their loved one's trauma as a result of the closeness of the relationship. An example would include the partner or spouse of a rape victim.

Here I would like to clarify what I now see as an error in the first edition of this book: There I included witnessing a traumatic incident in the category of secondary traumatization. Witnessing is now moved to where I (and the *DSM*) believe it rightfully belongs, in the paragraph on primary traumatization, above.

With regard to psychotherapists impacted by working with traumatized individuals, the term *vicarious traumatization* is used. It has now been widely recognized that psychotherapists can vicariously experience their client's trauma in their own nervous systems. The result is similar to feeling vicarious excitement while reading about a narrow escape during war, or hearing a breathless, detailed description of a horseback ride. The listeners did not actually experience the event, though they felt as though they did, often profoundly. A pornographic novel has a similar mechanism and sometimes a more recognizable effect.

An additional note of clarification: When a psychotherapist suffers from, or is more vulnerable to, the effects of a client's trauma due to their own personal history of trauma, the historic trauma is primary traumatization. In this instance, traumatic stress resulting from hearing descriptions of a client's trauma can be either, or a combination of, vicarious traumatization or uncontained or unconscious countertransference, per the section on countertransference below.

Any of these phenomena can affect you. Compassion fatigue and burnout may have their roots in the psychotherapeutic relationship, but can also arise independently of the issues your clients bring to therapy. Sometimes problems of workplace administration can be a contributing factor. Of course, any helping professional who neglects to satisfy their human needs for companionship, rest, reasonable working hours, free time, vacations, and so on, can eventually succumb to burnout. Vicarious traumatization, in contrast, is a sign that a client's history is having an extreme effect on you.

### COMPASSION FATIGUE

Compassion fatigue happens when you become (any combination of) mentally, emotionally, or physically exhausted from doing compassionate work. All health and mental health professionals as well as caregivers of all sorts are at high risk for compassion fatigue. Though always a challenge for therapists, compassion fatigue is usually easily managed through attention to scheduling and basic self-care. However, when the pull is to compassionately help everyone, compassion fatigue is an even greater risk. Take a minute to consider: Does this sound like you? Do your needs get put aside all too often, or even completely forgotten? If so, you are in good company. It is very easy, sometimes even habitual, to overextend by helping others at the cost of your own well-being. And during chaotic times such as the COVID-19 pandemic, when travel may also be reduced, making space to take breaks or any sort of time off may be difficult. In addition, longer breaks such as vacations may become prohibitive for a time. During 2020 I often heard colleagues and supervisees say, "I can't really take a break because my _____ [fill in the blank: kids, spouse, friend, parent, neighbor] needs me when I'm not working, so I might as well keep going," or "If I cannot go on vacation, I might as well work and get paid for that time."

**Caution:** Attitudes such as those promote perfect scenarios and quick routes to compassion fatigue and even burnout (see below). During times of crisis, it is especially vital to remember: If you do not care for yourself, eventually you will become unable to care for anyone else. So if you truly want to be of help to others, *you absolutely must pay attention to your own needs*. That is the only way you will ensure that you can keep going for the sake of others as well as yourself. This is the same vital principle every airline uses when instructing passengers on the use of oxygen masks in the event of a loss of cabin pressure. I suspect you will remember that they always say, "Put on your own oxygen mask first before helping anyone else." The reason? If you do not take care that you can keep breathing, you may not be able to help others do the same.

When times are stressful or traumatic, you may have noticed in yourself the pull or habit to:

- Push aside your own feelings to prioritize those of others
- Isolate and not seek support for yourself
- Skip meals
- Neglect hydration
- Reduce or avoid breaks and rest periods
- Postpone normal time off such as weekends and holidays
- Feel guilty about taking any time out for yourself
- Work beyond the hours you are actually paid for on your job
- Delay or stop taking vacation time

When you notice any of these behaviors in yourself, or similar behaviors that you are particularly vulnerable to, ask yourself, "What would I advise my friend or colleague in a similar circumstance?" Be honest. Would you be advising someone else to keep going past hunger or exhaustion? Would you recommend they skip bathroom breaks or hydrating? Would you suggest they forget about sleeping? I suspect you would not. And, if I am correct, it might be time to consider why you are more compassionate toward others than you are toward yourself. In fact, compassion fatigue might just as well be called inadequate self-compassion—a relatively new concept first promoted by Kristin Neff (2011) in her groundbreaking book of the same title, *Self-Compassion*. Further, in her more recent volume, *Fierce Self-Compassion*, Neff (2021) applies the same vital concept to those, including helping professionals of all sorts, who are endeavoring to make the world a better place.

Of course it certainly compounds matters if you do not get support from your place of employment. I recently had a phone chat with a colleague, Mark, who is employed by a local mental health clinic. His is a 40-hour-per-week job. Typically, all 40 hours, except for daily 30-minute lunch breaks, are direct service, that is, client therapy hours. During the best of times it is an exhausting schedule. But, as you may relate to, time management for routine and crisis phone calls, writing up notes, and so on usually overflows beyond those paid 40 hours. And, of course, when a community or world crisis also includes an economic crisis, complaining to the boss or asking for any leeway could feel (or be) too risky. In this case, my colleague does not feel he dares to rock the boat at this time. His solution to his bind is to continue sacrificing his all-the-more scarce time for self-nourishment.

Though he is not always successful, Mark has told me that he aims to regularly walk or bike ride most evenings before dinner, either alone or with as many of his family members as he can recruit. Not only does he find the exercise helpful in modulating his stress, it also serves as quality time with whoever joins him. In addition, when schedules align, he enjoys family dinners. Both of these strategies allow him to check in with multiple family members at once, freeing some of the precious hours between dinner and bed for attending to some of his own needs, checking in with friends, and eking out some quality time alone with his husband.

## ENERGY ECONOMY

During crisis times, whether global or personal, just about everyone gets overly tired. Stress impacts sleep cycles. Some stay up later, others sleep fewer hours, many crave more rest than during calmer times. And even when possible, sleeping longer hours may impact time management during the day.

Take a minute to think and then jot down some notes: How does added stress affect your need for rest and your energy levels?

My friend and colleague, Michael Gavin, a somatic and trauma therapist in the United Kingdom, developed a useful strategy for managing excessive tiredness some decades ago when he was recovering from chronic fatigue syndrome (better known in the United States as fibromyalgia). He noticed that on the rare day when he had a burst of energy, he would get excited, believing that he was recovered, and would proceed to spend every minute of the day active, accomplishing whatever he had been putting off. He would then be shocked and discouraged to find himself severely fatigued again, ending up back in bed for several days or a week. Frustratingly, that pattern repeated many, many times. Eventually, it dawned on him that using up all of his rare energy burst compromised any forward progress. In an effort to break the cycle, he decided to try something different, if counterintuitive. On those rare energy-burst days, instead of using up all of his energy, he decided to think of his energy like a bank account and endeavor to stay in the black rather than letting his energy balance go to zero or even into the red (exhaustion). That meant he had to learn to stop and rest often, even while he felt he had energy to keep going, and that he could never use up all of his energy burst no matter how tempting that was. Over time he learned there was a sense to his idea: When he could stick with the discipline, each day saving energy, he found that his overall energy level improved. His days of exhaustion gradually decreased and then virtually disappeared. As long as he kept his energy account in the black, he never again ran out.

Michael's strategy has had meaning for me when recovering from illness, particularly a period of postviral exhaustion. And I have passed his wisdom on to many others. It is a strategy that works if one has the patience to stick with it, actually a good example of the principle "less is more." There is no reason why you could not apply the same principle to combating compassion fatigue: Never spend 100% of your energy, compassionate or otherwise, on any one day. Always keep at least a tiny percentage in your account. Stop giving while you still have a little bit more to give, and save that for yourself. Mindful self-awareness, which is discussed at the end of this chapter, will help you in monitoring your energy levels and could help you to build rather than deplete your energy reserves.

### VICARIOUS TRAUMA

Vicarious trauma becomes a risk when you overidentify with someone else's trauma (client, family member, friend). Overempathizing or overresonating is the major foundation for vicarious trauma. Whatever you call it, overidenti-fying with another's pain, fear, anger, and so on, trying to feel in your body what their emotions or body sensations may feel or have felt like, envisioning whatever it was that happened to them, all will put you at enormous risk for suffering a degree of stress, even trauma, similar to that person's. Thoughts such as, "That could have been me [my mother, my child, and so on]" also increase the possibility of developing vicarious trauma. And when family, community, or world events are causing unprecedented amounts of trauma, it is very easy to find yourself relating too strongly to the crises of one or more of those in your sphere. Think of trauma as being just as contagious as, if not more than, COVID-19, although the means of infection as well as the symptoms are quite different.

Many therapists and other helping professionals feel obligated to feel another's distress to the same degree as those who are suffering. Sometimes it is a natural affinity or the school of thought in their professional education. But it can also be caused by how someone was raised, the result of an acquired coping mechanism. However you learned it, or if it is just your natural habit, I would strongly advise you to learn to be aware of and then temper that tendency so you can gain mastery over with whom and how much you identify or empathize with another individual or group. Skill building in this area is offered in Chapter 2.

As much as it may seem like a good idea at first glance, overempathizing can handicap the therapist as much as the client. Consider that your clients are suffering to the degree that they are because, in part, their suffering has reduced their access to the clear thinking necessary for problem solving as well as at least some of their belief in the possibility of overcoming their circumstances. If you are resonating and identifying with their pain and suffering, you are at risk for the same deficits in clear thinking and hope. As a result, not only can you end up with vicarious trauma, but your capacity to help that other person is actually diminished when you become nearly or as affected by their circumstances as they are.

Alesha consulted with me following difficulties treating one of her clients. At one of the Black Lives Matter protests, the client had been tear-gassed and then pushed to the ground by a couple of riot police. This was, of course, highly traumatizing for the client. Though Alesha participated in the movement in multiple other ways, she did not take to the streets and attend protests. Nonetheless, a few days after hearing the experience of her client, she began having similar symptoms of acute traumatic stress.[5] She became nervous, had trouble sleeping and concentrating, and even had a nightmare of that client's traumatic incident.

Exploring this in supervision, Alesha was able to recognize that while listening to her client's experience, she had been picturing similar scenes she had watched on the news, imagining herself in her client's place. And in her mind she kept thinking, "That could have been me!" Since Alesha had not experienced anything like that in her own life, we agreed that this was not countertransference (see below), but clearly vicarious traumatization. Once Alesha learned to control those visual images (see Chapter 3) and change her self-talk to, "Thank goodness that was not me!" the vicarious trauma symptoms abated, and she found herself in a better position to help her client.

The skill-building sections of Chapters 2 and 3 will provide you with specific tools and strategies to take control of and regulate the degree to which you empathize with others (clients and patients as well as in personal relationships).

## BURNOUT

Burnout occurs when inadequate self-care—from any combination of risk factors—becomes so extreme that your ability to function normally becomes severely compromised. It is not only therapists and helping professionals who are at risk for burnout. Accountants, stockbrokers, teachers, home caregivers (family or hired), and so on are also at risk. Think of burnout as a potential anytime someone is overloaded with responsibility to the point of mental and physical collapse. In that way, it makes sense

---

[5] Similar to PTSD, though it occurs in the first months following an incident. If symptoms do not resolve within that time, the diagnosis changes to PTSD.

that burnout can be an even greater risk during times of community and world catastrophe including pandemics, war, civil and racial unrest, natural disasters, and so on.

Even when the world is relatively calm, it is easy to get too busy and forget about yourself. With the extraordinary demands of family, community, and global crises, the vulnerability to burnout increases multifold.

Janelle, a trauma therapist, was due to begin her annual vacation, and she looked forward to it very much. She desperately needed the break and the rest. However, the world lockdown due to the COVID-19 virus began just a week before she was due to leave. Travel everywhere was drastically restricted or even halted. To say she was disappointed is a huge understatement. However, rather than continue with her plan to take time off, Janelle figured that as long as she could not go anywhere, she might as well keep working. Tired and spent as she was, she soldiered on. She gradually began to disintegrate physically, mentally, and emotionally. Both her professional process notes and personal checkbook revealed multiple (sometimes costly) errors. In addition, she was short tempered and was losing her sense of humor. Each morning she was increasingly reluctant to get out of bed. Eventually, she just stayed there, canceling clients as well as social engagements. She remembered that her chosen work was valuable to her, an important contribution to helping others, and she usually loved spending time with her friends. However, more and more she became depressed and indifferent.

Janelle's situation is just one portrait of burnout. Of course there are broad variations. The sum total that leads to burnout is a combination of factors, as above, including physical exhaustion, mental overload, and, often, doses of vicarious trauma and uncontained countertransference. Although it is definitely possible to recover from burnout with a period of rest, prevention is much preferable. For example, even though Janelle could not take a vacation, she still could have taken one or more weeks off from her work to indulge in activities she usually had little time for, including taking naps, walking in the woods, reading novels, and so on. It would not be an exciting week, but the change of pace and rest would likely have helped her to significantly reduce her risk for burnout.

### Countertransference

*Our difficulty here is to get one word [countertransference] not to mean as many different things as there are people using it.*
—Margaret Little, "R"

For many, countertransference is a confusing and highly debatable concept. There are widely varying definitions of the term, as well as wildly divergent strategies for managing or making use of it. Before discussing countertransference, a brief review of the concept of transference will help to put it into perspective.

In the early days of psychoanalysis, Sigmund Freud wanted the mental state of his analysts to be like a blank screen. That way, he believed, patients could project or transfer their feelings from past experiences onto the analyst. Freud wanted this process to be uncomplicated by the analyst's own feelings, history, or biases. Through analysis of the patient's transference, analysts would be able to confront and come to terms with fears and other feelings that often emanated from experiences in their own pasts.

As almost every psychotherapist now knows, it is impossible to keep one's mind blank and remain completely objective when facing a client's difficulties and emotions. Even the best-trained and most experienced psychotherapists are vulnerable to being touched or stirred by their clients. Freud eventually recognized that the reactive feelings of analysts were inevitable and coined a new term in 1910: "We have become aware of the 'counter-transference' which arises in the Physician as a result of the patient's influence on his unconscious feelings, and we are most inclined to insist that he shall recognize this counter-transference in himself and overcome it" (1910/1953, pp. 141–142). In the same paper, he went on to indicate that he expected the analyst to rise above countertransference reactions. He asserted that those who could not do so should not become practitioners of psychoanalysis. In a later paper, Freud went on to reinforce the idea that countertransference must be kept "in check" (1915/1953, p. 164).

Definitions of countertransference vary. Some believe it only involves the unconscious feelings stirred up in the therapist by the client. Others hold that countertransference encompasses the totality of the therapist's reaction to the client. Informally, many therapists think of transference as baggage from the client's past carried into the therapy room, and countertransference as the therapist's past baggage likewise brought into the room.

Not every therapist response to a client is a countertransference reaction. There are many other possible sources for a therapist's response to his clients. Three examples follow.

Some therapist reactions are appropriate responses for the circumstances, such as a therapist who becomes anxious or angry in response to an angry client who is acting in a threatening manner. Another class of reactions has roots in somatic empathy (discussed at length in Chapter 2), for example, getting a stomachache when a client has one. Still other reactions may be responses to client projections that have no echo or hook in the therapist's current or earlier life, as when a soft-spoken therapist becomes frustrated at a client's continued accusations that she is yelling.

Of course, today most practitioners disagree with Freud's assertion that countertransference must be overcome or kept in check all the time. While it can stir uncomfortable feelings, it is generally acknowledged that countertransference is sometimes desirable in the therapeutic relationship. At the least, it can help therapists enhance empathy or give them clues to understanding what is going on with their clients.

Many interpersonal analysts have questioned the traditional concept of transference (Gill, 1983; Gill & Hoffman, 1982; Stern, 1992). They believe transference experiences are related to current therapeutic interactions and are not solely distortions or projections from the past. Gill and Hoffman (1982) say transference operates much like a Geiger counter, sensitizing an individual to ascribe meanings that might not be apparent or meaningful to anyone else.

Contemporary interpersonal psychoanalysts view the therapeutic relationship as an intersubjective one in which client and analyst are influencing each other all the time (Stolorow & Atwood, 1992). Transference and countertransference are seen as arising from the relationship jointly created by both, an interpersonal rather than intrapsychic experience. In other words, in this view, the client's transference creates the analyst's countertransference; and conversely, the analyst's countertransference creates the client's transference. Marlene's situation illustrates one constructive use of countertransference as well as a risk.

Marlene knew that she felt deeply for her clients, especially the ones struggling with depression. She realized that some of her feelings had roots in memories of her mother's depression. Countertransference from that aspect of her own history helped her to gain a deep empathy with her depressed clients. Over many years, she became more successful with those types of clients than some of her colleagues who did not have a depressed parent. At the same time, Marlene needed to learn to monitor and prevent herself from relating or reacting to her clients' depression in similar ways as she had to her mother's, and to be alert for the times that memories of her mother's struggles could trigger feelings of sadness or resentment.

For the purposes of this book, the simplest definition is the most useful. From here on, the term *countertransference* will refer to a practitioner's reactions to the client that have roots in the practitioner's own past. For example, if a therapist becomes sad when their client expresses grief because of their own unresolved grief, that is countertransference. If she becomes sad when a long-term client reports being diagnosed with cancer, that is a response to the current client-therapist relationship, not countertransference.

## COUNTERTRANSFERENCE IN THE THERAPEUTIC RELATIONSHIP

The therapeutic relationship usually consists of two people: the therapist and the client. However, at times it may seem as if there are others in the room, ghosts from each person's past. Thus the therapeutic relationship actually consists of two people and two personal histories. Essentially, transference and countertransference exist in any relationship, not just the therapeutic relationship: parent–child, teacher–student, employee–employer, between friends, and with couples. Interpersonal and relational patterns and dynamics from the past that have been internalized by each person may inevitably arise and be reenacted within relationships. Transference and countertransference elements in a relationship can be positive or negative, healthy or unhealthy, or a benefit or detriment to the relationship (Kohut, 1981). For example, if your blue eyes remind me of my mother, and that brings up a warm feeling in me, then I may be more sympathetic or compassionate toward you. If I perceive your distant attitude as being like my father's, I may think you do not like me. If your academic prowess reminds me of my older brother, I may feel competitive and resentful toward you. And so on. These old patterns arise in a current relationship though they are actually reflections from the past. Managing countertransference to the best advantage is facilitated by mindful self-awareness, including body awareness.

Ellen, a child psychologist, worked in a neighborhood agency. She had lost her mother when she was three years old. Her father subsequently married a woman with two daughters. Ellen never felt that she was treated fairly by her stepmother. As a result, she was particularly anxious about her child clients who had stepparents. As much of her caseload involved (not surprisingly) children of divorce, her anxiety was persistent and gradually increased to uncontainable levels. During a much-needed leave of absence, she sought therapy for herself. She became aware that unresolved issues from her own childhood were infringing on her ability to effectively help her young clients. Becoming aware of the corollaries and how they affected her was adequate to enable her return to work. However, sticking with her own therapy proved to be important. Once she resolved the issues of her own that were provoked by her clients, she was better able to help them without suffering along with them.

Countertransference can be identified from several sources. It is usually identified from thoughts and emotions; however, body sensations, mental images, and behaviors can also be important indicators. Body sensations, including temperature changes, shifts in areas of tension and relaxation, skin sensations, and so on can be part of a countertransference response. If you have ever felt your skin crawl or become tense in your shoulders while with a client, you have likely experienced a somatic aspect of countertransference. Having pictures in your mind's eye or dialogue or songs in your mind's ear might also be part of such a response. Finally, noticing changes in your breathing or heart rate, or finding yourself moving or behaving in an unexpected way, may be the result of countertransference (though some might call the latter projective identification, which is discussed below).

Bobbie was usually a very calm and patient therapist. Every once in a while, though, she would find herself reacting harshly to a client, particularly those who were judgmental of others. With guidance from her supervisor, she realized that these episodes began with a growing tension in her chest that restricted her breathing. She then would become very impatient and sometimes lash out. Bobbie's supervisor helped her to identify that this somatic and emotional scenario followed a course that was familiar. During Bobbie's high school years, she endured many lectures from her judgmental older brother. The supervisor suggested Bobbie work on this memory in psychotherapy, which helped her to separate her judgmental clients from the judgments of her brother. As a result, Bobbie gained improved ability to help her clients and, as a bonus, also improved her relationship with her now adult brother.

## UNCONTAINED OR UNCONSCIOUS COUNTERTRANSFERENCE

Your own personal background can be a help or a hindrance depending on how much awareness you have of your history and how it affects you. Can you imagine how much more difficult Alesha's symptoms would have been to deal with if she had, in fact, experienced the same type of police brutality as her client? And then take that a step further to consider if the triggering incident had not been recent, but something from her past that had a similar theme, for example being pushed down by a bully during her school years. If Alesha could easily make that connection, it would likely be a quick fix. But if the bullying incident was long forgotten, it might take some time for her to make sense of her symptoms. That is one example of just how disruptive uncontained or unconscious countertransference can be.

Under normal circumstances, countertransference is always something a therapist needs to be alert for, and, of course, it can also be advantageous for helping professionals of all sorts. Sometimes countertransference is handy for helping you to better understand or relate your client's experience. But more often than not, when unresolved past situations and circumstances of high stress and trauma are awakened, your ability to help can become severely compromised. In situations where catastrophe is shared by all, such as a pandemic or war, the chances of dreadful personal experiences being evoked by hearing similar stories from others can be increased significantly. The best way forward in such circumstances, both for prevention and for healing, is to, as Socrates famously advised,

KNOW THYSELF.

And I would add: know thy personal history. It is only by recognizing the experiences of your life that may unsettle you—whether past or current—that you can have control and power over them, including when triggered by a client. That means also paying attention during community or global crisis times to how circumstances are affecting you, which may include being honest that it is affecting you, just like everyone else. One of the ways in which countertransference can become an added challenge during crisis times is by denying the amount of distress you are feeling. With self-awareness, countertransference has the potential to be tamed and become a useful ally for yourself and those in your care.

> Sly found it difficult to listen to the grief of clients whose loved ones had, due to the COVID-19 pandemic, recently died alone in nursing homes. He wanted his clients to accept the deaths and move on in an insensitive way that was not characteristic of him. It took some patience, but he

eventually understood that his own loss of a dear uncle under similar circumstances was still very fresh in his emotions. He had tried to push away how hard that loss had hit him. In doing so, compassion for the losses his clients had experienced was not adequately available.

## COUNTERTRANSFERENCE EXERCISE

Here is a quick exercise that will give you more clarity about some aspects of countertransference. Choose one of your clients to focus on during this exercise. It may be helpful to write down your responses.

First, mindfully check in with yourself to establish a baseline of how you are feeling right now. Then remember being with that client and notice the following:

- Sensations you feel in your body (hot, cold, achy, prickles, etc.)
- Visual or auditory images that arise in your mind (pictures, colors, sounds, songs, etc.)
- Movement or muscular impulses in your body (head turning, sitting back, legs tensing, clenched fists, etc.)
- Changes in autonomic arousal (breathing, heart rate, temperature of hands and feet, etc.)
- What you feel emotionally (angry, irritated, sad, happy, scared, turned on, disgusted, etc.)
- Any thoughts that occur to you

Next, take a few minutes to consider which of your responses could be mirrors of your client's experience (sensations, images, behaviors, feelings, thoughts). Which could more likely be reflections from your own past?

There is no right or wrong answer for this (or any) exercise in this book. Each point, however, is significant: how you feel about your client and what that client elicits in you. Feel free to try this exercise with other clients. It might be interesting to see how your experiences differ from client to client. You are also welcome to share this and any exercises in this book with your colleagues as well as your supervisees. It may be a good basis for fruitful discussions and perhaps even increased mutual support.

### Projective Identification

Projective identification is a major psychoanalytic theory. It attempts to account for how and why analysts sometimes find themselves having feelings and physical reactions similar to those of their patients, or experiencing emotions and behaviors their clients may be blocking or split off from. Further, analysts use principles of projective identification to guide their therapeutic reactions. Therefore, it is not possible (or sensible) to write a book on vicarious trauma and emotional contagion—theories that also endeavor to understand these phenomena—without paying attention to projective identification.

While projective identification is a cornerstone of psychoanalysis, there is a good deal of professional disagreement regarding its existence, what it is and is not, how it occurs, and whether it is useful or harmful. In this section, the history of projective identification and its current status are discussed. In Chapter 6 the concept is revisited. There I take a critical look at it in light of the new theories, concepts, and procedures discussed in the pages between.

Projective identification was first introduced to psychoanalysis by Melanie Klein (1946). She saw it as a primitive mental phenomenon, a form of communication that could occur in any interpersonal relationship, beginning in the contact between an infant and its primary caregiver. Basically, it involves the belief that someone can project parts of themselves onto—or into—another person. Klein believed that an infant is not psychologically equipped to identify its own emotional states as something occurring within its tiny being. Instead, it projects those states into the mother or other primary caretaker. (As the caretaker is usually the mother, for shorthand, I will refer to "mother.") As a result, it is thought that the infant perceives the mother as the cause of its emotions, believing that they originate outside of the infant's self. This trend is assumed to persist through life as the child, and later the adult, continues to project those states and traits that it does not like or cannot accept in itself onto others. Klein and her followers believe that an individual—infant, child, or adult—puts (projects) those states, those emotions, into the other person. In Klein's understanding, it is not merely that the projecting individual perceives the states or emotions in the other person, but that they are also able to cause emotions or actions that are consistent with the projection. When projective identification occurs in the psychoanalytic relationship, it becomes the analyst's job to process the projections and give them back to the patient in a more palatable form.

The notion that unwanted emotions or behaviors can be put into another person appears to be the major difference between Klein's idea of projective identification and Anna Freud's (1937) earlier concept of projection. In basic projection, the unwanted emotions are perceived as being a part of the other, whether or not that person is feeling or expressing them. Denying your own anger while accusing your spouse of being angry with you would be a common example of Anna Freud's understanding of projection. Klein's projective identification would instead suggest that you put your feelings of anger into your spouse because you will not feel them or cannot identify yourself as an angry person, causing your spouse to become angry with you, seemingly for no reason. In Klein's view, the angry spouse is not feeling his own anger, that is, becoming angry as a reasonable or unreasonable reaction to the situation. Instead Klein believed you unconsciously make your spouse feel and act out your anger. In the psychoanalytic relationship, if the therapist becomes distressed, it is the client who is believed to have unconsciously put uncomfortable, unwanted, and disowned feelings into the analyst. Further, as a result, the analyst may be induced by the client to behave in certain ways, such as acting angrily toward him. When the client is dealing with traumatic events, vicarious traumatization may be viewed as inducing the therapist to feel the horror of their trauma.

According to Grotstein (1981) and Kohut (1959, 1971), projective identification may form the basis for empathy. Intersubjective theory originated in Kohut's work on empathy (discussed in the next section). He believed that the client projects missing functions of the self (soothing, calming, understanding, etc.) onto the therapist, and the therapist then provides those functions for the client until the client can integrate and perform them himself. From this viewpoint, projective identification facilitates a therapist's empathetic understanding of the client's needs.

## PROJECTIVE IDENTIFICATION IN THE THERAPEUTIC RELATIONSHIP

Psychoanalysis utilizes an integrated, if complicated, application of projective identification. Martha Stark's (1999) *Modes of Therapeutic Action* has excellent in-depth examples of this process in action. In the hands of an adept analyst, the principle of projective identification may facilitate healing in a psychoanalytic patient. However, when it is not well understood, in the hands of the less experienced, or applied generally within other types of therapeutic models or therapeutic relationships, it can become problematic. While it originated in psychoanalysis, the theory of projective identification has been widely, if sometimes inaccurately, adopted by many other disciplines. The consequences include therapists blaming or holding their clients responsible for their own uncomfortable feelings. For example, "My client wouldn't feel her anger, so I ended up with it." Usually, psychoanalysts regard projective identification as a normal and desirable part of the psychoanalytic process. Some analysts, however, as well as many psychotherapists from other disciplines, view projective identification as something that detracts from, or even harms, the therapeutic relationship or even the therapist. Outside of psychoanalysis, it is often regarded as an inconvenient or undesirable defense mechanism associated with psychopathology and early developmental trauma (Grotstein, 1981).

Many believe that projective identification holds the power to provoke countertransference in the practitioner. In this view, nearly all negative and positive feelings toward a client may be disowned by the therapist as being caused by the client (Hedges, 1983). This tendency can be very problematic, not just because of the risk of hurting the client. The therapist who is unable to distinguish her own feelings from those of her client, and who also feels at the mercy of her client's feelings, may increase her risk for compassion fatigue, vicarious traumatization, unmanageable countertransference, and burnout.

The case example of Bobbie, above, can be used to illustrate and contrast some of the differences between countertransference and projective identification. If you will remember (or review), with the help of her supervisor, Bobbie discovered her feelings toward her client had roots in her own family and high school history. Projective identification could be another possible interpretation for the same situation—particularly if Bobbie was unable to find (or unwilling to look for) a link in her own past. Then it would be easy to interpret her harsh reaction toward her client as being induced by the client's unconscious rejection of her own feelings of harshness toward others. If Bobbie were on the right track, that could be helpful to the client. But if she is on the wrong track, such an interpretation could be detrimental for them both.

Schore (1994) speculated that projective identification is relevant to empathy, the main topic of Chapter 2. Perhaps it is even more than that: Maybe projective identification is empathy, or a category of empathy, something that therapists tune into rather than something that happens to them. Theories that support such a premise are discussed throughout the rest of this book. In Chapter 6, I will take another look at projective identification, together with the additional insights developed through the intervening chapters. By then I hope you will be well equipped to understand—and take charge of—the mechanisms underlying those shared feelings and states that regularly occur in the therapeutic relationship.

### How About You?

Now that you have read the varying definitions and descriptions of therapist risk factors in this chapter, take (or set aside) some time to consider (if you have not already) where your areas of risk lie. Is there one in particular or a combination? Did you choose this book because you are already suffering from or on the edge of compassion fatigue or burnout? Do you now realize that those nightmares you have been having may be due to vicarious traumatization? Is your own history at the root of periods of difficult countertransference? As mentioned before, knowing yourself and your history is going to be your first line of defense in identifying your vulnerabilities in your work and planning and taking steps to better caring for yourself so you can better care for your clients. The more honest you can be with yourself and the more active and proactive you can be to help and protect yourself, the longer you will be able to continue the work you love. Longevity in the helping professions is much dependent on increasing self-knowledge and self-care.

## Skill Building

### Mindfulness

Mindful self-awareness is going to be your best, or at the least one of your best, means to your self-care. It is just plain logical: If you are not aware of yourself, for example, when you are beginning a slide toward compassion fatigue, vicarious trauma, burnout, or unmanageable countertransference, how would you be able to help yourself head off disaster? And if you have missed the first cues that you are headed for such difficulties, mindful self-awareness can help to guide you out of those depths toward regaining your balance.

I know, I know, some of you are probably rolling your eyes and thinking, "Again?!" Of course it is not news that mindfulness is a popular topic included in just about every current psychology and psychotherapy book and workbook. For that reason, I am not going to dwell on the basics, as I have useful tools to offer you. Nonetheless, I do want to make a pitch for you to be sure to include simple mindfulness and mindful practices in your self-care tool kit. Truth be told, those I know to be best at managing their self-care, also in the most turbulent times, implement mindfulness in one form or another prominently, and regularly, in their lives.

Brief reminder: Being mindful means anchoring your awareness in now, the present moment. You accomplish that by focusing on something, often called a *target*, that you use to hold your attention. A common target during meditation, for example, is the feeling of your breathing going in and out. However, it is important to note that your target does not need to be a body process. You can just as well notice your environment—something you see or hear, or even something you touch (like petting your cat), taste (as letting a candy slowly melt in your mouth), or a simple activity you are engaged in (washing dishes, brushing your teeth, taking a walk). The trick is to catch when your mind wanders (which it will) to the past or future and bring your attention back to whatever it is you have chosen as your awareness anchor in the present. It is that exercise in bringing your wandering mind back to now that is the core of mindfulness. More on target choices below.

Training your ability to hold mindful attention can be extremely useful in helping you to cope with stressful situations, whether a brief episode (e.g., meeting a deadline) or ongoing crisis (e.g., war, pandemic). At times, it is difficult enough, stressful enough, to endure the present moment itself. Adding fear and anticipation about the future or regrets or longing for the past risks handicapping your ability to respond to what is happening now. In addition, mindfulness can enhance any precious moments of calm in the storm. It can give you the chance to take full advantage of rare blessed breaks by holding your attention on the (albeit temporary) relief of the absence of stress or pressure—even if only for a few minutes, hours, or days. In those, albeit brief, oases, mindfulness can help you realize space to breathe, possibly rest, and perhaps even regroup. During the COVID-19 crisis, I was particularly dependent on mindfulness when my attention habitually flew to worries about the future, the what-if's that things could get even worse. At those times, I endeavored to stop and shift my focus to pay detailed attention to the fact that whatever I was fearing for the future was not happening at that present moment. Many a night that mindful strategy helped me, gratefully, to fall asleep.

## MINDFUL DUAL AWARENESS: CHOOSING TARGETS BEST SUITED TO YOU

Usually, mindful practices advocate choosing targets from your internal senses, particularly the breath or other internal (interoceptive) body sensations, to bind your attention to the present moment. And while that works for plenty of people, there are, nonetheless, a good many who, particularly when under added stress, find that attention to their inner sensations actually will increase their anxiety and stress rather than ease it. If that sounds familiar, you might try instead to attend to one or more external (exteroceptive) sensations, what are more commonly referred to as the five senses: sight, hearing, taste, touch, smell. They may help you more effectively hold your focus on *now*. It is completely legitimate to have mindful moments and even to meditate by focusing on something in your external environment. You can look at a painting or the view outside your window, listen to a sound, music, or even nearby traffic. You can feel the texture of an object (e.g., stone, cloth, fur), smell a favorite spice, or taste a favorite flavor in your mouth (such as melting chocolate). In fact, often during my professional trainings, I devote an after-lunch exercise to a chocolate meditation. I created the exercise as an application of my own discovery that I sometimes enjoy what I call a "chocolate walking meditation" from time to time.

My idea for a chocolate meditation was initially inspired by the well-known raisin exercise that is usually part of the introduction to a mindfulness-based stress reduction course.[6] I simply adapted the instructions I remembered as follows:

- Choose a piece of pure chocolate (dark, milk, white, ruby). This works best if the chocolate is free of nuts or other ingredients that must be chewed. Alternatively, you can choose a nonchocolate candy that melts, or even a small piece of flavorful fruit if you do not like or cannot have sweets. But, of course, do not do this exercise if it does not appeal to you.
- Whatever food item you choose, this is your target for this exercise in mindfulness. As with all mindful targets, this is what you will return your attention to when your mind wanders (as it will). Follow the instructions below at an easy, unrushed pace. In addition, as well as following the instructions to attend to the external sensations, you can also choose (or not) to notice what happens elsewhere in your body as you look, touch, smell, hear, taste. At each step you might notice, for example: Does the moisture of your mouth change? Does your stomach react? Is there a shift in your breathing? And so on.
- Sit or stand in a position that is comfortable for you (with food in your mouth, this would not be particularly safe to do lying down). Take your time and do not rush through each of the next steps.
- Place your chocolate (or other food) on your hand (or a plate, napkin, etc.) and just look at it. Without thinking about it, use your sense of sight to simply notice its shape, color, edges, and so on.
- Apply your sense of touch to feel the texture of it between your fingers.

---

[6] As inspired by John Kabat-Zinn (2013) in his book *Full Catastrophe Living*.

- For your sense of smell, raise it to your nose and take a whiff, noticing the aroma.
- Next, bring it close to your ear and observe if your sense of hearing recognizes a sound.
- And then, finally, for your sense of taste, place it in your mouth, but do not chew it.
- Notice also through your sense of touch the feel on your tongue. And then the taste.
- As you feel it melting (or softening if your food choice does not melt), notice when your attention wanders, and keep bringing it back to the mouth sensation and taste. You might also check if simultaneously you have sensations elsewhere in your body.
- Eventually the piece of chocolate or food will be small or soft enough that you might want to finish it with a chew and a swallow.
- And then pay attention to the lingering taste as well as feel in your mouth. Observe how those sensations fade—like the sound of a bell— until they disappear completely.
- Last, bring your attention to your surroundings and notice anything that comes to mind from this experience. Write down whatever is useful for you.
- And notice if this mindful exercise provided you a pause of some sort in your day or period of stress. Do you feel any different (for better or worse) from this experience? Is it something you would like to do again?

## KEEPING A MINDFUL EYE ON YOURSELF

Another reason mindfulness can be so useful for therapists is that a growing body of research demonstrates that therapists who practice mindful self-awareness during sessions with stressed and traumatized clients have significantly lower incidences of vicarious trauma and compassion fatigue (Harrison, 2007; Thompson et al., 2014). This means that mindfulness can help you to prevent your client's stress from compounding your own— during normal as well as catastrophic times. This does not mean that you should constantly be paying attention to yourself when working with clients (though that is not a bad idea). All that mindful awareness seems to require to be effective in this way is periodically checking in with yourself. For example, when you ask your client to notice the temperature of their hands, check yours too. When you see your client's respiration, pay attention to yours. And so on. Also, mindfully monitoring your own autonomic nervous system (ANS) arousal (see Chapter 2) will be a great help to alert you to slow things down or take a break when you feel your own stress rising.

Here are a couple of strategies you can try. If you find them useful, practice will ensure they are available to you whenever you need them.

1. When you are with your client, check in with yourself at regular intervals. You might set a soft alarm on your phone or invest in a meditation type of alarm clock or phone app (they chime at programmed intervals). Do not worry about this disrupting your clients, as it is likely just as good for them to check in with themselves at regular intervals as it is for you. Just make sure to warn your client that chimes will interrupt occasionally and explain the purpose. Sometimes I have negotiated with a client that each time we hear the chime we will stop what we are doing or talking about and take two or three breaths before continuing. Particularly for clients working with trauma, this can be a useful opportunity to reboot both your and their arousal levels, resuming in a calmer or steadier state.

2. When you are with your client, periodically notice if you can keep mindful awareness of yourself and your client at the same time. Usually therapists are more aware of their clients than of themselves. Nevertheless, with practice, you can learn to tune in to both, either simultaneously or sequentially.

I offer both these exercises in my self-care trainings to good result. If you would rather gain facility with these skills prior to trying them when you are with your clients, arrange to practice with one or more colleagues.

### NOW I AM AWARE

"Now I am aware . . . " is the typical beginning to many an exercise in Gestalt therapy. Fritz Perls, the creator and founder of that movement and method of psychotherapy, was experienced in mindful practice and the importance of the present moment from his studies of Zen Buddhism. It was Perls (1968) who first introduced those concepts into psychotherapy. The "now I am aware" exercise will help you to anchor yourself in the reality of your current surroundings and state of being. When worries about the future or regrets of the past intrude, a few minutes of "now I am aware" can help you to create a space for calm and clear thinking. Of course, you must tell the truth. So if the present moment is actually fraught with tumult or danger, do not focus on an exercise—instead prioritize seeking safety. But most of the time, the present moment, even if only 60 seconds, has potential to be an oasis.

Periodically throughout your day, or as often as you feel it useful, stop to identify *now*. Settle on your feet or into your chair. Take a breath or two. And then just start saying and then finishing the sentence "Now I am aware . . . " as many times as you like. I will write a set of my current experience right now to demonstrate:

Now I am aware of the text tone ringing on my phone.

Now I am aware of seeing my fingers moving on the keyboard.

Now I am aware of the feeling of the keys under the tips of my fingers, particularly the ring fingers of each hand.

Now I am aware of the sound of traffic outside my window.

Now I am aware of the feel of the breeze [coming through the window] on my face.

Now I am aware I just sat back a little and took a deep breath.

Now I am aware of wondering what I will type next.

And so on . . .

Try a set, yourself, right now where you are reading this book.

# CHAPTER 2

# Managing the Ties That Bind

What are the mechanisms of both body and brain that underlie the phenomenon of empathy? The theory section of this chapter strives to answer that question by first defining and then exploring the neurophysiology of empathy, the distinct features of somatic empathy, and the inevitable human tendency for mirroring and mimicry. In the skill-building section, you will be given tools to help you to increase your mindful awareness and control over your personal empathy dial—to be able to easily adjust your level of empathy (increase and decrease) with others.

## Theory

### Empathy

The only area of agreement in the literature on empathy is that there is wide disagreement about what empathy is. This disagreement also extends to the concept of sympathy. In many articles and books, sympathy and empathy are virtually interchangeable terms for the same concept. Others, however, make a clear distinction between the two. In nearly every article and book on the topic, both terms are subject to differing definitions. For the purposes of this book, I have decided to depend on the definition of empathy in the authoritative *Merriam-Webster's Collegiate Dictionary*:

> *The action of understanding, being aware of, being sensitive to, and vicariously experiencing the feelings, thoughts, and experience of another of either*

*the past or present without having the feelings, thoughts, and experience*
*fully communicated in an objectively explicit manner.* (Merriam-Webster,
n.d.)

Empathy is necessary for survival of the species. It is what alerts us to the
needs of others and draws us to respond. Empathy is the foremost tool in
the hands of every psychotherapist. None of us would have much success as
therapists without our capacity and facility for empathy.

Empathy also triggers gut sensations that can advise on who can be
trusted and who should be feared. Conscious empathy is a desirable capacity, making it possible to relate to the experiences of others, to walk in their
shoes, so to speak. It is part and parcel of being human. Empathy leads to
compassion by providing insight into another's state of being. "I know how
you feel" is a common expression of empathy.

However, empathy also has a downside, particularly when it is not conscious and is therefore beyond your ability to moderate. When, as proposed
in the definition above, you are vicariously experiencing the state of another
unconsciously, there can be a strong emotional and somatic impact. A common, if benign, example could go as follows. Judy says to her husband at
dinner, "No, I did not have an enjoyable lunch. My colleague, Susan, was
in a funk, and it really got to me. I felt badly for her and tried to help. But
when we parted, she was still upset, and I've felt lousy all afternoon." Obviously Judy was trying to be a good friend. So why did she end up suffering
too? Before answering this question, a look at the roots of the concept of
empathy is in order.

## THE HISTORY OF EMPATHY

As I began to peruse the existing literature in research for this book, I
assumed that the idea of empathy was a theory exclusive to psychology.
Actually, I discovered, it is not. I was surprised to learn that the notion of
empathy was first applied in the context of art appreciation. In the late 19th
and early 20th centuries, empathy was considered essential to understanding
aesthetics, the idea that a person could be deeply affected by the mood of
something else—a painting, a sculpture—and the term *empathy* was applied

to that effect. The earliest writings on the topic appear from Theodor Lipps (1903/1964) who, in German, used the term *Einfühlung* to name the kinds of feelings that could be noticed in the body, including proprioceptive changes and sensations.

Since the early 1900s, psychologists from a variety of disciplines, including social psychology, neurophysiology, and folk psychology, have studied empathy. Though empathy has been studied for decades, many of the early findings were not always taken seriously. Prior to the Decade of the Brain in the 1990s, psychology was often considered a soft science, its research not readily accepted. New technologies, including various types of brain scanning, have turned the field of psychology into an accepted hard science. However, empathy remains an elusive and complicated concept, even for psychotherapists.

There is no better resource on the early history of empathy than Gladstein's (1984) "The Historical Roots of Contemporary Empathy Research." Reviewed below are some of the most salient points from that article, interspersed with a few additional points from other sources.

The earliest definitions of empathy were anthropomorphic; that is, *empathy* referred to people infusing objects and art with human qualities (Gladstein, 1984). By the late 19th and early 20th centuries, this view was superseded by an interpersonal view of empathy. While E. B. Titchener coined the actual term *empathy* in 1909, it appears he based it on Theodor Lipps's (1903/1964) earlier concept of Einfühlung. Some researchers began to notice an interpersonal element to empathy. The contagious nature of laughter is one example. "Emotional contagion" (MacDougall, 1908) and "fellow-feeling" (Scheler, 1912/1972) were terms coined to describe the effect of interpersonal empathy. Sullivan (1947, 1954) observed that a child quickly picked up the tension of an anxious mother and called it "contagion of emotion." Others soon added to these basic observations.

Applications of empathy in psychotherapy slowly evolved through the middle of the 20th century. In 1948, Theodor Reik wrote, "the analyst must oscillate in the same rhythm with his patient. He vicariously lives his patient's experiences and at the same time looks upon them with the factual regard of the investigator" (p. 116). Similarly, Carl Rogers (1946) suggested that the therapist should use "deep understanding" and try to perceive the client "as the client seems to himself." By 1951, Rogers had begun using the terms *empathic attitude* and *empathic understanding* in his discussion of the counselor-client relationship. Heinz Kohut (1978), the psychoanalyst who founded the movement of self-psychology, believed that the field of psychology itself should be defined by the concept of empathy, that classical psychoanalysis failed to help patients who had preoedipal (before 3 years of age) trauma. He set out to develop a therapeutic method that involved verbal reflection (as opposed to psychoanalytic interpretation) of the client's subjective experience. His aim was to help the client to feel understood by the therapist walking in the client's shoes, so to speak (Kohut, 1959, 1971, 1978, 1981).

### EMPATHY IN THE THERAPEUTIC RELATIONSHIP

In the earlier example, I asked: Why, when Judy was trying to be helpful, did she end up suffering along with her friend? Here is one possible answer: Judy was unaware that she took on so much of Susan's feelings and that her empathy could have consequences. As a result, she was infected by Susan's upset without having the tools to identify or intervene in that automatic process.

Unconscious empathy is the mechanism of emotional infection. This is the same mechanism that is at work on a regular basis in the therapeutic relationship: Therapists commonly catch the upset feelings of their clients. Often the effect is short-lived. But sometimes the impact is lasting, persisting long after the end of a session. For example, if you find yourself feeling down during or following work with a depressed client, or hungry during or after a session with an anorexic client, empathy may be the culprit. Of course, empathy is very important in the therapeutic relationship and is by no means always a problem.

About 20 minutes into one session, Lillian, a marriage and family therapist, gained an important insight into the plight of her client, Isaac. He was struggling with an irrational anger toward authority figures that had caused problems at his workplace. Frankly, Lillian was somewhat irritated with him, thinking he should have better impulse control. And she was frustrated that she was unable to get him to think more clearly. But today, as Isaac ranted about a coworker, Lillian flashed on a surprisingly similar conversation she had recently had with her 8-year-old son. He had come home crying after being rebuffed by another child. Of course, the particulars were different, but the feelings and themes were similar. When she made that link, that Isaac was feeling and responding as her young son would, her feelings toward him softened and her irritation receded. She could now see underneath his anger and resonate with his unexpressed hurt feelings. As a result, she felt more in contact with him, not so antagonistic. Lillian then changed her tactics and began to talk with Isaac as she would with her son, to that young part of him. For the first time in several sessions, they really connected. Isaac felt heard and supported, and he calmed down. That made it possible for him to look at the situation with his coworker differently. Both Lillian and Isaac felt good at the end of this successful session.

That example illustrates one of the ways in which empathy can be a critically useful tool for the psychotherapist. Lillian tapped into her own memory and feelings for a link to Isaac. When they connected, she was better able to help him. Lillian was aware of the link and the change in her feelings. The session left no residue in her system. However, empathy's mark is not always so positive.

Hans was a psychologist at a refugee assistance center. Though he had never been homeless or displaced himself, he still had a deep empathy for his clients. He would often imagine what it would be like to be them. Of course, sometimes this facilitated his work. But over time, his energy began to flag and his optimism faltered. Empathy with a particular client accelerated Hans toward the edge of burnout. He had been working with Kabil for about six months. Kabil had fled his country during a political upheaval. Like many of Hans's clients, Kabil had been in mortal danger because of views that were sympathetic to the previous regime. He was forced to leave family and friends behind to settle in Hans's country once he was granted refugee status. Typical of many refugees, Kabil was depressed and greatly missed his home country, family, and friends. The therapy sessions were often laden with sadness and frustration. Hans was often greatly affected by Kabil's feelings. If Hans had been able to observe one of these sessions, he would have been surprised by what he saw. Invariably, as he listened intently, he would gradually slip into deeper and deeper resonance with Kabil. It was easily observable not only in Hans's demeanor but also in his posture, his breathing, and his facial expression. His empathy was so deep that for the duration of a session, Hans was, in essence, one with Kabil. Of course this deep affinity provided Kabil with a very sympathetic ear and an ally who had a deep understanding of what it was like to be Kabil. But there was a disadvantage: Hans was losing his ability to be objectively helpful, and feelings of hopelessness and depression were beginning to spill into his private life. His wife was becoming concerned. By resonating so deeply (and unconsciously) with Kabil (as well as other clients), Hans was losing the optimism he needed to help improve Kabil's life, as well as to live his own.

### The Neurophysiology of Empathy

Empathy helps us to share joy with our clients, families, and friends. It also facilitates our sharing in their fears and their pain. Consider: Have you ever felt uncharacteristically or unexpectedly nervous in the presence of someone who was anxious? Or has another's anger possibly infected your own mood to the point where you became angry about something you had been more neutral about, or angrier than you had been in the first place? How about this: Are there movie scenes that make you cry, your heart pound, your muscles tense, or turn you on? All of these responses are possible because of empathy. Anytime you are sharing in the emotional or physical state of another, whether pleasant or unpleasant, in person or at the movies, empathy is operational.

The benefits of empathy are fairly obvious. Empathy facilitates human care and support for other humans. It helps us to form relationships with family, friends, and colleague groups, as well as to bond, help each other, and work together toward common goals. And, obviously, it helps you in your work as a psychotherapist.

Disadvantages of empathy are usually less apparent. It is also empathy that is, for example, at the root of mob violence, the glue of cults, and so on. In response to the COVID-19 pandemic, whether you were a mask wearer or antimasker was, to some degree, determined via empathy with those you most sympathized or associated with. Empathy is also at work when you find your good mood has disappeared in the presence of someone who is in a distressed state.

This section illuminates the neurophysiology that makes empathy possible, that is, to vicariously feel what another person is feeling (as illustrated by Hans, above). To be able to understand how such a feat is possible, it is first necessary to be familiar with some basics of the human nervous system, its structure and function.

## THE HUMAN NERVOUS SYSTEM

The term *central nervous system* (CNS) commonly has two usages. The first is (incorrectly) as the name of the body's entire nervous system. More accurately, however, the term describes that portion of the nervous system that is most central in the body: the brain and spinal cord. It is from that core that all of the body's nerves emanate.

The nerves of the CNS originate in the brain and spinal cord. From there they distribute to all points in the body as the *peripheral nervous system*. Nerves communicate throughout the body via hormones, neurotransmitters that facilitate the transfer of information across synapses, the junctions between nerve endings. Efferent nerves transmit instructions from the brain to the body (e.g., "Contract the left flexor digiti minimi brevis" to bend the little finger of the left hand). Afferent nerves broadcast sensory information from the body to the brain (e.g., "Moving that finger hurts"). Grasping the basics of this two-way communication system is integral to understanding the vicarious nature of empathy: the brain communicates to the body and the body communicates back to the brain. More on this later.

The peripheral nervous system has two divisions: sensory and motor. They each also have two divisions. The motor (muscle) division is divided into somatic and autonomic branches, and the sensory division is divided into exteroceptor and interoceptor branches (see Figure 2.1). In Chapter 3, the motor division's autonomic nervous system is discussed in depth. This chapter focuses on the somatic nervous system and both branches of the sensory division: interoceptive and exteroceptive.

## MOTOR DIVISION: SOMATIC NERVOUS SYSTEM

The nerves of the body's skeletal muscles make up the somatic nervous system. Stimulation to one of these nerves causes a muscle to contract; in the absence of stimulation, there is no contraction; nothing happens in the muscle. The common term for this nonaction or noncontraction is *relaxation*, which sounds like an active process ("Just relax!"), though it is not. So relaxation of a muscle is when it is doing nothing. In general, it is the contractions and noncontractions (relaxation) of a muscle, regulated from the brain or spinal cord, that create physical movement.

The somatic nervous system is composed of efferent nerves, which carry instructions from the brain and spinal cord to the muscles. For example, when your eyes move to follow the printed text in this book, your brain is signaling nerves to stimulate muscles on one side of your eyes to contract. At the same time, there must also be a signal to nerves on the opposite side of your eyes to stop stimulation so that those muscles do nothing (relax). As your eyes sweep from left to right, muscles on the right side of the eyeball are contracting while the ones on the left side are not contracting. It is this interplay of contraction and noncontraction that makes the eye movement (or any movement) possible. When your eyes sweep back to the left, the opposite is happening. If you are wearing progressive (multifocus) eyeglasses, it will not be your eyes that are moving but your head that is turning from side to side as you read. In that case, it will be muscles at the sides of the neck that are alternately contracting and noncontracting to make possible the head movement that facilitates reading. The commands from the brain to the muscles of the eyes or neck travel along efferent nerves, brain to body.

On rare occasions, efferent nerves in the spinal cord can instruct body

## The Body's Nervous System

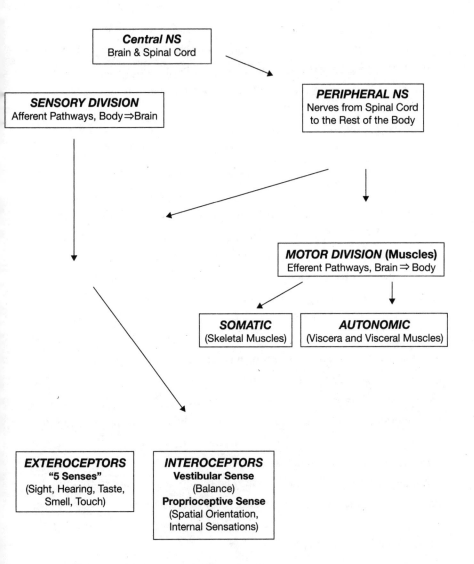

**FIGURE 2.1**    The Structure of the Human Nervous System

movement without a directive from the brain. The quick jerk your arm and hand make in reaction to inadvertently touching a hot stove (set in motion by sensory feedback from your fingers or hand) is an example. That instantaneous reflex, yanking your hand out of danger, is directed from the spinal cord; the brain is bypassed. As can be seen from this and later examples, the sensory and motor divisions of the nervous system interact all the time. In fact, without sensory feedback, much successful movement is not even possible. Think about trying to walk without being able to feel the bottom of your foot or the weight of your body on your knees.

## SENSORY DIVISION: EXTEROCEPTORS

Sensory nerves are afferent nerves. They are constantly communicating information from the body's periphery to the brain and spinal cord. There are two main categories: exteroceptors and interoceptors. Exteroceptors are nerves that relay the sensory information with which we are most familiar—sight, hearing, taste, touch, smell—what are commonly called the five senses. Communication of exteroceptive nerves connects us to our external environment. In the previous example, it is the exteroceptive sense of touch that is activated by contact with the hot stove.

No single branch of the nervous system functions independently. Information from the sensory nervous system will often generate activity in the somatic nervous system. Continuing with the example above will clarify this interplay: The sensation of endangering heat is quickly communicated to the spinal cord (afferent), where the instruction to contract hand and arm muscles (to jerk the hand away) is sent immediately in response (efferent). A split second or two later, as the sensation of pain reaches the brain (an afferent process that is much slower), further instructions are sent from the brain (efferent), which result in additional muscular movements: shaking the hand, blowing on the fingers, dashing to the freezer to get ice, and so forth.

## SENSORY DIVISION: INTEROCEPTORS

Though it is equally important, most people are less familiar with the interoceptive branch of the sensory nervous system. It includes three main senses:

- Vestibular: regulates your sense of balance, including the relationship of the body to gravity
- Proprioceptive, spatial: tells you where the parts of your body (including head, trunk, and limbs) are in space at any time
- Proprioceptive, internal: communicates information about the state of your organs and connective tissue (butterflies in the stomach, muscle aches, etc.)

The proprioceptive spatial sense is sometimes a difficult concept to grasp. Three simple exercises will give you a clearer understanding:

- Standing or sitting, stretch your arms out to your sides and point the pointer finger on each of your hands. Then with your eyes closed, alternate touching the tip of your pointer fingers to the tip of your nose.
- Right now, without looking, identify the position of your legs and feet. Include the angle of each and the proximity of one to the other. Once you have an idea, look and see if you are correct.
- Put on some music and dance a little. Stop suddenly and, before looking, identify how your legs, feet, arms, hands, head, and so on are positioned (in front of or behind your trunk, bent or straight, tilted or upright, etc.). If you do this with others, ask for their feedback. If you are doing this alone, it can help to check in a mirror.

Like the exteroceptors, the interoceptors also interact with (and influence) other divisions of the nervous system. The nerves of the somatic nervous system, discussed above, do not act alone in moving our bodies around in space. To walk across a room, for instance, requires a cooperative effort across several divisions of the nervous system:

- Somatic nerves contract (and release) the muscles of the legs to facilitate movement and to hold the trunk and head upright.
- Proprioceptive nerves send feedback to the brain on where the legs and feet are in relationship to the body and the floor.

- Exteroceptive nerves communicate when the bottom of the foot contacts the ground (sense of touch).
- Interoceptive nerves communicate when weight is shifted to the knees, ankles, and feet.
- Vestibular nerves tell the brain whether or not the body is upright.

The internal sense is the core of neurologist Antonio Damasio's (1994) theory of somatic markers. He proposed that the experience of emotion consists of gut sensations that are elicited in response to various stimuli. For example, if you eat something that makes you ill, the next time you see, smell, or are offered it, you may feel some degree of nausea (an internal sensation that has become a somatic marker for the previous experience with that food). After a time the strongest reaction will likely fade, but you may continue to have an involuntary aversion to that food (the somatic marker), perhaps even forgetting the origin of your dislike.

## EMPATHY AND THE NERVOUS SYSTEM

Individuals in close interaction with others (including psychotherapists) commonly, spontaneously, and unconsciously copy each other's facial expressions and postures (as demonstrated by Hans above). Reflexive smiling in response to another's smile is just one example of this. When facial expressions associated with particular emotions are copied, both people may experience the same feeling. This tendency is rooted in afferent feedback from the internal sense and is related to Damasio's somatic marker theory. This idea is expanded in the next two sections, Somatic Empathy and Mirroring and Mimicry.

Try turning down the sides of your mouth, lowering the outer edges. At the same time, notice what happens in your gut. Do you feel any sensation there? What about any changes in your breathing or sensations in your chest? Do you associate those sensations with a particular feeling?

Many people who try this exercise will sense a kind of heaviness in their gut or chest and will associate it with the feeling of sadness. That is the result of the somatic marker we all have for how sadness feels, both on the face (proprioceptive awareness of my downturned mouth) and in the gut. It is because of this feedback system (à la Damasio's somatic markers) that adopting an empathic facial expression or posture with your client—consciously or unconsciously—can dramatically affect you.

Empathy can also be set in motion by any part of the sensory nervous system. Visual, auditory, and tactile senses are particularly vulnerable. It is commonplace to visualize stories in the mind's eye or hear dialogue in the mind's ear when reading or listening to stories—whether from literature, news (written and broadcast), or direct communication with another. Provocations can also occur in other senses, such as touch when you feel cold observing or hearing about a snowstorm, or taste when you see a cooking show on television or listen to the description of a scrumptious meal. Just as Lipps (1903/1964) found that viewing a painting could stir empathy, so can exposure to other types of sensory stimuli.

Here is another exercise to try: Think of a piece of favorite music from your college years (for this, I often call up songs by the Beatles or Simon and Garfunkel). Listen to it in your imagination (or put it on your phone) and notice what happens in your sensory memory. Do you have memories of smells, tastes, movements, and so on from the time when you most often listened to that music? I have given lectures and workshops on topics from this book over the years since the first edition was published. In teaching about somatic markers, I have sometimes played a clip of the Beatles' "Come Together" for the audience. When it stops, I routinely ask the group to call out any sensory memories they experienced. There is usually a lot of giggling in response because (as I came to learn) many people (of my generation in particular but not exclusively) will recall the aroma of marijuana and feel a (usually) pleasant spaciness when they hear that piece of music.

For another experience, imagine your spice rack and remember the smell of each spice, one at a time. Alternatively, you can try actually smelling the spices. Notice if pictures arise in your mind's eye or sensations in your mouth or stomach in association with your memories of the different fragrances.

Once you have experienced this firsthand, you are on the way to comprehending how listening to and observing a client could elicit sensory memories in yourself.

## THE NEUROLOGY OF EMPATHY

Neuroscience is attempting to explain the interpersonal phenomena of imitation, resonance, simulation, and the somato–emotional results of those processes that are called empathy. Of particular note are the theories that emerged in the mid-1990s with the discovery of what are now called *mirror neurons*.

When *Help for the Helper* was first published in 2006, few had yet heard of mirror neurons. It is likely that by now you have. Nonetheless, I will briefly review the concept and history for those who are not familiar with these unique, and relevant, neurons.

Mirror neurons are just what their name implies: brain cells that reflect the activity of another's brain cells. They were first discovered by Italian researchers (Gallese et al., 1996; Rizzolatti et al., 1996) at Universitá Degli Studi di Parma (the University of Parma). Actually, the discovery was accidental—a common occurrence in the evolution of scientific ideas. These researchers were studying grasping behaviors in live monkeys. They observed activity in the monkeys' brains via electrodes connected to a monitor, so they could identify which neurons were firing at any given time. Specifically, they were investigating which individual neurons fired when a monkey reached out and grasped a raisin. During a break, something amazing—and never before detected—happened with one of the primate subjects: Neurons in the monkey's brain associated with grasping lit up when one of the researchers reached out and grasped a raisin himself (Gallese, 1999). That is, the neurons that fired when the monkey itself grasped a raisin were the same ones that fired when the monkey observed the researcher's similar grasping movement. The same neuron activated by performing the action was also activated by seeing the action.

Of course the researchers were amazed. Nothing like this had been seen before. There had been some previous speculation about a motor matching system (Fadiga et al., 1995), but proof had not yet been obtained. In this case, the neurons in the monkey's motor system were actually recorded responding to the action of the researcher. Through that simple grasping movement, the monkey and the researcher essentially became connected to one another. Rizzolatti and Arbib proposed that mirror neurons "represent the link between sender and receiver" (1998, p. 188). For an action to elicit the response of mirror neurons, it must be seen (or perhaps imagined) in process. The visual stimulus of the actor activates the same neurons in the observer (Gallese, 2001).

This accidental occurrence was the first hard evidence for the existence of a neuronal mirror system, meaning that the monkey might feel the researcher's movement. The mirror response in the monkey's neurons was not just simple recognition, the monkey felt what the researcher was doing. That kind of thoughtful perception is activated elsewhere in the brain. What happened between the monkey and the researcher necessitated a new concept, a new theory. The monkey's neurons fired as if it had made the same movement itself. Actually, our bodies frequently recognize another's movement; it just had not been documented in the brain before. You have probably experienced the same thing yourself—a time you cringed when seeing someone get hurt, or felt your thighs tense or your breathing accelerate while you were watching sports or a passionate love scene on television.

Renowned neuroscientist V. S. Ramachandran (2000) voiced extreme excitement at the discovery of mirror neurons. He enthusiastically predicted that mirror neurons could revolutionize psychology in a manner similar to DNA's revolution of biology. Ramachandran speculated that phenomena such as ESP—which has stumped scientists for eons—might be explained by mirror neurons.

Usually discussed within the context of observation and imitation of movement, including the development of spoken language, mirror neurons actually appear to be involved in many more areas of the brain and many more aspects of interaction. The role of mirror neurons in language development is simple to grasp (pun intended) as it likely underpins the evolution of human communication, beginning with gesticular language. It has been shown, for example, that Broca's area, the major center for the production of speech in humans, is also important for the production of gestures (Chollet et al., 1991; Parsons et al., 1995). Moreover, several studies have observed a mirror response to hand gestures in the neurons of Broca's area (Arbib et al., 2000; Rizzolatti & Arbib, 1998). This implies that communication among humans was likely dependent on gesture in earlier times. Moreover, modern day language development in children often includes hand signals. For example, toddlers are able to point at something they want long before they are able to express their desire in words.

International travelers also know, firsthand, the importance of gesture in communication. How many of us have found our way in a foreign land by depending on hand signs? Finding a place in a strange city can almost always be facilitated by stating the name of the place you are looking for while simultaneously raising your shoulders with hands upturned—connecting a place name with that gesture is universally understood as asking where it is. This is actually how I have found my way to a bathroom in many countries, raising my shoulders and asking, "Toilet?"

From these beginnings, interest in mirror neurons has grown rapidly. Scientists are now looking at mirror neurons as a possible explanation for common phenomena. For example, it is possible that mirror neurons will help us understand the obvious infectiousness of laughter and yawning. Platek and colleagues (2003) conducted several experiments on the contagiousness of yawning. Among other things, their data suggested that yawning is a kind of empathic response quite possibly mediated by mirror neurons. They are not the only ones to study and to speculate about the relationship between empathy and mirror neurons. A growing body of literature focuses on that very idea (e.g., Cozolino, 2002; Decety & Chaminade, 2003; Gallese, 2001; Harris, 2003; Preston & de Waal, 2002; Wolf et al., 2000, 2001).

### Somatic Empathy

> Empathy is deeply grounded in the experience of my lived-body, and it is this experience that enables us to directly recognize others, not as bodies endowed with a mind, but as persons like us.
> —Gallese, Ferrari, and Umilta, "The Mirror Matching System"

> [Empathy is] an autonomic nervous system state which tends to simulate that of another person.
> —Ax, "Goals and Methods of Psychophysiology"

A situation that occurred in my first job as a new social worker in the mid-1970s will help to illustrate how vulnerable we are to being infected by the states of our clients. While I sat in my office with particular clients, I would observe things happening in my body that I did not notice with all clients. The pleasant sensations did not concern me, and I did not pay much attention to them. However, I found that I did need to do something about sensations that were not so pleasant. Some of my uncomfortable responses could be blamed on newbie jitters, but I strongly sensed that there was more to it than that.

> I distinctly remember my bodily reactions to Allison. As she recounted the crises of her week in a spacey, disconnected way, she kept her body very still. I had to lean forward to hear her whispery, nearly inaudible voice. As we worked together, I often noticed that I felt light-headed, which I did not like. When I began to pay attention to what was happening in my body, I found that my breathing had become very shallow—in fact, nearly undetectable. No wonder I was feeling light-headed and spacey; I wasn't getting enough oxygen.
>
> Turning my attention back to Allison, I noticed that her chest was barely moving. I was taken aback—we were breathing alike! Was I copying her respiration style? I wondered if my light-headedness and general feelings of disconnectedness were just the result of new-therapist nervousness or the direct result of my imitation of Allison's breathing. If (as it appeared) our respiration had actually become synchronized, I thought, it was totally unconscious on both our parts.

In all of my graduate school discussions on the therapeutic relationship, including the fine points of transference and countertransference, I could not remember anyone ever mentioning the possibility of "catching" bodily behaviors. Intrigued and a bit bewildered, I took my observations to my supervisor. I still remember her look of startled skepticism. "What an odd hypothesis," she finally remarked, her cool tone clearly implying that my experience was not to be taken seriously. I was dumbfounded by her lack of curiosity and did not bring it up again in our supervision, but I never doubted my own sensations.

The following pages highlight a mere fraction of the research that leads to the conclusion that the body is centrally involved in empathy. A surprisingly large quantity of hard scientific evidence indicates that empathy is definitely more than a cognitive phenomenon. Empathy is, in fact, a highly integrated process involving both cognitive and somatic, brain and body. The cognitive aspects have been studied at length and are fairly well known, as discussed previously. The somatic side, how empathy is communicated and expressed through the body and from one body to another, is less well known. Neuroscience is the latest entrant into the study of empathy. This discussion includes areas of research that appear to have promise in helping us to further understand how the body, mind, and brain interact in the phenomenon of empathy.

## BODY TO BODY

Most of us automatically smile when another smiles at us. It is a normal human response that often has nothing to do with whether or not we know the other person. Our bodies (in this case, the muscles around our mouths) respond without any thinking being involved. Something similar happens when we see someone yawn—it is nearly impossible to stifle a sympathetic yawn. In fact, our bodies respond to other peoples' bodies all the time. Face-to-face contact is not even necessary. Can you remember the last time you enjoyed a sexy scene in a movie? Your body's response to that scene is an example of somatic empathy.

Freud's original ideas about conversion hysteria were among the first psychological theories to recognize the relationship between mind and body. Wilhelm Reich, one of Freud's most famous (and infamous) students, went off on his own tack to further Freud's early somatic theories and to develop Orgonomy, a mind–body integrated approach to treating mental illness (Reich, 1972). Since then, many well-known models and methods of both psychotherapy and body psychotherapy have given attention to the interconnectedness of mind and body (including bioenergetics, gestalt, cognitive–behavioral, somatic experiencing, sensory motor, body–mind psychotherapy, and eye movement desensitization and reprocessing). However, while psychological theories of empathy have existed for a long time, it is only recently that the body has been acknowledged as a significant player in the phenomenon of empathy.

Early on the scene were Elaine Hatfield and her colleagues at the University of Hawaii (Hsee et al., 1990). Hatfield became interested in how people seemed to catch the emotions of others and called the phenomenon *emotional contagion*. While the term had been used by others in a few previous articles (Gladstein, 1984; Schoenewolf, 1990; Stiff et al., 1988), it was Hatfield and her colleagues who fully developed the concept (Hatfield et al., 1994). Emotional contagion differs from previous definitions of empathy by identifying it as a circumstance of shared feelings. That is, in emotional contagion, I feel what you feel; I have "caught it." Pertinent to the thesis of this book, Hatfield acknowledged the body as a central vehicle for emotional contagion. Her theory includes the hypothesis that facial, vocal, and postural mimicry are centrally involved. The result of emotional contagion is a convergence of one person's emotions with another's (Hatfield et al., 1992). Further, Hatfield believed that emotional contagion is an inevitable consequence of human interaction. In the final theory section of this chapter, Mirroring and Mimicry, I will argue (and teach skills to demonstrate) that we can actually, easily, learn to choose whether or not we are infected by another's feelings; you are not a victim of another's feelings, but can decide yourself how much to feel with someone. But first the theory of somatic empathy needs to be clarified.

## DEVELOPING THE CONCEPT OF SOMATIC EMPATHY

In English, the terms *emotion* and *feeling* are nearly interchangeable. Many have endeavored to distinguish them, but none of the distinctions has really caught on. To date, Damasio has been the most successful. He proposed a very useful differentiation between emotion and feeling. According to him, emotion is composed of all things bodily: sensations, autonomic and somatic muscular changes, movement, and so forth. Feeling, on the other hand, is the label that describes the summation of these body states once they are recognized by the mind. Therefore, a feeling is the cortex's name for an experience, or awareness, of emotion (Damasio, 1994, 1999, 2003). Next time you identify that you are sad, angry, or happy, take a minute to notice the bodily sensations and muscular tensions that underlie that feeling. For example, when angry, you might detect tension in your shoulders or jaw, and heat in your face. According to Damasio, those are exactly what constitute emotion.

There is a logical progression to understanding the existence of somatic empathy. My nine-point progressive argument is summarized and then discussed in detail below.

1. Each feeling (happy, sad, angry, surprised, afraid, etc.) has a specific, observable somatic manifestation: Facial expression and body posture (or movement) are achieved through a distribution of muscular tension and relaxation.
2. Every feeling is associated with a particular pattern of nonobservable activity: autonomic nervous system (ANS) changes in heart rate, skin temperature, and so forth, as well as the common physical sensations that are normally associated with feelings.
3. The observable characteristics of facial expression and posture can be consciously copied (mimicked or mirrored) voluntarily, muscle by muscle.
4. Copying the muscular changes associated with a particular feeling induces the associated ANS reactions. One body intentionally empathizes with the other.
5. Muscle patterns also can be (and often are) imitated unconsciously. During normal situations of interpersonal contact, it is common for people to mirror one another's facial and postural muscular patterns (more about this, below).
6. Unconscious mirroring will also induce associated ANS reactions and feelings. One person is feeling what the other is feeling but does not realize it.
7. Instinctive synchrony of affective and ANS states in others may have an evolutionary role for survival of the species.

8. Sometimes somatic empathy manifests as what seems to be mind reading, intuition, or ESP, which can of course be useful. However, it can also have negative consequences for the unconscious participant.

9. The activity of the brain's mirror neurons may account for some portion of unconscious mimicry.

## DISCUSSION

1. **Each feeling (happy, sad, angry, surprised, afraid, etc.) has a specific, observable somatic manifestation: Facial expression and body posture (or movement) are achieved through a distribution of muscular tension and relaxation.**

The commonality of emotional facial expressions has been researched for nearly 150 years. In 1867, Charles Darwin surveyed missionaries and others who were living around the world in different cultures: Australian Aboriginal, Indian, African, Native American, Chinese, Malayan, and Ceylonese. He wanted to find out if affects, as well as their observable expressions, were consistent across various cultures. When visiting each culture, he asked to be shown how individuals looked when angry, sad, happy, and so forth. The results of his survey showed consistency for all ranges of affect across unrelated and often isolated cultures, as well as common somatic expression of those affects (Darwin, 1872/1965). That is, the world over, people smile when happy, frown and shed tears when sad, grit teeth when angry, open mouths wide in surprise, and so on. Since Darwin's groundbreaking study, others have followed suit to demonstrate the universality of emotional expression.

Paul Ekman (2003) confirmed Darwin's early findings. In 1965, he took photographs of Americans expressing a variety of feelings to an isolated tribe in Papua, New Guinea. He showed the photos to many of the natives—some who had had contact with other cultures and some who had not. All of the natives were easily able to identify the feelings being expressed in those pictures. This was possible, of course, because the natives in that isolated tribe also showed their feelings in the same ways.

2. **Every feeling is associated with a particular pattern of nonobservable activity: ANS changes in heart rate, skin temperature, respiration, and so forth, as well as the common physical sensations that are normally associated with feelings.**

   Again, Paul Ekman and his colleagues conducted studies both in the United States and in West Sumatra, and found a commonality of ANS changes across cultural bounds (Ekman et al., 1983; Levenson, 1992; Levenson et al., 1990, 1992). In particular, Ekman and colleagues (1983) were able to demonstrate specific changes in heart rate and skin temperature. They found elevated heart rates for anger, fear, and sadness, and decreased heart rates for happiness, disgust, and surprise. Skin temperature increased the most with anger and lowered the most with fear and sadness.

3. **The observable characteristics of facial expression and posture can be consciously copied (mimicked or mirrored) voluntarily, muscle by muscle.**

   This one you can try for yourself. Together with a friend, partner, or client, mimic as closely as you can the facial expression, posture, or movement of the other. Pay attention to what happens in your own body during each step in the process.

4. **Copying the muscular changes associated with a particular feeling induces the associated ANS reactions. One body intentionally empathizes with another. (Structured mirroring exercises follow in the sections Mirroring and Mimicry, Facial and Postural Awareness, and Postural Mirroring.)**

   Studies in this area are very compelling, as the subjects in most of them had no idea that the researchers were interested in emotions. For instance, Strack and colleagues (1988) made subjects simulate a smiling position of the mouth by having them hold a pen between their teeth. When the subjects subsequently read humorous material, they tended to rate it as more amusing than those subjects who did not have their mouths surreptitiously forced into a smile. Levenson and colleagues (1990) conducted three studies instructing subjects precisely which facial muscles to move and how to move them to replicate specific affects. They found statistically significant correlations between the artificially instructed expressions and the feelings the subjects reported. They further discovered that the subject's ANS responses were consistent with the target emotions. For both results, subjects who were the most precise in their replication of the specific movements or expressions showed the greatest correlations. In addition, body posture has been studied. Duclos and associates (1989) directed subjects into specific postures. Unbeknownst to the subjects, each posture was typical of fear, sadness, or anger. Their results clearly demonstrated that emotional postures have an effect on feelings. Duclos concluded that when people copy another's emotional posture, they are more likely to share the same feeling (aka empathy). There is clearly an afferent feedback system (body to brain) involving body position and muscle tone that may correspond to Damasio's (1994) concept of somatic markers.

In the early 2000s, Dr. Maggie Shiffrar at Rutgers University in New Jersey and I conducted two studies on postural mirroring and somatic empathy (Rothschild & Shiffrar, 2003, 2004). Our subjects copied the postures of models who were silently remembering emotionally charged situations from their pasts. Not only did the subjects come to experience many of the same body sensations and feelings as the models, they were also prone to see or hear associated imagery and also often appeared to be mind readers, correctly guessing the situations that were being remembered (but never spoken about) by the models. Exciting as these preliminary data are, our samples were far too small and variables all too difficult to control to draw any hard conclusions. However, added to the research that has gone before, our premise still looks promising. (See later in this chapter as well as the appendix for a more detailed description of this pilot project.)

5. **Muscle patterns also can be (and often are) imitated unconsciously. During normal situations of interpersonal contact, it is**

**common for people to mirror one another's breathing, facial, and postural muscular patterns.**

This is the area of research that is the most comprehensive. Numerous studies confirm that people unconsciously mirror each other all of the time. Morris (1979) called it a *postural echo*, while Hatfield and colleagues (1992, 1994) called it *emotional contagion*. Hess and Blairy (2001) surreptitiously filmed the faces of subjects while they observed videos of people expressing various feelings. They found that the subjects consistently unconsciously mimicked the happy, angry, and sad expressions on the faces of the people in the videos. You may also have observed what Zajonc and colleagues (1987) confirmed: Many couples who stay together over many years grow to look like each other. The most logical explanation for this phenomenon is that couples tend to mimic each other's expression habitually, eventually leading to an actual observable, physical change. I have noticed that long-term couples often have the same mannerisms—how they use their hands or nod when they talk or listen—regardless of whether I am seeing them together or individually. Interestingly, I have even noted that able-bodied spouses can take on some of the mannerisms of disabled partners, making them look somewhat disabled themselves even though they are not. And this may be at least some of the reason that children often share the same facial expressions, gait, and other behaviors as their parents or older siblings.

Researchers have also observed that individuals chatting together in pairs often mirror each other's movements (Hatfield et al., 1994; Kendon, 1970; LaFrance, 1976, 1979). This one you can easily confirm yourself. At your local café or favorite restaurant, or even across the dinner table, observe those who are in close conversation and notice how often one copies the other's facial expression (e.g., smile, frown), gesture (e.g., drumming fingers, nodding), or postural element (e.g., resting head on hand, crossing legs). Remember also to pay attention to their feet, as foot tapping and leg swinging are also often shared behaviors.

Can facial mirroring occur even when subjects have no idea they are being exposed to emotional facial expressions? In an intriguing study, subjects were shown a series of faces with neutral expressions interspersed with very quick flashes of faces with happy or angry expressions. The emotional faces were shown with such speed that it was not possible for the subjects to register seeing them consciously. Nonetheless, they mimicked the emotional facial expressions (Dimberg, 1982; Dimberg et al., 2000).

6. **Unconscious mirroring will also induce associated ANS reactions and feelings. One person is feeling what the other is feeling but does not realize it.**

   In the aforementioned study by Hess and Blairy (2001), it was also found that subjects noticed changes in their own moods that corresponded to the expression they were unconsciously mimicking. Levenson and Ruef (1997) found that when one person copies another's facial expression, both the feeling and emotional (physical) responses are set in motion. They identified a direct link between facial expressions and feelings, smiles being particularly powerful for eliciting pleasant feelings. In two simple experiments, Paccalin and Jeannerod (2000) demonstrated that sedentary spectators synchronize their breathing with the respiration of a performing athlete. They also noted that people experienced muscle contractions in sympathy with the effort of others, for example while watching someone exert great effort to loosen the lid on a well-sealed jar, or when watching downhill skiing on television. These usually unconscious tendencies are so universal that you will likely notice them in yourself when you are paying mindful attention. It is also common to react to another's pain. Hodges and Wegner noted, "observing a person who touches a stove and winces causes us to wince, and, via physiological feedback from the set of muscles required to wince, I too can almost feel the burn" (1997, p. 316).

7. **Instinctive synchrony of affective and ANS states in others may have an evolutionary role for survival of the species.**

   Because facial mimicry makes it possible to experience the emotional and feeling state of another, Levenson and associates (1990) saw it as more than a simple social signal. They believed that such behavior may serve as the basis for the creation of empathy, including attachment and bonding. In other studies, a clear connection between postural mimicry and rapport was found. As people copy one another's postures and movements, they get to know each other better and feel more positive about each other (Levenson & Ruef, 1997). When in danger, a whole group of people can instinctively synchronize their nervous systems to better respond to the danger. The phenomenon of menstrual synchrony may have an evolutionary purpose (McClintock, 1971; Weller & Weller, 1993). Perhaps it served the needs of primitive clans for women to be fertile at the same time. Though I could not find scientific references, I have begun to wonder about the function of the highly contagious gag reflex. Perhaps it played a significant role in the survival of early hunter-gatherer tribes. Imagine a starving group coming upon a new plant or a dead animal. They all begin to eat hungrily. Then, one vomits and they all reflexively follow in turn. If the plant was poisoned or the meat contaminated, lives may be spared and the survival of the tribe protected.

8. **Sometimes somatic empathy manifests as what seems to be mind reading, intuition, or ESP, which can of course be useful. However, it can also have negative consequences for the unconscious participant.**

As described above, one person's emotion can be caught by another, when facial or postural mirroring creates a similar internal experience, This hypothesis is supported by several studies which demonstrate that emotions can be created by mimicking muscle contractions associated with particular emotions (Adolphs et al., 2000; Blairy et al., 1999; Duclos et al., 1989; Hess & Blairy, 2001). Further, in the aforementioned pilot studies, Shiffrar and I documented preliminary evidence that more than emotion may be received via the action of mimicking another's posture. Many of our subjects intuited actual information, correctly guessing themes and actual situations in the memories of the models whose postures they were copying (Rothschild & Shiffrar, 2003, 2004).

A 1988 study by Miller, Stiff, and Ellis predicted the current wave of interest in compassion fatigue. They found that emotional contagion was a precursor to burnout among human service workers. Predictably, workers who were most easily infected by the feelings of those they were assisting were the most vulnerable to burnout.

9. **The activity of the brain's mirror neurons may account for some portion of unconscious mimicry.**
   As early as 1995, Fadiga and colleagues were speculating about the existence of a visual–motor matching system. The discovery of mirror neurons confirmed their hunch. Such a system accounts for the common automatic reactions we all have when we observe actions in others. Yawning and laughter are the most familiar behaviors that people habitually copy.

Considered in their entirety, the nine points outlined above make a solid case that empathy is more than just a cognitive and emotional mechanism. Body processes are intimately involved. Somatic empathy is expressed through the motor division of the nervous system (somatic nerves control the skeletal muscles, and autonomic nerves control the visceral muscles) and is perceived through the sensory nervous system: the five senses (exteroceptors) and balance, internal sensations, and proprioception (interoceptors).

The following is a rather extreme example of what body-to-body empathy may look like during a therapy session.

Gavin, a new child psychologist in private practice, particularly enjoyed using play therapy and the sand tray with his young patients. Observing one of his sessions through a one-way mirror was a fascinating experience. The interaction between Gavin and his patient was akin to watching a game of emotional "Follow the leader." When the child smiled, Gavin smiled. The child frowned; Gavin frowned. The patient raised her eyebrows, and Gavin followed suit. No facial expression was initiated by the girl that was not mimicked by her therapist shortly thereafter. Gavin also mimicked his young client's breathing at times. Sighs appeared to be particularly contagious. Meeting with Gavin later that day, I asked him what the child had been feeling and what his own feelings had been during that hour. His oral report was congruent with what I had seen. He was catching the child's feelings. When I asked him how that might be possible, he had no clue. But when we looked at a video of the session together, he began to laugh. He saw it immediately: "My face is always an exact copy of hers!" Once I pointed it out, he could clearly see when he mimicked her breathing. By copying the girl's facial expression as well as breathing pattern, he tuned into and caught her feelings. It was unconscious; he was not trying to do it. He was truly surprised when he saw himself.

Of course, not all therapists mimic to the same degree that Gavin demonstrated. Some are especially self-aware and body aware and notice when they are and are not copying the client's expressions and breathing. Others may mimic purposefully to empathize with or to get a taste of the client's feelings. But plenty of practitioners, like Gavin, habitually and unconsciously copy client facial expressions, breathing patterns, and postures. Not only are they unconscious of the process, most important, they are clueless about the price their mimicry may be exacting from them. In Gavin's session, the risk was minimal as the shared feelings were pleasant. But what if the client had been feeling fear or anger? The next sections build on the hypothesis of somatic empathy with additional illustrations of active postural and facial mirroring. Guidance in becoming more aware of somatic empathy between you and your clients is offered, including exercises for practice. It is hoped that by the end of this chapter, you will be better equipped to identify when your feelings, body sensations, and actions are the result of empathy with your client and when they are not. Subsequent chapters offer additional practical tools for putting you in charge of how—and how much—you empathize with your clients, giving you the choice, increasing empathy when you want a greater sense of the client, turning it down when you want to maintain a more objective perspective.

### *Mirroring And Mimicry*

*Help me never to judge another until I have walked*
*in his moccasins.*
　　　　　—Native American prayer

As the saying goes, "Imitation is the most sincere form of flattery." It is also the quickest way to be infected by what another person is feeling. As discussed above, the human tendency to copy facial expressions, postures, respiration, and mannerisms is a common, if usually unconscious, feature of interaction with others. Chartrand and Bargh (1999) called it the *chameleon effect*. In fact, it has been found that people with a high tendency for empathy will copy others in these ways more than those who test low for empathy (Lakin et al., 2003). Mimicry is also the basis for many things we learn including speech, table manners, and tying our shoes. You might even consider whether your therapeutic style has elements of mimicking a therapist you have admired or whether any of your colleagues resemble one of their mentors. Recently, an old colleague actually confided to me that it took her years to lose the foreign accent she had unconsciously acquired from her favorite supervisor. The unique styles, mannerisms, and speech inflections of popular clinicians have often (and sometimes unfortunately) been copied; examples include Sigmund Freud in the 1950s, and Fritz Perls and Carl Rogers in the 1960s and 1970s.

Though facial and postural mimicry are usually automatic, by increasing your self-awareness and body awareness you can learn to observe for yourself how much you imitate those around you and how often they imitate you. The next time you see a client, have lunch with a friend, or talk with your spouse, check how often aspects of your posture have become the same as theirs. Also try leaning your head on your hand or crossing your legs. Then see how long it takes for the other person to do the same. You can become a scientist, testing imitative behavior in your own professional and social circles.

## ROOTS OF THE HYPOTHESIS

In the late 1960s, one of my closest friends, Nancy Curtis, was studying to be a physical therapist. Sometimes, while we were strolling down a street, she would notice a stranger walking in a manner she considered interesting. Unabashedly, she would proceed to mimic the gait of that stranger as I followed behind. She would then tell me what she felt in her body, where that person might have an injury, or some such. At first I was embarrassed by her behavior and worried about what would happen if she was caught, that is, detected by her subject. I did not want her to shame anyone. Nancy insisted she knew what she was doing and no one would get hurt. She was careful, she reassured me, only to mimic at a discreet distance; her subjects never saw what she was doing, never noticed. After witnessing her actions several times, I became reassured that she never exaggerated her mimicry; it never became mockery. She was subtle enough that anyone looking at her would, if they even noticed, just think she had the different gait herself. I was more aware of it because she told me what she was doing.

Nancy's strange behavior, purposely mimicking another's movement, was her way of practicing gait diagnosis (analyzing how someone walks), a critically important tool for a physical therapist. She found that she could make the most accurate evaluation if she could feel in her own body what was going on in the hip, ankle, or foot of her subject (and later, her patients). As a novice, for her, mere visual observation was not enough.

I became fascinated by the practice and, just for fun, asked Nancy to teach me how to do it. Actually, it was quite easy, and I caught on quickly. So I learned to copy (mimic) the gaits of people walking in front of me. At first, gait mimicry was a game for me, just an interesting way to find out what was going on in someone's body as well as to learn more about what my friend was studying. It also stirred some fascinating conversations about body mechanics with Nancy. I became pretty good at it, and my diagnosis was often in agreement with hers.

A few years later as I began to study psychotherapy and body psychotherapy, I became generally more self-aware as I practiced various training exercises and remembered what Nancy had taught me. That piqued my interest in body mimicry even more, and I applied her method sometimes on my own. Eventually I began to realize that copying a stranger's gait changed more than just my way of walking. Sometimes an unexpected emotion stirred in me, and I would suddenly find myself in a different mood. For example, following behind a youth with a confident stride, I might feel a little cocky myself. Following others, I might feel sad, angry, irritated, happy, and so on. On some occasions, visual images and thoughts emerged that I could not account for. I began to wonder: By copying another's manner of walking, was I actually getting a little peek into what it was like to be them? When I copied a gait, was I walking in their moccasins, so to speak?

As discussed in the previous section, it is well documented that observation of another's movement alone can influence the same behavior in the observer. Chartrand and Bargh (1999) showed that experimental subjects sitting with a research associate who was cued to scratch his nose tended to follow suit. The same resulted when the associate shook his foot. Imitation is innate. Infants as young as 42 minutes old have been seen to mimic the facial expression of a parent (Meltzoff & Moore, 1983, 1989). Even more crucial, my discovery has also been found by researchers: observing another's movement can also influence emotions as well as more complex behaviors. In their classic studies, Bandura and colleagues (1963) demonstrated that children who watched a film showing aggressive behavior increased their levels of aggression through imitation. Just the experience of adopting an emotion-associated posture can stimulate a change in emotional experience (Duclos et al., 1989). All told, it is undeniable, as Niedenthal and colleagues (2005) concluded: The body is an integral repository for social and emotional information processing.

What more might be happening when people imitate each other's behavior and expressions? Based on the study by Bandura and colleagues and the like, we know feelings are communicated through imitated actions. Hess and Blairy (2001) found that happiness and sadness were exchanged when a subject observed and then mimicked a facial expression. On these bases, it becomes reasonable to wonder just what information might be exchanged between two people when each emulates the other's behavior, posture, or facial expression. Perhaps you already have an idea; you may have experienced something similar yourself. Have you ever known by your own sensations or feelings how your client, child, friend, or spouse was feeling before they told you? Have you ever seen in your mind's eye what your client later described? The next section further clarifies at least one of the mechanisms at work in these phenomena and the basis for my pilot research with Maggie Shiffrar, as discussed above and below.

## POSTURAL MIRRORING

*Postural mirroring* is the term that has been coined for the mimicry of another's physical posture, including facial expressions, and the communication of emotional and other information that often accompanies such behavior. It appears the term was used first by dance therapists. They have long utilized postural mirroring as a common tool of their trade. A dance therapist will use it to get a feel for her clients, and also to give feedback on what is observed and felt (Siegel, 1984). When a client stands or moves in a certain way, the dance therapist will follow suit. The practice was likely inspired by Wilhelm Reich, the father of body psychotherapy (now often called somatic psychology). In his classic *Character Analysis*, he wrote, "The patient's expressive movements involuntarily bring about an imitation in our own organism. By [actively] imitating these movements, we 'sense' and understand the expression in ourselves and, consequently, in the patient" (Reich, 1972, p. 362).

Postural mirroring involves mimicry—whether conscious or unconscious. Sometimes we do it on purpose. Anytime we copy a posture, an expression, or the breathing pattern of another person, we are using postural mirroring. As children, we mimicked our parents, teachers, and older siblings in order to learn many tasks: holding a pencil, playing hopscotch, and so on. Anytime a parent, teacher, or sibling said, "Watch and then do it like me," we were being encouraged to mimic. We also mimicked others as we learned how to behave in different milieus: at the table, at school, on the playground, and so forth. (While living in Denmark, I was often—sometimes too often—admonished to mimic those around me rather than "behaving like a typical American.") Sometimes children take their behavioral mimicry a step further toward actual postural mirroring when they try to take on the movement, mannerisms, or speech of a parent, friend, actor, or pop star they admire, trying to act and be just like them.

Next time you are at a park or a shopping center, take a look at pairs of parents and children. How does the child sit, stand, or walk like the parent? Posture depends somewhat on build, but it is also habituated through (conscious and unconscious) mimicry. Some families walk erect, some slump. Not only does bone structure determine a common family posture, but mimicry also plays a role. Notice your own children at the dinner table. Whom do they sit like? Whom do their manners remind you of: their friends, you, your spouse? Manners are also learned through mimicry.

Consider for a minute or two how you sit or stand in relationship to the individuals you help—you might want to pay attention in one or two sessions to get an idea. Start to notice when you assume their posture, wholly or partially. Do you have a tendency to cross your legs, sit on the edge of your seat, slump, or breathe like your client? Do you copy their expression onto your own face in an attempt to communicate that you understand what they are feeling—smiling, lowering your eyebrows, clenching your teeth? Have you ever slowed your breathing in the hope that your panicking client would follow suit, calming his own panicked gasps? If you answer yes to any of these questions, then you already know (or are learning) something about mirroring. Continuing to pay attention to your own posture and expressions when you are with your clients will further increase your awareness of how much you do or do not mirror. In a few pages, I will begin to look at how you might use that awareness to better care for yourself during and following therapy sessions.

## POSTURAL MIRRORING AND EMPATHY

As mentioned previously, empathy has to do with feeling what another is feeling. Since mirroring appears to enhance that likelihood, it just may be a major mechanism of empathy. You can try this yourself with a client, friend, or family member: Consciously mimic his respiration pattern, posture, or facial expression. Then guess what he is feeling and ask if you are correct. You can also try the following more structured exercise with a friend or colleague.

Both of you stand up and each take stock of your own physical and emotional state to establish a baseline. What sensations are you aware of (temperature, aches and pains, tension, relaxation, etc.)? What are you feeling emotionally? Next, follow, literally, in the other person's footsteps. Have your friend walk normally just ahead of you. To the best of your ability, copy their posture and gait, remembering to include placement of arms and hands, if you can see them. Do this for a minute or so. Notice what you have to do with your own body to walk like your friend. How are you using your muscles and balance differently? Be as specific as possible. Then take stock of what you are feeling emotionally. Is it the same or different than before you walked like them? Compare with each other what you were sensing in your bodies and feeling in your emotions while walking in this way. Then you can switch and have your friend copy you. It will not happen every time, but you may find quite a bit of correspondence in what each of you were sensing and feeling.

This exercise demonstrates the essence of postural mirroring: mimicking another's posture or movement, which usually results in empathizing with the other's physical and emotional state. It is that simple. Actors have been doing this for centuries, often using postural mirroring to become the person they are to play on screen or stage. Some actors will spend many hours observing, in person or on film, an individual they are to portray, consciously mimicking posture, mannerisms, and speech. One of the most successful of these was Jamie Foxx in his portrayal of Ray Charles in the movie *Ray*, for which he won a Best Actor Oscar in 2005. Some viewers said they could not distinguish the two.

## FEELING WHAT THE OTHER FEELS

I have informally instructed the above exercise and a more formal mirroring exercise (see the chapter Conscious Mirroring) with hundreds of psychotherapists and body psychotherapists. Predictably, physical experiences are consistently parallel because the exercises involve the mimicking of posture and movement. Also predictably, based on the research reviewed in previous sections, there is consistent emotional resonance—partners experiencing the same feelings. What accounts for this? Do physical movement and posture also communicate somato-emotional states that underpin feeling? Experiments on posture mimicry by Duclos and colleagues (1989) support this premise. They do not, however, explain the mechanism. We need to look further.

Antonio Damasio's (1994) concept of somatic markers, as discussed earlier, may account for at least some of this phenomenon. To review his theory, Damasio posited that the experience of emotions is composed of body sensations that are elicited in response to various stimuli. Those sensations, and their related emotions, become encoded and then stored as implicit memories associated with the stimuli that originally evoked them (possibly similar to classical conditioning). Remember: Damasio clarified a distinction between emotion and feeling. The former includes all things physical: sensations, facial expressions, muscle contractions, autonomic fluctuations, and so on. When the aggregate of that body information reaches awareness in the frontal cortex, a label is then applied—angry, scared, sad, happy, or some such—which is what he calls feeling. According to Damasio, a feeling is the awareness of emotion. Following Damasio's theory, it becomes logical that feelings could be communicated through mirroring. For example, when I mimic the posture and expression of my sad client, I am mimicking much of what constitutes his emotion (for example, furrowing my brow, dropping the sides of my mouth, lowering my head, depressing my chest, etc.). As noted previously, adopting expressions and postures associated with emotions can stir the same familiar internal sensations (ache in the gut, fullness in the throat, even tears, etc.). My own frontal cortex assesses the information from my body and applies the label *sad*. That is one way (if not a major way) that I could "know" what my client is feeling at any one time. There are quotation marks around the word *know* because it is, of course, possible to misjudge. I would rarely (if ever) want to tell a client "I know what you are feeling" before he had told me—both because I could be wrong and because I prefer not to lead a client in that way. Nonetheless, the information can be useful at times.

I can take this a step further, though, because an additional phenomenon is common when one mirrors another. Often (though not as consistently as with physical and emotional correspondence) a strong correlation of imagery, thoughts, and actual knowledge is communicated between two people. Sometimes we call it intuition or ESP.

## MIRRORING RESEARCH

During a pilot study conducted in 2003 (Rothschild & Shiffrar, 2003) as part of a training course in Europe, I asked one of the group sponsors to silently model his posture after something reminiscent of an emotional situation from his life and to hold it steady for a few minutes with no movement. He struck a pose with one arm elevated behind him, the other reaching outward and down in front of him; his feet were about a foot and a half apart, placed one in front of the other, his torso bent slightly forward.

No words or verbal information of any kind were communicated to the group members. Half of the group was instructed to copy his posture, the other half just to observe it. Following the exercise, the group members filled out questionnaires indicating the physical sensations, feelings, thoughts, and images they experienced, and to guess what the model may have been remembering. After the group members had a chance to note their personal responses and fill out their questionnaires, the sponsor was allowed to speak. He told us that he had remembered being a teenager, saving a younger sibling from drowning in a stream in the woods. The responses to the questionnaires from the mirroring half of the group were fascinating. No one had known what the situation was—none had any similar life experience, so no somatic markers for anything similar. However, several in that half felt a powerful effort or struggle in their own bodies and a sense of urgency. Generally they reported feeling strong and focused. Fear was the predominant affect. Some had visual images of being outdoors and of water or trees. Considering that the remembered scenario was something totally outside any of their life experience, and for that matter outside of the average person's experience, the results were quite astonishing.

We did a second experiment with the same group, same procedure as above. The second sponsor modeled a posture in memory of something that would be quite familiar to almost anyone (i.e., most would have somatic markers for it): feeding her infant grandchild. The results were intriguing. Among both the mirroring and the observing halves, there was an extremely high correlation of sensations, emotions, and images (the mirroring group having the highest). In addition, the majority easily guessed that the situation had something to do with caring for a young child. Likely, these higher correlations could be predicted since just about every adult has somatic markers for caring for a baby in some way or another.

## USING CONSCIOUS POSTURAL MIRRORING TO GAIN INFORMATION

Though the aim of this book is to reduce risks to therapist well-being, including unconscious mirroring, it is important to at least mention the possible advantage of conscious postural mirroring as an aid to the therapeutic process. When you want to get a literal feel for what it's like to be in your client's skin, you can consciously mirror some aspect of his or her behavior or expression. I tried this when I worked with Fred, a new college graduate who had come into therapy to address his anxiety about dealing with authority on his first professional job. Though he'd grown up with a violent father who had beaten him regularly as a child, Fred did not see or feel any connection between his childhood trauma and his current fear of standing up to his boss.

One afternoon, Fred arrived for his weekly session deeply (and unusually) depressed. He had been thinking about suicide, he said, but had no idea why. Admittedly, I was not sure either. To explore what might be going on, I asked him to describe what "suicidal" felt like in his body. To see if it could help my understanding, as I listened to his somatic report I tuned in by copying his flat facial expression and slumped posture. Almost immediately, I began to experience in my own body the sense of deadness Fred had just described to me. It reminded me of the freeze response that is an instinctive reaction to inescapable threat. All at once, a light bulb flashed in my mind. "Fred," I asked, "have you ever seen a mouse that's been caught by a cat?" He nodded. "What does the mouse do?" I prodded. "It plays dead," he replied, his face beginning to brighten with interest. We then discussed the protective function of freezing for all prey, both animals and people. Finally, I asked Fred if he'd ever reacted that way himself.

"Yeah," he said softly, "when my dad beat me." As his father hit him, he told me, his body would lose all power and "go dead." For the first time, he made both a cognitive and felt connection between his childhood horrors and his current emotional state. It seemed a light bulb had also come on in Fred's mind. As he began to talk thoughtfully about his own "internal mouse," his body posture gradually became more upright and animated, and by the end of the session he reported that his thoughts of suicide had receded. Could I have helped Fred make this breakthrough with talk alone? Perhaps, but it would likely have entailed several more sessions full of the usual conversational roundabouts, byways, and detours. Instead, by mirroring him, I was able to quickly feel and then understand Fred's deadness.

I have found this to be a useful therapeutic tool. However, there is an important caveat: While purposefully synchronizing with your client can often provide added insight or even jump-start a stalled session, be aware that the data you pick up are not infallible. Just as gaps can occur between speaker and listener in verbal communication, so can somatic communication be distorted by your own filters. If, for example, you mimic your client's head tilt and get a feeling of anxiety in your chest, your client may indeed be anxious. But it also could be that you habitually tilt your head in that way when *you* are anxious, so that mirroring the client's head tilt triggers your own somatic markers for anxiety. Be sure to check out your bodily hunches with your clients and not jump to conclusions.

### THE RISKS OF UNCONSCIOUS POSTURAL MIRRORING

I learned about some of the risks of postural mirroring the hard way, through discomforting and distressing personal experiences with my clients. While there were several difficult incidents, one in particular stands out (Rothschild, 2004b).

I had been seeing Ronald for about a year when, one day, he came to his session absolutely furious with me. He was so angry he could neither face me nor speak. He had scheduled a double session, and during the first hour he sat turned away from me with his head bowed, the rest of his body very tense and slightly shaking. I tried to make contact with him using my usual supply of therapeutic phrases: "You seem very angry." "It must be very difficult for you." And so forth. He would not respond to any of it. Each effort at contact and empathy seemed like a cartoon bubble, departing my lips, floating out into the room a foot or so, and then falling flat on the floor with a thump. Finally, I told myself to keep quiet, let him be in his anger, and wait for him to be ready to contact me. It seemed as though it was going to take a while and, frankly, I began to get a little bored. Remembering an exercise I had learned during body psychotherapy training, I decided to mimic his posture, just to see if I could gain any insight into what was going on with him. However, I wasn't prepared for the physical and emotional impact it would later have on me.

Shortly after I copied Ronald's posture, he began to speak to me and tell me how angry he was. Could he have sensed my mimicry even though he was not looking? Was it possible that my nonverbal empathetic posture communicated something to him more potent than words? Or was the timing coincidental? Actually, I do not know. But what Ronald perceived is not pertinent here. Most important is that I forgot: I had first mirrored him consciously, but I continued unconsciously as I became absorbed in his words and emotional expression. We went on with the session, resolving some (but not all) of his anger. He felt better when he left.

When he closed the door and I had only myself to focus on, I found I did not feel better. In fact, I was in a rage. I was furious. It was very uncomfortable, and I became quite distressed. I tried to work it out by yelling, stomping, and hitting a pillow, but it would not abate. I tried to figure out why I was so angry. Was I angry with Ronald? Something in my life? Something from my past? I could not figure it out. My upset went on for several hours, barely containable as I saw other clients. Finally, when

I was free in the late afternoon, I called a close friend and colleague. I had to tell someone how upset and confused I was and get some support. My friend grasped the situation immediately. She asked me, "When did it start? What were you doing?" When I recounted the session with Ronald, she simply said, "Oh, Babette! You were mirroring him." As soon as she said it, I remembered what I had begun doing consciously and then had forgotten. With that awareness, my body shifted, automatically regaining my own posture. I exhaled deeply. I immediately felt better. It was as though my friend had thrown warm water on me; the anger just melted off. That feeling of anger had not belonged to me—I had adopted it from Ronald!

I learned an important lesson that day: Never take postural mirroring for granted. Always pay attention, whether conscious or making the unconscious conscious. And make sure to reverse it during sessions or, at the latest, immediately after a client leaves. Never forget its power.

## MIRRORING VERSUS PROJECTIVE IDENTIFICATION

To some therapists, what happened between Ronald and me might look like a textbook example of projective identification—a case of Ronald putting his uncomfortable feelings into me and thereby inducing my fury. I could not disagree more. I was a full participant in the process: Only after I actively mirrored Ronald did I begin to feel angry. But while my mimicry was entirely conscious—if later forgotten—I believe that this kind of brain-to-brain/body-to-body communication occurs at an unconscious level between clients and therapists all the time. The next time you feel that you may be suffering from the impact of a projective identification, you may need to look no further than your own body to discover whether you have mimicked your client's posture, facial expression, or breathing pattern. Routinely adding such a simple step could eliminate blaming clients for feelings that are, in fact, rooted in your own naturally responsive neural circuitry.

There is liberation here, particularly for therapists who often find themselves on the edge of emotional overload. Active awareness of your own role in absorbing clients' feelings can help you to control the contagion. Once you become aware of your mimicry, any movement or inner dialogue that brings you back to the sensations and feelings of your own body—and out of synchronization with the client—will help you to apply the empathy brakes. You might stretch, take a drink of water, get up to fetch a pen, or write some notes. Alternatively or in addition, remind yourself that you have been sampling or resonating with your client's feelings, that they are not your own. These steps will not short-circuit your caring or compassion, but rather will allow you to return to yourself, to a place of clarity, presence, and helpful attunement to your client.

## MAKING UNCONSCIOUS MIRRORING CONSCIOUS

By now, you may have realized that postural mirroring is something you do with clients habitually and unconsciously. You might even be beginning to wonder if some of the feelings you have during and following client sessions have something to do with postural mirroring. So, if the process is unconscious, you may be wondering, what can you do about it? How do you make it conscious?

Basically, mindfulness (being aware in the present moment) is all that is needed for you to pay attention to yourself. Constant attention is not necessary. Just make sure to check in with yourself from time to time. Start with something doable. For instance, with each client this week, take a mini-break to check on your own posture, breathing, and such midway through each session. You could negotiate with your client to set a mild-sounding alarm (I use one called "meditation bell") to remind you both to stop what you are doing and each check in with yourself—it is a good thing for the client to do also. You might do the same, for that matter, during meetings with your colleagues and time spent with family and friends. If you find doing that once in each hour is useful, you might consider increasing it to two or three times. Do not try to do too much at once; small steps will be better. In several of the skill-building sections that follow in this chapter, additional techniques and strategies for increasing body and self-awareness are described in detail.

## WHEN A CLIENT FEELS YOUR PAIN

Somatic empathy, of course, is a two-way street. Our clients often unconsciously adopt our body patterns and take on our corresponding emotional states. Many therapists instinctively foster this process. When, for example, you slow your own breathing and your anxious clients subsequently slow theirs, you are likely engaging their capacity for unconscious mirroring, possibly their mirror neurons too. No words need be exchanged for a client to gradually match your slower respiration and begin to calm down. But beware: If your calm state is contagious, so too is your agitation. When a client is unusually out of sorts on a day when you have not been in a good mood, you might consider if your client is tuning in to you. Clients can pick up all sorts of feelings and states from the therapist. Here is a lighter example.

One morning, upon returning to Copenhagen (my then home) after a long visit to the United States, I was suffering from a particularly challenging case of jet lag. Though exhausted and headachy, I jumped right into my usual work schedule. At the end of my afternoon session with Helle, I asked her, per usual, "How are you feeling?" Helle proceeded to describe my jet lag in precise detail. "I feel very tired, and there's a feeling of pressure in my forehead," she said, rubbing her eyebrows. "I also feel an odd heaviness in my chest. And I'm hungry, though I shouldn't be. I ate a good lunch just before I came."

I suggested to Helle that she stand up and walk around the room, hoping that the physical activity would move her out of my somatic sphere of influence and back into contact with her own body. After pacing for a minute or two, she returned to her chair, noticeably more energetic. "My exhaustion and hunger have disappeared!" she reported. I then told her how I was feeling, that she had described my sensations precisely. We then had a discussion about how picking up other people's states affected her in her daily life.

Since awareness is an important part of the process for controlling the mirroring dance, we spent a few minutes tracking down how Helle had caught my state. In retracing her steps—and postures—she realized she had rested her head on her hand as I had tiredly done. That ordinary act of unconscious mimicry was enough to make her vulnerable to feeling my jet lag and the California-time-zone hunger that accompanied it.

As mentioned earlier, conscious mimicry can be used to facilitate a greater knowledge and rapport with your client. But whether it happens consciously or unconsciously, mimicry and the awareness of mimicry are "a kind of natural 'social glue' that produces empathic understanding and even greater [support] between people, without their having to intend or try to have this happen" (Chartrand & Bargh, 1999, p. 897).

## Skill Building

### Your Personal Empathy Dial

It may be helpful for you to think of your own empathy as being controlled by a dial. Turn the dial up and your empathy goes up; you feel more of what your client is feeling. Turn the dial down, and you gain distance from whatever is going on with your client. You gain the ability to think more clearly and be objective about what you can and cannot do to help yourself and your client when your empathy dial is turned lower. Each direction, more empathy and less empathy, has its own advantages and disadvantages. Likewise, one direction or the other will be most appropriate in varying circumstances. If you experiment and practice with turning your empathy dial up and down, you will eventually find that a spot somewhere in the middle is ideal in most, but not all, circumstances. That will be the place where you can resonate with your client enough to know what is going on without your own clear thinking becoming compromised.

Empathy is never a constant. There are degrees of empathy, and you can learn to adjust your level of empathy just as you are able to adjust the volume on your radio, television, or cell phone. To do so, it might help to think of your capacity for empathy or resonance as having a control mechanism, something like the volume dial on an old-fashioned stereo or radio or a button volume control on a newer gizmo, such as your phone or computer. Maybe something like one of these:

And, of course, feel free to choose or create whatever image helps you to grasp and apply this concept of adjusting your level of empathy up and down, more and less. Just make sure that the control mechanism you choose supports the idea that you can both dial up (increase) and dial down (decrease) your empathy and resonance whenever you want to.

Most of you will not need instruction in how to turn your empathy dial up. Helping professionals of all types, including psychotherapists, are usually very strong on empathy, often too strong. That is why, I believe, we are at such high risk for compassion fatigue and vicarious traumatization. Therefore, learning strategies and tricks to monitor and adjust your empathy dial can be very handy. Then, at the least, you will gain a degree of choice from situation to situation. You decide whether it is most advantageous—and involves the best care for yourself—to dial your empathy up or down. Turning it up means you resonate stronger emotionally, somatically, and intuitively. Turning it down will give you increased emotional and energetic distance, making objectivity and clearer thinking more possible.

Being aware of and taking control of your level of empathy can help you to avoid the dangers of unconscious empathy, including mistaking the emotion or stress symptoms from your client as your own, as I did with Ronald, above. That kind of confusion can truly make you nuts, as I inadvertently demonstrated.

Be reassured, dialing down empathy and resonance does not mean that you stop caring. Not at all. It is completely possible to maintain compassion while reducing empathy. Medical professionals, for instance, do this all the time, particularly dentists and surgeons. Consider if your doctor, knowing a particular necessary procedure will cause pain, hesitated to proceed because of empathizing with you. You could actually be harmed as a result. Such professionals know full well they must put their resonance aside while at the same time caring very much about your well-being. I have had a few conversations about compassion without empathy with several of my physician friends. They agree that they definitely want to help, even when it causes pain, but know they dare not feel that pain along with their patient lest they not be able to follow through.

It may help you to think about it this way:

EMPATHY = FEELING *WITH* SOMEONE

COMPASSION = CARING *ABOUT* SOMEONE

Mindfulness, as discussed previously, is one handy tool to use to check on the degree of your empathy at any point in time. Mindful awareness can assist your decision of when to adjust your empathy up or down. It will also help you to know when adjustments are warranted, advantageous, or unnecessary.

TAKING CONTROL

The most straightforward mechanism for turning down your empathy dial with another human is simply to feel your feet on the ground or the seat of your chair under your bum. Another is to notice when you are sitting forward (as many therapists do automatically with clients) and then just lean back so that you can feel the back of your chair. Tell yourself "sit back" from time to time to help you decrease resonance during therapy sessions. You can try it now: Take a minute to remember how you usually sit with one of your clients and then imagine telling yourself to sit back or to feel the cushion beneath your buttocks. Both as you imagine doing this and then when you are actually trying it with a client, pay attention mindfully to notice if sitting back gives you more breathing space and room to think. Also pay mindful attention to your client and see if you sitting back has a desirable or adverse effect. Usually you will find the client also gets more breathing space when you turn down your empathy dial in this way. And by "breathing space," I mean that both figuratively and literally. I often have seen a client's breathing ease or deepen when there is more space between us.

Mindful self-observation will help you know when to make a change. Once you catch yourself mimicking, you can then shift (your breath, face, posture) to lower your empathy dial and feel what you are feeling yourself. You can get practice by yourself using the same strategies described below while watching a movie or television program. One of the ways we get sucked into dramas, sitcoms, romcoms, sports, and the like is by involuntarily mimicking the facial expressions and breathing patterns of the actors. Hit the pause button on your remote control from time to time to check on yourself. Once you get the hang of your own tendencies during entertaining programming, you will be better able to apply your knowledge and skills in personal and professional situations.

### Facial and Postural Awareness

*The sight of a face that is happy, loving, angry, sad, or fearful can cause the viewer to mimic elements of that face and, consequently, to catch the other's emotions.*
—Hatfield and colleagues, *Emotional Contagion*

Humans routinely mimic the facial expressions of others. This is readily observable in public places and at gatherings of colleagues, family, or friends. You will find that the expressions on the faces of people in pairs or small groups often match. Facial mimicry is a reflex that usually happens outside our awareness. But even when we are paying attention, it can sometimes be difficult to stop it. As you walk down the street or through a store, for example, how often do you reflexively smile in response to the smile of a stranger? Probably often, perhaps even more often than you know. Have you ever tried to not smile back? I have tried myself many times, going to the store determined not to smile at everyone who smiles at me. And then . . . drat! I did it again. I will say that it is easier to resist the smiling reflex when I am in a grumpy mood. But if I am feeling good, it seems nearly impossible. The reflex to smile back is so automatic and hardwired into our brains that it requires a good deal of effort to counter it, but it does get easier with practice.

In the therapy room, psychotherapists will sometimes consciously adjust their facial expression to express empathy to a client, a nonverbal message: "I understand what you are feeling (or going through)." Usually the effect is temporary, but sometimes it can be long-lasting and can deeply affect the therapist, particularly when copying the client's facial expression is not conscious.

Marlene was a clinical social worker at a shelter for battered women. She had grown up in a relatively cohesive family and believed she had many resources for tackling her difficult job. Generally, she was emotionally and physically healthy, taking regular vacations, working out, eating well, and making use of her very supportive network. Though Marlene had not had the same kinds of life experiences as the women she was helping, she felt she was able to relate deeply. She genuinely cared about the residents of the shelter, crying and laughing with them, worrying for their safety when they were discharged, celebrating their triumphs, and grieving for and with those who met tragedy.

As much as she loved her work, after three years at the shelter, Marlene began to feel she was burning out. She found it increasingly difficult to get up and go to work. Sometimes, when she was by herself, she found herself crying about the hopelessness of life. She had never thought of herself as prone to depression before, but she was considering asking her doctor for antidepressant medication.

What happened to Marlene? Her depression was not due to counter-transference or her current life situation. Nothing in her past or present life linked her to the experiences of these women except her work with them. Could it be that her level of resonance was so great that her ability to work was becoming compromised? The key here lies in the depth of her empathy, likely deeper than she ever realized. Understanding how the empathy dial is turned up and down automatically will point to ways that it can also be turned up and down purposefully, that is, within Marlene's, and your, control.

## FACIAL FEEDBACK HYPOTHESIS

> *Facial mimicry is arguably the expressive behavior most closely tied to emotional processes in general and to emotional rapport and knowledge in particular. . . . Both theory and data suggest that the synchrony of interactants' facial expressions can lead fairly directly to the commonality of emotional states across individuals.*
> —Levenson and Ruef, "Physiological Aspects of Emotional Knowledge and Rapport"

Before you read on in this section, try a quick experiment:

1. Briefly scan your body and mind to assess your current emotional and physical state. What are you feeling emotionally? How are your breathing and heart rate? And so on.
2. Turn down the sides of your mouth and notice if there are any changes in you. Is there a difference in emotion, respiration, tension, or relaxation anywhere?
3. Next turn up the sides of your mouth and scan yourself to assess the same features.
4. Take note of anything that changed in Steps 2 and 3. There may have been a difference and there may not have.

Though it is not 100% effective, many people experience a change in mood when the position of their mouth changes. Mouth turned down in what is usually called a frown often corresponds to a dampening of mood, restricted breathing, sometimes sadness or an edge of depression. Likewise, turning up the sides of the mouth into what is usually called a smile will often lead to a lifting of mood, ease of breathing, and so on. This is the reasoning behind the old song, "Put on a Happy Face," or parental cajoling of a child to smile in an attempt to quell a tantrum. For an applicable theory, read further.

Adopting a particular facial expression communicates emotional information to the brain. The same process is involved whether the facial expression is generated from inside you or is set in motion by copying the expression of another. The facial feedback hypothesis was first proposed by Silvan Tomkins (1963). He found that the position or pattern of facial muscles leads to subjective feelings of emotion, so that mimicking the look of an emotion will activate the same emotion. For example, turning down the sides of the mouth will generate an internal feeling of sadness. Actors use the principles of this hypothesis to produce and communicate the emotions they portray. Simply put: How your face is arranged affects how you feel.

Paul Ekman agreed that altering facial expression can actually cause emotion. He found that induced facial expression changes physiological responses throughout the body, specifically in the ANS, affecting such factors as heart rate and skin temperature. Each facial expression produces a different pattern. For example, anger raises heartbeat and skin temperature; disgust lowers them (Ekman et al., 1983). Recalling the earlier discussion on the sensory nervous system and Damasio's somatic marker theory, the facial feedback hypothesis makes more sense. The change in muscular position activates interoceptive nerves, which are linked to somatic markers and give feedback to the brain on the experience of emotion. In a corroborating study by Ulf Dimberg (1982), college students showed increased activity in their cheek muscles while viewing happy, smiling faces and increased activity in their brow muscles when viewing angry, scowling faces. Dimberg also found that ANS activity in the students was altered per Ekman's findings. It is relevant for practitioners that Dimberg observed that ANS reactions to happy faces were short-lived, while reactions to angry faces were longer lasting. Maybe that is a partial explanation why my reaction to Ronald, above, persisted over so many hours.

Back to Marlene:

In a consultation session, she talked about her work and her growing burnout. The more she talked, I noticed, the more she adopted the facial expression of someone who has lived through terrible trauma. She really began to look beaten down. As this was not actually the case for her, I became curious about how she related to her clients. "How much of the time," I asked, "do you feel your client's experience?" "Most of the time, I think," she replied. "In social work school I was taught that empathy was my primary tool for connecting to my clients." I asked if she knew how she accomplished such a resonance. She was not sure, so I suggested that in the next week she pay greater attention to her body and her face when working with clients.

At the next consultation, Marlene was eager to tell me that she had paid a lot of attention. She often noticed her face adopting expressions similar to those of her clients, or at least it felt that way from the inside. She could feel her jaw clench and her eyes harden when a client was expressing anger, and she recognized a softness around her eyes and a catch in her throat when one cried.

Next, as an experiment, I asked her to remember a particular client's expression, adopt it on her own face as she felt it, and then look in the mirror to see if that was correct. When she looked, she was surprised to see just how much she looked like that client. "I didn't know I could be so accurate!" she exclaimed. "And what do you feel emotionally when you adopt that expression?" I asked. She answered rather quickly, "Anxious and depressed." I probed further: "Does that have any correlation to that client's feelings?" Marlene nodded slowly. I could almost see the light bulb turning on over her head. "Do you think this has something to do with why I am feeling so depressed?"

Yes, I did. Marlene and I spent much of that consultation going over facial feedback theory. I then suggested that during the following week she experiment with the same client, sometimes consciously adopting a different facial expression. We discussed what kinds of expressions she might adopt that would convey understanding and concern, without being a copy of the client's expression. In addition, I wanted her to notice how she felt, herself, before and after each session.

At our next meeting, Marlene was enthusiastic. Consciously changing her facial expression, while difficult, had definitely had an emotional impact. She had felt in a better mood following the session with her target client than she did with other clients that week. She decided that she wanted to take the experiment further and try paying attention to and altering her facial expression with more clients. Over the next few months, Marlene found that her depression lifted significantly. She was still distressed by the severity of trauma her clients had to deal with, but her own day-to-day functioning improved significantly.

## CONTROLLING FACIAL MIMICRY
The exercises below will help you to increase awareness of, and control over, your own propensity for facial mirroring.

### ──── OBSERVING AND CONTROLLING THE SMILING REFLEX ────

1. On your next trip to the grocery store, or on a neighborhood walk, see how many people you can catch smiling in response to your smiling at them. As you pass another, purposely smile and notice how people respond.

2. During an average day or outing, count how often you smile in response to a smile from another.

3. Then, on several more outings, practice not smiling automatically in response to some of the strangers' smiles. You may find this harder than you would think, so do not be discouraged if it takes you many tries to get the hang of it.

## ———— CONTROLLING FACIAL MIMICRY IN RESPONSE ————
## TO ATHLETES AND FILM ACTORS

1. Either watching television or at the movies, pay attention to your facial expression when an athlete or actor is expressing a strong emotion.
2. Identify which expressions are the most habitual for you to copy.
3. Practice not copying one or more of those expressions during subsequent television programs or films.

APPLICATIONS WITH YOUR CLIENTS:
AWARENESS OF FACIAL MIRRORING

Videotaping one or more therapy sessions with at least one client is an ideal way to gain awareness of your propensity to mirror client facial expressions. The camera should be angled to take in both of you. The steps below can be used instead of or in addition to videotaping.

## ———————— PRE-SESSION INVENTORY ————————

1. Start by choosing one client whose feelings you seem vulnerable to or one who tends to hang around or hitch a ride home with you in your feelings or thoughts after sessions (like the Haunted Mansion ghosts I mentioned in the introduction).
2. Immediately prior to the next session with that client, take an inventory of how you are feeling emotionally. Include what your facial expression feels like from the inside. It will probably be helpful to write this down so you remember exactly.
3. Before you go to meet your client, look in a mirror and see what your facial expression actually looks like pre-session. Include the muscles around your forehead, mouth, cheeks, and eyes, and the expression of your eyes. Jot all of this down or take a selfie.

─────────────── **DURING THE SESSION** ───────────────

1. Include in your session notes—several times during the session—the client's feelings and facial expression.

2. At least twice (even better, three or four times) take a quick inventory of your own feelings and what your facial expression feels like. Make a note.

3. Also during the session, write down when you notice your facial expression changing, and check to see if the client's expression has also changed.

─────────────── **POST-SESSION EVALUATION** ───────────────

1. Immediately following the session, make note of your post-session feelings, indicating if any are similar to the feelings your client was expressing or suppressing during the session.

2. Next, look in the mirror to see what your facial expression looks like. How is it different than before the session? Is it reflective of your own mood or your client's?

─────────────── **POST-SESSION INTERVENTION** ───────────────

1. If your facial expression is a mirror of your client's, move your facial muscles around, making faces at yourself. Notice if or how that changes your mood.

2. Think of something or someone pleasant and notice if or how that changes your facial expression.

─────────────── **NEXT-SESSION INTERVENTION** ───────────────

1. At the next session with the same client, consciously change your facial expression to something different than your client's three times during the hour. Of course you will not want to smile if your client is feeling upset, or make an angry face at a skittish client. But

you can adopt a neutral expression, neither happy nor upset (you may need to practice this with a mirror before the session), change the position of your brows, crinkle your nose, or some such. Notice your mood during the session and after your client has left. Is it the same or different than you usually feel after seeing this client?

2.  If you find it difficult to change your expression when you are with your client, practice first in other encounters: friends, family, and so on. You could also role-play with a colleague.

3.  When you are successful in controlling your facial expressions with one client, move on to another and start again at the beginning, above.

4.  Do not forget that you can always adopt the same expression as your client when you feel that is of benefit to the client and poses little or no risk to your own well-being. Learning to control automatic facial mirroring gives you more choices: to mirror or not to mirror, depending on what is most useful for the therapy and what benefits the well-being of both you and your client.

It is easy to assume that clients want us to feel along with them, and some surely do. However, many clients much prefer for the therapist—and others—to stay out of emotional resonance (to stay in your own chair, as I discuss in Chapter 6). I remember a particular group therapy session when a young woman arrived in tears, reporting the breakup of her marriage. As she sobbed her story, the other group members were deeply touched, many crying along with her. At the end of the session, the woman thanked everyone for the support. She also reported that she appreciated the empathy of the group but found that she kept her eyes riveted on me—the one person in the room who was not distressed along with her. She felt she needed to anchor herself with someone who was solid and unmoved. I asked if she had felt me to be indifferent. "Oh, no," she replied. "I know you care, but I was relieved you didn't look upset like everyone else. Their feelings were validating, but I'm going to need stability to get my footing back."

### Conscious Mirroring

*When I wish to find out how wise, or how stupid, or how good, or
how wicked is anyone, or what are his thoughts at the moment,
I fashion the expression of my face, as accurately as possible, in
accordance with the expression of his, and then wait to see what
thoughts or sentiments arise in my mind or heart, as if to match or
correspond with the expression.*
—Schoolboy in Edgar Allan Poe, "The Purloined Letter"

As has been discussed, in addition to facial mirroring, humans frequently and habitually copy the postures of others. This can also be readily observed in public places: couples both resting their heads on hands, legs crossed in the same way, looking down or away at the same time, simultaneous stretching, leg rocking, finger drumming, and so forth. It can also be useful to notice groups of teenagers, how they stand, slump, and make gestures alike.

Postural mimicry follows a route similar to the facial feedback hypothesis. That is, copying postures can also trigger somatic mechanisms that give emotional feedback to the brain. When I sit like you sit, I can experience what you are feeling. Unconscious postural mirroring can wreak the same havoc as unconscious facial mirroring. However, when brought into awareness and used consciously and purposely, postural mirroring can be a powerful route to increased empathy.

Conscious mirroring is used in many body psychotherapy (somatic psychology) programs (and some psychotherapy programs) to facilitate the therapist's capacity for insight into the client's situation and emotional state. As mentioned previously, the idea originated in dance therapy (Siegel, 1984). When conscious, time limited, and undertaken (and interrupted) with full awareness, it can be an extremely useful way to gain insight and enhance understanding in a psychotherapy setting.

The following exercise serves several purposes. First, it demonstrates what postural mirroring is and how to do it consciously. Second, it provides guidelines so you can practice it yourself if you so choose. Third, it will increase your awareness of any postural mirroring you might already be doing unconsciously.

─────────────────── **MIRRORING EXERCISE** ───────────────────

As discussed above and also in the appendix, this exercise is similar to the one Maggie Shiffrar and I used to study postural mirroring. It is best done with a colleague who would be able to review the results with you in a meaningful way. Eventually, you may want to experiment with conscious mirroring with one or more of your clients using some of the principles here, but this structured exercise is not advisable for client use. This exercise can be used with a single colleague, or as part of a group training or consultation session.

1. In pairs, designate one person as A and the other as B.
2. From this point on, *do not talk*. At the end of the exercise an instruction is given for discussion and comparing notes.
3. Prior to starting, both partners should check their self-awareness to get a baseline to compare with. Notice any particulars in your body: temperature, muscle tension, breathing pattern, internal sensations, and so on. Also assess what you are feeling emotionally and your mood in general.
4. Then, A thinks of a situation with some emotional charge. It can be a pleasant or *mildly* unpleasant emotion (happy, sad, irritated, anxious, lust, etc.), so long as it is not traumatic or highly stressful. Keeping the emotional material low-key will make it easier to focus on the nuts and bolts of the skill building without being distracted by upsetting material.[7]
5. Next, A adopts a physical posture (sitting, standing, or crouching) that has something to do with that situation and maintains it without moving. For example, if the situation has to do with driving a

───────────────────

[7] Caution: Please take care with your choice of memory. Even when I have used this in training programs and have been very careful to repeatedly specify that the emotion should be low-key, therapists still choose car accidents, hospital emergencies, and the like. As a result of those kinds of choices, both partners have often ended up very upset—one remembering trauma and the other feeling vicarious trauma. This really is a powerful exercise.

car, A might sit in a chair with raised arms feigning holding a steering wheel.

6. While A maintains the position, B mirrors (copies) A's posture, getting into the exact same position as A.

7. Then B takes note of the following:
   — What do I have to do with my body to assume this posture? Which muscles do I tense, relax? Where do I twist, turn? Do I bend or tip in any way?
   — What sensations do I become aware of? What is my body temperature and how is it distributed? Is there tingling, numbness, pain, pleasure? Where?
   — Do any images come to mind? What are the pictures, sounds, tastes, smells that emerge?
   — What am I feeling emotionally? (happy, scared, sad, etc.)
   — What thoughts (or other verbalizations, e.g., songs) are running through my head?

8. Once B has checked those five points, B silently guesses what kind of situation A is remembering.

9. Then, B signals A that they both can relax their postures and sit down facing each other. B then gives A a specific report. At this point A only listens and does not talk yet.

10. B uses this structure for the feedback:
    — "When I was standing/sitting/crouching like you . . . "
    — "I did . . . with my body [describe what B had to do to assume A's posture]."
    — "I sensed in my body . . . [describe physical sensations]."
    — "I saw/heard/smelled/tasted . . . [describe images]."
    — "I felt . . . [emotion]."
    — "I thought . . . "
    — Lastly, B tells his guess.

11. When B is finished, then it is A's turn to speak: A shares with B the situation that A was remembering, including what was happening in A's body, sensations, emotions, images, and thoughts.

12. A and B discuss the similarities and differences in their experiences.

When giving feedback, remember to talk about your own experience. You may be accessing information about the other person, but what you are picking up is going through your own filters. There may or may not be correspondence. Information gained in this manner will likely provide you with some hunches about the other person's experience, but not knowledge until you have checked your accuracy. This is an important distinction: Sometimes therapists confuse intuition with fact, which can cause difficulties for the client.[8] Always check out your hunches and take the other's word for whether or not you are on target.

Based on your discussion with your partner, take note of which elements you were most accurate with. Are you more sensitive to body sensations, emotions, visual images, auditory images, or thoughts? You may want to try this exercise several times, possibly with several people, before you reach a conclusion. Once you know your areas of strength, you can maximize them by focusing on those elements when you want to tune in to your client. It will also tell you which elements are your vulnerability if you are picking up too much or having trouble letting it go (which is addressed in the section Unmirroring).

## APPLICATIONS OF POSTURAL MIRRORING IN PSYCHOTHERAPY

Once you have grasped the tools of conscious mirroring, you can take them into your office. The first step is to check in with yourself before you meet with a client. Take note of your breathing pattern, style of sitting, tilt of your head, and so forth. After you have grasped your own style, you will be ready to notice when your posture or aspects of your posture match your client's. Also notice your breathing pattern.

Next you can experiment with consciously mimicking the client's posture (or one aspect of it). Maybe at first just cross your legs the same way, synchronize your breathing, or put your head in the same position. Once you do that, check in with the elements that were the focus of the previous exercise and see what you come up with. It is not usually a good idea to

---

[8] I have experienced this myself as a client, a few times getting into an argument with my therapist who was certain, because of her intuition, that I was feeling something I was not. I can tell you, it is a very, very unpleasant situation.

completely mimic a client's posture when you are sitting face-to-face. Some clients could feel shamed if they notice.

Most important, check with your client about any hunches. It can be very tempting to assume that the changes in your sensations, emotions, images, or thoughts are accurate details about your client, which they may be. However, they can also be aspects of yourself that have become triggered through the mirroring process. You will not be able to tell the difference unless you check.

If you like the idea, use conscious mirroring as a tool to enhance intuition, but never mistake it for knowledge until you have checked it out with your client. And make sure to stay aware of what you are doing and shift out of the mirroring into your own posture and breathing—otherwise you could end up confused and distressed as I was with Ronald, above.

### ADDITIONAL APPLICATIONS

You can apply the same idea with others. For example, at dinner try mimicking the posture of your spouse, friend, or child, and then make some guesses about what they might be feeling or what kind of day they had. You can make a game of it. Conscious mirroring might also be used to help someone who has a low empathy IQ. It could help them learn how it feels to be in another's moccasins for a while.

Postural mirroring can also be a powerful tool for supervision and consultation. Role-playing one of your own clients is an oft-used and valuable technique for gaining insight into a client and revealing areas of counter-transference. This tool is enhanced by paying particular attention to how the client sits and moves. The process is similar to an actor getting into a role. When you can accurately copy the client's bearing and movements, both you and your supervisor will have more hunches to work with. Again, just make sure to "de-role" before you leave the supervision so you do not carry your client home with you.

### *Unmirroring*

> *Thinking of the transmission of moods as akin to the transmission*
> *of social viruses, it seems reasonable to suppose that some*
> *people . . . stand especially vulnerable to contagion.*
> —Hatfield and colleagues, Emotional Contagion

In the previous section, you learned about using postural mirroring con-sciously to increase your empathy with a client or other person. Actually the emphasis was on your somatic empathy with that person, as the connection is body to body. For the psychotherapist, that may enhance your resonance with and intuition about your clients. That is the upside of somatic empathy. There is also a downside.

When unchecked, somatic empathy can be problematic. As discussed earlier, unconscious somatic empathy may be a major factor underlying your risk for compassion fatigue, vicarious traumatization, and burnout. However, mitigating that risk is fairly easy and mainly requires self-awareness and common sense. Somatic empathy only becomes a danger when the therapist is not aware of it, and therefore not in control of it, unconsciously tuning into the sensations, emotions, images, and thoughts of clients. Under such a circumstance, the therapist will not be able to distinguish client states from her own. Actually, it is this confusion that is usually most problematic.

This is a good place to look back at my situation with Ronald earlier in this chapter. The problem generated for me by postural mirroring was obvi-ous: I confused Ronald's anger with my own. I mirrored Ronald and then forgot what I had been doing. When I felt rage, I could not locate the source and resolve it, because it had not been a response to my own life situation. By accurately attuning to Ronald, I had picked up—been infected by—his rage. Had I stayed aware of what I was doing, the distinction would have been clear to me. However, because I forgot, I confused the rage infection with a true rage of my own. When I looked to my own life for the source of my anger, I became confused and agitated. Once my colleague reminded me of the postural mirroring I had been doing, the distinction between Ronald and myself—between his feelings and mine—was instantaneously clear, and the rage I had inadvertently adopted melted away. As it dissipated, so did my discomfort and confusion. It is important to note that unconscious postural mirroring happens all the time in and outside of therapeutic relationships. The following consultation transcript will help illustrate strategies to maintain awareness and alter habitual unconscious mirroring.

## BREATHLESS HANK

Hank is an experienced psychologist in private practice. He gets most of his supervision from a peer group, but periodically seeks additional input. During the following consultation, he discussed physical symptoms that had arisen in working with a particular client.

> **Hank:** I read your article in the *Networker* [Rothschild, 2004b]. The story you told about losing your breath with a client resonated with my experience with a current client. I hoped you might be able to help me with him and with my reactions.
>
> **Babette:** I'll be glad to try. Tell me what happens.
>
> **Hank:** When I work with this client, about 15 minutes into most sessions, I find myself feeling light-headed. I've noticed that my breathing is very shallow and so is his. I've tried changing my breathing pattern. That works for a few minutes, and then I'm light-headed again.
>
> **Babette:** Have you looked into content triggers; is what he talks about disturbing for you?
>
> **Hank:** I did think of that. But this happens no matter what he is talking about. Often we are just addressing his daily life, no sort of distressing material.

It would be ideal to have Hank videotape a session with his client. That way we could look together at what was happening with him. We discussed this idea, but for several reasons, Hank did not think this was possible. Mainly, the client was very concerned about privacy and would probably not give permission. Due to the client's stress level, Hank did not even want to ask. Next I suggested a possible alternative.

> **Babette:** Then here is what I would like to suggest: I'd like you to imagine that you are in your therapy room with your client. Assume your typical posture, and then remember your client as he talks about various things. I am going to pay attention to what I see in you and may stop you from time to time.

As Hank began to imagine a session with his client, I noticed that he was sitting up fairly straight. A minute or so later, I saw his posture begin to change. He seemed to collapse a bit across his middle, and he slid down in the chair.

> **Babette:** I want to stop you for a moment. I notice something changing in your posture. Can you identify the change? If you can't, I'll tell you what I see, but I want to check first if you can feel it.
> **Hank:** Well, my posture isn't as straight as when I started. Is that what you mean?
> **Babette:** Yes. Can you describe the difference more precisely?

The more Hank could feel and describe for himself, the better. If I only told him what I saw, he would not gain facility in self-observation. I wanted him to be more able to observe himself during sessions.

> **Hank:** Well, I've slid down in the chair a bit and my head is slightly forward.
> **Babette:** What's happening in your midsection?
> **Hank:** Oh! I'm sort of folded.
> **Babette:** That's what I see. To me it looks like you are actually slumping. How is your remembered client sitting?
> **Hank:** Oh, he always slumps!

I was not surprised. It is very common for the therapist to slip into a mirrored posture of the client. Hank inadvertently demonstrated this tendency very well.

**Babette:** So, is it possible that as the session continues, you gradually slip into mirroring his slump more and more?

**Hank:** I guess that's possible. If that's the case, then just changing my breathing wouldn't be enough to help me, would it?

**Babette:** Nope. Not only because of the mirroring, but also the actual posture. In that slumped position, notice your breathing. Then straighten up, sitting as you were a while ago, and see if there is a difference.

Trying out the two postures and focusing on body awareness would help teach Hank's body as well as his mind the difference between the two positions.

**Hank:** Of course, when I am sitting up straight, it is much easier to breathe deeply. Do you think that it's this simple? Keep from slumping and I'll keep my breath and no longer be light-headed?

**Babette:** It may be. What you just said is common sense. At least I think it is worth a try. For the next two sessions, would you pay attention to your posture? It might be difficult to stay out of that mirroring. It looks to be very automatic.

**Hank:** I'm sure I can do it for two sessions. I'll make a note to myself and post it on my side table.

Two weeks later Hank sent an email to say the change in posture worked very well. He was no longer light-headed with that client. Every time he found himself slumping, he pulled himself up straight again. Unmirroring both his client's breathing pattern and posture worked to keep Hank from being affected by the somatic states of his client.

## PUTTING YOU IN CHARGE

Mediating the negative risks of somatic empathy first involves mindfulness: becoming aware of when and how you gain access to information about your clients, how you attune with them, and how you become vulnerable to being infected by their states.

─────────────── **UNMIRRORING EXERCISE 1** ───────────────

For the next week, in one or more sessions, pay attention to your own body posture, facial expression, and breathing pattern. Stay alert for times when you drift into patterns that mimic your client.

Occasionally, consciously change one aspect of your position, your breathing, or your expression. Then see whether you feel differently and notice if there is any change in your client. Most clients will not notice at all. Certain clients will feel more comfortable when you mirror them. However, as mentioned above, many will feel relieved when you do not and are less in tune with them. Many of your clients will be better able to stay in touch with themselves when you stay in touch with yourself.

─────────────── **UNMIRRORING EXERCISE 2** ───────────────

This exercise requires a partner. It can be done informally with a friend or colleague, or as part of a group training or consultation. Again, it is not recommended to use this (as written) with clients.

1. In pairs, designate one as the client and the other as the therapist.
2. The client tells a personal story. It can be about anything with a positive or mildly negative emotional charge, but not trauma or great distress.
3. As the therapist listens to the client's story, he consciously mirrors the client's posture, facial expression, or breathing and notices what happens in his own body, emotions, and thoughts.
4. Next, the therapist evaluates what he must do to unmirror:
   — Change his posture?
   — Change his breathing?
   — Tense up or relax? Where?
   — Change position? How?
   — What else? Feel free to be creative.
5. The therapist then shifts between mirroring and unmirroring, tak-

ing a minute or two with each. Both therapist and client notice changes in their own body and emotions as the therapist shifts.

6. Finally, let go of the roles and discuss what happened.

Note: Usually in this exercise the one in the client role is very alert, often uncomfortably, to the therapist's shifts between mirroring and unmirroring. As a result, some therapists become reluctant to try unmirroring with their clients. However, the majority of your clients (who have not participated in the exercise or heard the instructions) will not notice whether you are mirroring them or not, at least consciously. So do not hesitate to try unmirroring in actual therapy situations.

Of foremost importance is mindfulness (awareness), so that you do not take on client states that will put you at risk. If you worry about unmirroring with your clients, remember: Many clients experience mirrored attunement as intrusive, feeling that they do not have their own space or experience. So feel free to experiment. Use your common sense. If unmirroring helps you to reduce your work stress, use it. If some clients are more uncomfortable when you unmirror, find ways to strike a balance between mirroring and unmirroring. If you do not think it is helpful to you and your clients, use other tools.

Therapists in my training courses have come up with many ways to unmirrror. Here are some of their ideas:

| | |
|---|---|
| • Sit up straight | • Visit the restroom |
| • Cross or uncross legs | • Tense specific muscles |
| • Change breathing | • Move around |
| • Take a drink | • Blink eyes |
| • Write some notes | • Take a deep breath |
| • Stretch | • Exhale |

You are welcome to send me your ideas or strategies that have worked for you, to share in future editions. My email address is on the copyright page.

### Controlling Empathic Imagery

Imagining the stories you hear from clients can boost your empathy with them. However, it can also cause problems. Visualizing the distressing and traumatic events of others puts you into the position of eyewitness—one of the categories in the *DSM-5* that qualifies for PTSD (American Psychiatric Association, 2013). It can really turn up your empathy dial. Moreover, many who habitually imagine client stories (consciously or unconsciously) tend to do so in the first person, imagining as if their client's experience was happening to them (Maxfield, 1997). You may have been doing this so automatically for years that you may or may not know if it causes you difficulty. However, if you are having symptoms of vicarious trauma, considering if imagery is causing problems for you might be wise. If you discover it is, or even might be, an issue, some simple, commonsense interventions will help to put you in charge of your imagery and, along with it, the adjustments of your empathy dial.

Following his graduate studies, Bob worked at his local Department of Veterans Affairs, first as an intern and later as a staff psychologist. He had never been in the armed services himself, but he enjoyed the opportunity to provide service to the VA. However, when he married and began his family, he felt the need to earn more money and left the VA to go into general private practice. That did not end his ties to the military, though. Yearly he received several referrals, from the VA and privately, of military personnel—enlisted and officers, those actively serving as well as veterans.

During the first eight years of his therapist career, Bob heard many accounts of the kinds of horrors that military men and women face during war and peacetime. He thought he managed well. During a particularly newsworthy time during the long war in Afghanistan, he began to "work overtime." He often found himself thinking excessively about his military clients during his free time. He also became edgy and developed sleeping difficulties, sometimes waking from nightmares of war.

Bob struggled a long time, trying to figure out why his clients' stories were getting to him now. One evening, while watching the news, he had an epiphany: The pictures he saw of the Afghan war on the television screen were similar to the ones he was seeing in his dreams with his clients' faces. The next day, while he was listening to one client's experience, he realized he was picturing them in his mind's eye, using film clips from last night's news as his template.

Can you relate to Bob's experience? If so, the next step for you, as it was for Bob, is to gain control, be in charge, of the imagery in your own mind. A few simple interventions (described in the additional cases below) could give you a secure sense of control over what are often believed to be uncontrollable intrusions.

## TO PICTURE OR NOT TO PICTURE

The next case illustration typifies how a common practice that aims to enhance therapist performance can actually detract from it.

Therkild was a counselor for a Holocaust research project. As part of his job, he conducted sessions with Holocaust survivors, detailing their experiences and helping them make sense of their lives. The stories he heard were, of course, horrific. Therkild believed that this project was highly significant, and he was proud to participate. However, he regularly suffered as a result. Though he wanted to continue with this work, he was having increasing trouble sleeping and bouts of severe agitation (hyperarousal)—typical symptoms of vicarious traumatization. Moreover, he was becoming hopeless about the future—a common symptom of burnout. He knew the source of his difficulties but did not want to quit. On the advice of a friend, he sought consultation.

With help, Therkild was able to zero in on his vulnerable points. Among other issues, the consultant identified Therkild's habit of visualizing the stories he was being told as a possible source of his difficulties. Therkild felt it was his duty to try to imagine what his clients had experienced. He would consciously visualize during sessions, trying to see the details of the horrific events the client had gone through; he hoped it would make him a more sensitive counselor. Unfortunately, however, the images he conjured during the interview sessions continued to appear unbidden at other times, often in his dreams. He was not able to shake the pictures or the feelings they stirred in him.

The consultant suggested Therkild might examine whether his habit of visualization actually enhanced his abilities as a counselor. They discussed the common assumption that sharing another's experience would always be helpful. It was the consultant's notion that this was not necessarily the case, that this practice could actually hamper Therkild's ability to help. At the least, he was clearly and admittedly suffering because of it. The only way to know if visualization was the key to his vicarious trauma was to make an experiment: try it both ways, alternating from session to session. He was instructed to pay attention to his body awareness and emotions before and after each session. Only then would he be able to determine what was best for him.

They agreed that for the next week, Therkild would keep his visual focus in the room for some sessions and continue to visualize the client's reflections for others. He would keep a log of what happened from session to session. Ahead of time, they discussed strategies to help keep Therkild alert in the here and now if he found himself falling into habitual visualizations. The consultant suggested that paying closer attention to the client's words and gestures, and periodically looking around the room, would be helpful in keeping Therkild focused. During the sessions, Therkild listened to his clients as always and asked appropriate questions. For half of the sessions he was mostly able to refrain from making pictures in his mind, relying on the strategies he and his consultant had come up with.

Though he felt a bit awkward in restricting himself, Therkild noticed a difference immediately. He did not become nearly as anxious as usual during sessions where he was not visualizing, and he was much calmer after those sessions. He had no doubts that what was described had been horrific. He felt very sympathetic. But without visualizing alongside them, he was not suffering with those clients. On the first night of his experiment, he slept more peacefully than he would have expected. Moreover, in reflecting back, he judged that the sessions where he had kept from visualizing had gone at least as well as usual. During those sessions, he had actually remembered a couple of important questions that he often forgot.

After a week of experimentation, Therkild weighed the pros and cons of visualizing his client's stories. He concluded that, for the most part, he would permanently change his habit and stop requiring himself to see the stories. He knew he could still use that tool if material came up that he could not otherwise understand. But generally he wanted to relieve himself of that added stressor.

This simple change was rather easy for Therkild to apply because, for the most part, his habit of visualization had usually been voluntary; he had chosen to create imagery. This is not always the case. Some therapists find themselves visualizing their clients' circumstances automatically. Stopping an unconscious habit is a little more involved, as the case of Tina shows below.

## CONTROLLING UNINVITED IMAGES

This example involves techniques inspired by neurolinguistic programming's concept of *submodalities* (Andreas & Andreas, 1987; Bandler, 1985). The idea is simple. A submodality is a feature or characteristic of an image. For example, volume is one submodality of sound; clarity and speed are others. Submodalities for visual images include size, shape, color, distance, and so on. The goal is to take control of any visual or auditory images that are invoked when hearing (or thinking about) distressing stories or reports. By changing elements of the images (the submodalities), they can be better managed.

Tina had been a therapist in a rape crisis center for about a year when she realized her lifestyle was becoming more and more restricted. Though she had never suffered physical violence, she was finding herself behaving and feeling in ways similar to many of her clients. Of course, like most who work with victims of violence, Tina had become more aware of danger and was more cautious. But in the last couple of months, what had been sensible caution had crossed the line toward debilitating limitations. She and her supervisor decided she needed counseling, and she engaged a psychotherapist.

Tina told her new therapist that she was behaving more and more like a woman who had been raped, and that scared her very much. She had also had a few anxiety attacks (racing heart, cold sweat, disorientation) while out at night and was becoming more and more concerned. The therapist helped Tina understand the concept of vicarious traumatization and suggested they find out what her particular vulnerabilities were. Among other things, the therapist focused closely on how Tina processed the information she was given by her clients, particularly how she heard their experiences of rape.

"Oh, I don't just hear it," Tina replied. "I see it." Upon close scrutiny, the therapist learned that images of the client's rape automatically appeared in Tina's mind's eye. She never planned to visualize the rapes. "It just happens." Actually, it was the one aspect of her job that she hated. Tina loved helping the women (and the occasional man), but she dreaded the images that would then fill her head. The psychotherapist believed there was an additional compounding factor: Tina's tendency to visualize her client's rape in the first person, as if it was happening to her, rather than watching it happen to the client.

This is a common occurrence with visualization (Maxfield, 1997). While first-person imagery can be useful in learning a new skill or sport, it actually can compound the therapist's risk for vicarious traumatization. Needless to say, it is a good idea to control imagery that is obviously distressing to you—during a session, immediately following a session, or between sessions with your client. If in doubt, being mindful and taking stock of your arousal level (discussed in Chapter 3) during sessions and when a client leaves can be helpful. As we will see in the examples below, it is common for psychotherapists to believe that visualizing client stories enhances empathy. Actually, that is probably correct. But at what cost? Is visualization necessary to empathy? And how much therapist empathy is necessary to be able to help a client? Probably the answer varies from practitioner to practitioner, and perhaps also from client to client. There is always a fine line to walk: maximizing useful empathy without endangering the mental health of the practitioner. For each of you, the balance will be slightly different, an individual matter for you to negotiate for yourself (or with the help of a consultant or your own therapist). Below are several exercises that will help readers with this tendency. First, back to Tina.

> Tina's therapist suggested that she could gain control of the images in her mind's eye. Tina was a bit dubious but was willing to try anything to feel better and be able to continue in her job. However, they did not jump directly to working with the debilitating, frightening images. Initially, they worked with neutral and positive images. For instance, the therapist first had Tina visualize a blue ball 12 inches in diameter floating in front of her chest, three feet away. Then the therapist instructed Tina to change aspects (submodalities) of the visualized ball—different color, distance, size, shape, and so on—changing one submodality at a time. When Tina became confident in her ability, the therapist gave more complicated instructions. Discovering that she was able to manipulate these simple images boosted Tina's confidence.

At this point it is relevant to mention that had Tina's (or Therkild's, for that matter) images been of an auditory or tactile nature, the same interventions could be used, changing the instructions to focus on sounds or skin sensations instead of visual images. The effect can be the same, though the adaptation of the instructions might be a bit more challenging. Sometimes the images are not actually seen but are sensed or felt. In those instances, the instructions can also be adapted. For example, a consultant could say, "Sense a 12-inch blue ball in front of you. Feel it shrink in size," and so forth.

At the next session, they continued to train Tina's sense of control. The therapist suggested that Tina choose a nontraumatic activity she had observed. As she liked to watch the Wimbledon tennis championship, she chose that. It was a plus for the purposes of the exercise that Tina did not actually play tennis. That way she could experiment with altering her first-person image with an activity her body did not actually recognize, just as she would eventually do with altering her imagination of a rape that she had (thankfully) also not experienced.

The therapist instructed Tina to start with one view, that of the player or that of the observer—and periodically switch her perspective. First she would imagine playing the game, how the swing of the racket would feel, or moving on her feet. Then she would change and imagine observing someone else playing the game as she did while watching television. The idea was for Tina to have the experience of controlling the imagery, without the stress of upsetting content. Once she became skilled at controlling images in this way, she could graduate to controlling the images that had been plaguing her.

This entire process took several weeks. Applying it in her working situation was gradual. At first Tina practiced being an observer, rather than a participant, in her mind's eye. Eventually, she learned that she could visualize other things when hearing the stories of rape. Like Therkild, ultimately, Tina found that she did not have to picture the violence to be sensitive and sympathetic to what her client had experienced.

### EXERCISES FOR IMAGERY CONTROL

If you think you could benefit from imagery control strategies in your own work, here are three exercises you can try. Remember, if you are not someone who has visual images, you can try the same procedure with the kinds of images you do have: auditory, tactile, body position and movement, and so forth.

────────── **IMAGERY CONTROL EXERCISE 1: VISUAL IMAGES** ──────────

In your mind's eye, imagine an everyday object. It does not matter what it is, so long as it is not associated with stress. If you are not able to visualize, you are welcome to alter the exercise, exchanging feeling or sensing for seeing or visualizing. As Tina did, manipulate your images (visual, sensory— whatever) of the object in as many ways (submodalities) as you can think of. One at a time, change its size, distance, color, shape, and so on.

────────── **IMAGERY CONTROL EXERCISE 2: AUDITORY IMAGES** ──────────

Imagine that you have a tape recorder beside you with a good selection of controls for altering the submodalities of volume, speed, pitch, direction, and so on. Choose something neutral or pleasant to start with: a song, dialogue from television, a story read aloud, or some such. Then play around with altering its features. Make it louder or softer. Raise and lower the pitch. Play it backward, play it forward. Try changing the speed. You can also change the voice to another speaker—such as John Wayne, Donald Duck, Madonna—any voice you like.

Next you can try the same tools with a sound or voice that has some emotional meaning for you. Just make sure to gradually increase the difficulty or emotional charge of the sound you are working with. Do not go to the next level of challenge until you have mastered the current level.

This is also a great technique for those who are plagued by critical voices in their heads. Just change the critical voice to Elmo or Mickey Mouse and see if the criticism has the same sting.

It is equally useful for, say, therapists who work with abused children and cannot get the sound of crying out of their head, or the veterans' counselor who keeps hearing gunfire. Learning to take command of the audio controls can help these distressing sounds and others that are replayed in your mind to diminish or even disappear.

## — IMAGERY CONTROL EXERCISE 3: ADDITIONAL APPLICATIONS —

Practice watching a pleasant or neutral image on an imagined television monitor. Assume you have a full set of controls for making the picture larger or smaller, changing the focus, changing the direction, altering the speed, changing the color palette, moving the television closer or farther from you, turning the sound up and down, or turning the picture on and off. One at a time, experiment with changing as many of the features (submodalities) as you can.

Once you become adept, you can try images that have more emotional meaning for you. Just make sure to take your time and gradually increase the difficulty of the images. Do not move on to something potentially more upsetting before you have mastered control of a less stressful image.

Eventually, you can apply the same skills with images from your work that plague you. When you find yourself imagining something horrible that you are being told about, move the screen farther away, blur the image, step out of first person and become the observer, look at something else, or turn off the image altogether and just listen to and watch your client. The idea is to reinforce for yourself that you have full control of whether and how much you will try on or witness the experiences of your clients.

Chapter 3 moves away from the emphasis on empathy but continues to focus on the therapist's body and therapist self-care. Arousal levels and boundaries are additional key components for a psychotherapist to manage in order to mediate the risks of compassion fatigue, vicarious traumatization, and burnout.

# Keeping Calm

Nearly every professional training on trauma and PTSD includes discussion of and guidelines for monitoring and regulating the client's ANS. But what about the therapist's? Could there be value for you in observing and regulating your own ANS? Absolutely! The aim of this chapter is to equip you to do just that so that you can reduce your risk for vicarious trauma and compassion fatigue.

In the theory section of this chapter I review two related views. First, what I am now going to call *old-school* was included in the original edition of this book as well as *The Body Remembers* (Rothschild, 2000). The *new-school* view was initially presented in *Revolutionizing Trauma Treatment* (Rothschild, 2021) and is illustrated by the full-color ANS table you will find following page 126. To my thinking, both views are interlinked and relevant today. Together, the basic knowledge they provide is your surest foundation for monitoring and then regulating your own arousal during therapy sessions—as well as in any situations where that would be advantageous for you.

The skill-building section includes strategies for regulating your nervous system during (and outside of) client sessions.

# Theory

### The Neurophysiology of Arousal

Chronic stress exacts a great toll on the body and mind. In the psychotherapist, that toll is usually referred to as compassion fatigue, vicarious trauma, or burnout. No better case can be made for learning about the nervous system and increasing awareness of one's own state of arousal than the personal story of my colleague Bonnita Wirth. In her own words (and with her permission):

After 32 years of direct service, I decided to close my psychotherapy practice. This was work that I loved and was quite successful at for many years. If I had waited much longer to make this change, my age would have put me out of the running for the kinds of administrative jobs that interested me.

For many, many years (beginning long before middle age), I had been a fitful sleeper. I would go to bed late (12:30 a.m. or later), wake several times in the night, and was up no later than 6:30 a.m. In spite of this, I did not feel tired or notice that my lack of sleep was impacting me one way or the other. I would sometimes refer to my "insomnia," thinking it was part and parcel of who I was. Even a close observer would never notice I was suffering any ill effects. I loved my work, enjoyed my patients, was successful, and never felt burned out. It seemed that my body and mind managed to adjust to the rigors of my work; I never noticed. Even the contrast of vacations was not adequate to alert me to the stress I was carrying. I had accommodated to the biological stress and just saw the consequences as my unique physiology. But a year after the closure, I got quite a surprise. I was talking about the changes over the past year with a colleague and reflected that within weeks of closing my practice, I started sleeping through the night for the first time in over three decades. This was an astonishing revelation and the first time I realized the connection. For all of those years I had never considered that my chosen and beloved profession had a cost: a significant impact on my body, my sleep, and my ability to fully relax. Having trouble falling asleep, sleeping fitfully, and waking had become my norm.

With that insight, I began to notice what had changed. I actually relaxed and felt tired when I got home from work. My nights are very different now: I am drifting off by 10 or 11 p.m., sleep solidly and peacefully, and first awaken at 5:30 a.m. or later. Amazing! I can't imagine what it must be like for those who are really burned out, burdened with compassion fatigue, or reeling from vicarious trauma.

## THE AUTONOMIC NERVOUS SYSTEM

Knowledge of the body is relevant for any psychotherapist. However, some will not be able to study all of it, and some will not be interested. If you only have time or brain space for a small portion, this is it. At the very least, becoming familiar with the autonomic division of the body's nervous system (the ANS) is a must for those who work with highly distressed or traumatized people. Grasping the ANS will give you key understanding and tools for both client containment and therapist self-care. Applications for clients are covered at length in *The Body Remembers: The Psychophysiology of Trauma and Trauma Treatment* (Rothschild, 2000) and *Revolutionizing Trauma Treatment* (Rothschild, 2017, 2021). Here the focus is on applications for you, the therapist.

The ANS regulates the body as it shifts through states of stress and calm. It is at the center of the body's response to all levels of stress, including when it prepares the body for fight, flight, or freeze when faced with a threat to life or limb. Lesser levels of arousal prepare the body to meet any demand—also those of difficult clients or workplaces. The racing heartbeat, cold sweat, and dry mouth associated with the effects of stress are all functions of the ANS. Likewise, the easy respiration, warm and dry skin, and lowered blood pressure associated with times of calm are also functions of the ANS. Understanding how the ANS works, and being able to identify the internal interoceptive cues that differentiate stress from calm, are critical for the therapist working with, and in proximity to, stress and trauma. The advantages extend beyond helping others. As, or even more, important is the benefit to psychotherapists themselves. Knowledge about the ANS can be used to protect you from the major risks of your job: compassion fatigue, vicarious traumatization, and burnout.

It is not only during a traumatic event that the ANS can activate toward fight, flight, or freeze, nor is it only the ANS of the victim that is vulnerable to activation. The therapist working with highly stressed or traumatized individuals is also vulnerable to heightened activation of the ANS, even when just sitting in an office and talking with a client. Vicarious trauma is a reality. Shindul-Rothschild (2001; no relation to the author) found "14% of mental health practitioners working with trauma victims reported traumatic stress levels similar to those experienced by victims with PTSD." Therapists who can track ANS activation in their own body are in a position to choose the amount of arousal that they each can manage or use to their advantage. They then also have the potential to halt or decrease their arousal, at will, to prevent adverse effects. Needless to say, that will be of huge benefit to your self-care.

## THE BASICS: OLD-SCHOOL ANS

In the original edition of *Help for the Helper* (Rothschild, 2006), I reviewed the basics of the ANS as they were generally understood at that time. I include that description here because the basics are still relevant. In the next section of this revised edition, I will update these old-school basics, weaving them together into a new-school synthesis of my own views along with those of Stephen Porges (2011) and Merete Holm Brantbjerg (2012, 2020), culminating in the six-column color ANS table that I first introduced in *Revolutionizing Trauma Treatment* (Rothschild, 2017) which is included also in this volume as an insert following page 126.

Simply put, the old-school understanding of the ANS has been the standard since at least 1900 (Johnson, 2013). It has two branches, the sympathetic nervous system (SNS) and the parasympathetic nervous system (PNS). They are understood to function in balance to promote survival of the individual and maintain homeostasis within the body. The SNS activates under conditions of stress, of which traumatic stress is the most extreme. The PNS is usually activated during rest and relaxation, though it is also active when some distressing feelings such as sadness occur. It can be elevated when shame, embarrassment, anger (not rage), and extreme terror are activated, as discussed below. Normally the SNS and PNS arouse and subdue, rise and fall, in complement to each other, like the pans of a scale—when one is more activated, the other is more suppressed. Neither branch ever ceases to function; they both are always on.

When the SNS is primarily aroused, heart rate and respiration quicken, pupils dilate, blood pressure rises, and blood flow is directed away from the skin and viscera into the muscles. As a result, digestion slows or stops. All of this action is nature's way of helping the body respond to demands. When quick and strong movements are needed, the bulk of the blood flow—with the nutrients and oxygen it carries—is directed to the muscles. Increased respiration ensures a greater supply of oxygen, and a quicker heart rate speeds it on its way. Nothing is wasted on the temporarily less important function of digestion, so the mouth goes dry as saliva is no longer needed. Warmth is also a lower priority, so the skin becomes cold and pale as the blood also flows away from it. The pupils dilate so that distance vision—toward the source of danger or goal of safety—is more acute. When threat is extreme, the bowel and bladder might empty, making the body lighter for quicker action, as well as leaving scent-rich scat to distract a pursuer.

The PNS is usually most aroused in states of rest and calm. The heartbeat and respiration slow, blood pressure lowers, pupils constrict, and the skin is warm and dry. When the PNS is dominant, much of the blood flow is directed away from the muscles, as their action is not as important. Instead, blood is directed toward the skin for warmth and the viscera to process nutrition through digestion and elimination. The mouth is moist with saliva, which, along with chewing, is necessary to begin the digestive process. Under the most extreme life-threatening danger, the SNS and PNS might be simultaneously hyperaroused to their most extreme level, pushing all systems to full throttle and causing the body to freeze—go dead like a mouse caught by a cat, or a deer or kangaroo caught in headlights. Figure 3.1, reproduced from *The Body Remembers* (Rothschild, 2000) and *Revolutionizing Trauma Treatment* (Rothschild, 2021), summarizes the old-school features of SNS and PNS activation.

| SYMPATHETIC BRANCH | PARASYMPATHETIC BRANCH |
|---|---|
| Activates during positive and negative stress states, including: sexual climax, rage, desperation, terror, anxiety/panic, trauma | States of activation include: rest and relaxation, sexual arousal, happiness, anger, grief, sadness |
| **Noticeable signs** | **Noticeable signs** |
| Faster respiration | Slower, deeper respiration |
| Quicker heart rate (pulse) | Slower heart rate (pulse) |
| Increased blood pressure | Decreased blood pressure |
| Pupils dilate | Pupils constrict |
| Pale skin color | Flushed skin color |
| Increased sweating | Skin dry (usually warm) to touch |
| Skin cold (possibly clammy) | Digestion (and peristalsis) increases |
| Digestion (and peristalsis) decreases | |
| **During actual traumatic event OR with flashback (visual, auditory and/or sensory)** | **During actual traumatic event OR with flashback (visual, auditory and/or sensory)** |
| Preparation for quick movement, leading to possible fight reflex or flight reflex | Can also activate concurrently with, while masking, sympathetic activation leading to tonic immobility: freezing reflex (like a mouse, caught by a cat, going dead). Marked by simultaneous signs of high sympathetic and parasympathetic activation. |

**FIGURE 3.1**    Autonomic Nervous System, Old-School Version    *Source: Rothschild, 2000, 2021*

## HOW THE ANS RESPONDS TO TRAUMA

The ANS is controlled by the brain's limbic system. It is this neural structure that coordinates or directs survival of the species, including the management of all levels of stress. The limbic system makes sure that food is sought when there is hunger, that liquid is found for thirst, that urges for sex are consummated so that the species continues to propagate. The limbic system also controls the stress response and directs the body to fight, flee, or freeze when faced with danger.

A small almond-shaped structure within the brain's limbic system, the amygdala, is responsible for all types of emotional response. It is best known for its role in perceiving danger. It gathers information from the sensory system—exteroceptors and interoceptors—and sounds an alarm. When that happens, a whole sequence of further activations ensues within the body. An alarm from the amygdala activates the hypothalamus, setting in motion two parallel actions: One activates the SNS while the other provokes the pituitary gland. The SNS triggers the adrenals to release epinephrine and norepinephrine, which mobilize the body for fight or flight. The pituitary action also stimulates the adrenals to release something different: cortisol. Following a successful fight or flight, cortisol will quiet the amygdala's alarm and return the nervous system to a state of homeostasis.

At least, that is how the system functions under ideal circumstances. Difficulties can develop in this sequence, however, when fight or flight are not successful, or if they are not possible. Under such circumstances, the amygdala continues to sound an alarm; the SNS continues to activate and prepare the body for fight or flight. The result is what I identify as the hall-marks of PTSD: persistent symptoms of hyperarousal in the ANS. These include hyper–startle response, hypervigilance, difficulty staying asleep, and others listed for PTSD in the DSM-5 (American Psychiatric Association, 2013).

Another difficulty can occur. When, under extreme threat, neither fight nor flight is possible, the limbic system can direct the body, instead, to go into a state of freeze, sometimes called tonic immobility (Gallup & Maser, 1977). Exactly how the freeze response occurs is not as well understood as fight and flight. The old-school belief is that it results from a simultaneous activation of the PNS and the SNS. When that happens, features of hyperarousal of the SNS (rapid heartbeat and respiration; cold, humid skin; pupil dilation; and raised blood pressure) persist while features of hyperarousal of the PNS (highly flushed skin, very slow respiration and heart rate, constricted pupils, and a drop in blood pressure) will also be present. This state can be identified by indicators of SNS hyperarousal (e.g., extremely rapid heart rate, very dry mouth) that occur with indicators of PNS hyperarousal (e.g., extremely slow respiration, very flushed skin)—a hodgepodge.

Freezing is characterized by paralysis, with either slack muscles (as when a mouse is captured by a cat) or stiff muscles (like a deer or kangaroo caught in headlights). During freezing there is an altered sense of time and space, reduced registration of pain, and dampened emotion. Those who have frozen under threat report a kind of dissociative experience: Time slows down and they are no longer afraid. As such, freezing is also an extremely valuable survival defense. However, it has greater consequences in the aftermath of trauma than does either fight or flight. Studies demonstrate that those who dissociate during trauma (including freezing) have a greater chance of developing PTSD than those who do not (Bremner et al., 1992; Classen et al., 1993; Shalev et al., 1996).

It is important to note that an individual does not have the luxury of choosing whether to respond to threat with fight, flight, or freezing responses. It is a subcortical (i.e., not thought out), automatic response mediated by the limbic system of the brain. There is no shame in freezing. It is the limbic system's best strategy for survival based on instantaneous evaluation of each situation and each person's unique resources and circumstances.

## THE BASICS: NEW-SCHOOL ANS

While the old-school basics still have relevance, they have also left gaps that have proved problematic for understanding the wider range of nuances in response that are seen both day-to-day and in extreme circumstances. It is for that reason that around 2014 I started toying with the old two-column table. First I added a column to represent *normal life*, when a degree of arousal is needed to tackle daily, but not traumatic, challenges. Next I pondered the two types of freeze response I was noticing and students were asking me about, the one with stiff muscles and racing heartbeat and the other with flaccid muscles and extremely slow heart rate. Third, I was concerned that the term *hypoarousal* was being used to describe two quite different phenomena, both the life-endangering collapse that accompanies the flaccid freeze state and the low energy of the person who is exhausted, depressed, grieving, or has given up on life in some way.

## UPDATING WITH THEORIES OF STEPHEN PORGES, DANIEL SIEGEL, AND MERETE HOLM BRANTBJERG

Stephen Porges provided important keys to two of the issues raised above. He has evolved an alternative understanding of the ANS and the reflexes of fight, flight, and freeze that became popular around the turn of the 21st cen-

tury (Porges, 1995, 2003). His innovative view continues to feature prominently in current ANS understanding, particularly among trauma specialists
and somatic psychology practitioners. In his *polyvagal theory*, Porges rejects
the concept of the PNS, replacing it with two types of *vagal nerve activation*: dorsal vagal, which underlies the collapsed, hypotoned (flaccid) freeze
state, and the ventral vagal, which he proposes underlies the calm state
necessary for social interaction. I do not disagree with him, though I see
those two vagal branches as synonymous with two differing levels of PNS
activation (as represented by PNS II and PNS III on my six-column ANS
table). It is therefore that in *Revolutionizing Trauma Treatment*, as well as
here in this revision, my aim is to incorporate Porges's valuable theory with
old-school foundations. Lacking in Porges's view is a differentiation between
the SNS activation necessary for tackling the challenges of normal life and
the more extreme SNS activation that underlies the hypertoned (stiff) freeze
response. I still firmly believe that familiarization with and ability to identify
the visible and palpable indicators of SNS and PNS activation is the best
tool available for monitoring both a client's and one's own current state of
stress and calm. That is why I set to work to expand and update the old-
school ANS table with my own synthesis. Bottom line: It is most important
to monitor your and your clients' ANS so you can each regulate your ANS
to avoid losing the ability to think clearly. Tracking PNS and SNS arousal
will make that possible. No matter which theory or synthesis you subscribe
to, being able to observe, identify, and distinguish SNS and PNS activation
in your own body is one of your very best hedges against compassion fatigue,
vicarious traumatization, and burnout.

The third issue I raised above, the possibility of two degrees of
hypoarousal, is further complicated by both Porges's theory and the concept
of a *window of tolerance* as proposed by Daniel Siegel (1999) in his first book,
*The Developing Mind*. It has been generally accepted, particularly by trauma
therapists, that there is just one type of hypoarousal, which is a response
to great threat. That is the one that Porges proposes is a collapse activated
by the dorsal branch of the vagal nerve. However, I and others, including
my Danish colleague Merete Holm Brantbjerg, have noticed a critical difference between the lowered arousal state that is a result of extreme threat

to life (associated with Porges's view of the dorsal vagal) and another quite different state of low arousal that is more likely a response to depression, neglect, bereavement, or a kind of giving up. Both are exhibited primarily by flaccid muscles.

For understanding the conundrum of hypoarousal, I believe you can do no better than to study Brantbjerg's theory (2012, 2020). She also has the most experience identifying and working with hypoarousal due to the somatic psychology tradition she was key in developing, Bodynamic Analysis, that was already working with hypoarousal as early as the 1960s.

## THE ANS, SOMATIC EMPATHY, AND VICARIOUS TRAUMA

Therapists working with very stressed and traumatized individuals are at particularly high risk for compassion fatigue and vicarious trauma when they ignore or are unable to distinguish their own signs of ANS arousal. This very common therapist hazard, however, is not necessary; it can be prevented, or at least greatly reduced.

We are most vulnerable to compassion fatigue and vicarious traumatization when we are unaware of the state of our own body and mind. We can become so focused on the distress of those in our care that we neglect our own growing discomfort. Actually, as my colleague whom I mentioned at the beginning of this chapter, Bonnita Wirth, discovered, we can even miss or misread the indicators that would tell us we are generally under stress. Sometimes it might be that your body is screaming in pain, fright, or exhaustion and you do not heed the signs. Of course there can be circumstances under which the needs of a client must supersede your own, but these should be rare instances. To be able to ensure your continued ability to help your clients and take care of yourself, you have to learn to watch for and recognize signals which tell you that you need to take a break, to rest, to talk to someone about your own experiences, to be with family and friends, to cry, to regroup, and so on. What are those signals and how do you recognize them?

### Autonomic Nervous System: Precision Regulation

Following page 126 you will find the full-color, six-column ANS table fold-out as premiered in *Revolutionizing Trauma Treatment*.[9] I created this table for two main purposes: (1) to improve your observation and regulation of your clients' dysregulated ANS states, to make trauma treatment safer; and (2) to provide you with a tool for observing and regulating your own ANS during sessions with your clients, to aid your self-care and help you to reduce or even eliminate your risk for vicarious trauma and compassion fatigue. (Note, a black-and-white rendering is included as Figure 3.2 for additional reference.)

I will not be providing such a lengthy discussion of the background or evolution of the table, nor applications to clients, as I did in *Revolutionizing Trauma Treatment* (Rothschild, 2021). If you would like information for using the table with clients, please look there. Hopefully, what I offer here will be immediately useful for your self-care in your current situation.

### BRIEF ADDITIONAL DISCLAIMER

In the introduction to this book, I mentioned the important role disagreement plays within a field of study. That is apropos here. While I am quite pleased with the table, I am definitely aware that it is not perfect. I believe I have been successful in improving on what was available previously, but I am sure this (and probably any) tool certainly can, itself, be improved upon. Whether it will be me who does that, or someone else, I do not know at this time. But, as I wrote in this book's introduction, no theory is set in stone; improving on or identifying what more could be done, subtracted or added, can only make any theory better.

### HOW TO READ THE ANS TABLE

As the title implies, the "Autonomic Nervous System: Precision Regulation, **What to Look For**" table has a twofold purpose. It is meant to be a tool

---

[9] It is also possible to obtain a stiff, laminated table from W. W. Norton's website or Amazon. Many therapists find it handy as a desk reference, and also because you can write on it with dry markers (like a whiteboard). Track yourself or your client, and then wipe it clean to start again. Just make sure to avoid permanent markers, as they will not erase.

# AUTONOMIC NERVOUS SYSTEM: PRECISION REGULATION
## ** WHAT TO LOOK FOR **

"Normal" Life →← Threat to Life

| | LETHARGIC Parasympathetic I (PNS I) | CALM Parasympathetic II (PNS II) *Ventral Vagus* | ACTIVE/ALERT Sympathetic I (SNS I) | FLIGHT/FIGHT Sympathetic II (SNS II) | HYPER FREEZE Sympathetic III (SNS III) | HYPO FREEZE Parasympathetic III (PNS III) *Dorsal Vagus Collapse* |
|---|---|---|---|---|---|---|
| PRIMARY STATE | Apathy, Depression | Safe, Clear Thinking, Social Engagement | Alert, Ready to Act | React to Danger | Await Opportunity to Escape | Prepare for Death |
| AROUSAL | Too Low | Low | Moderate | High | Extreme Overload | Excessive Overwhelm Induces Hypoarousal |
| MUSCLES | Slack | Relaxed/toned | Toned | Tense | Rigid (deer in the headlights) | Flaccid |
| RESPIRATION | Shallow | Easy, often into belly | Increasing rate | Fast, often in upper chest | Hyperventilation | Hypo-ventilation |
| HEART RATE | Slow | Resting | Quicker or more forceful | Quick and/or forceful | Tachycardia (very fast) | Bradycardia (very slow) |
| BLOOD PRESSURE | Likely low | Normal | On the rise | Elevated | Significantly high | Significantly low |
| PUPILS, EYES, EYE LIDS | Pupils smaller, lids may be heavy | Pupils smaller, eyes moist, eye lids relaxed | Pupils widening, eyes less moist, eye lids toned | Pupils very dilated, eyes dry, eye lids tensed/raised | Pupils very small or dilated, eyes very dry, lids very tense | Lids drooping, eyes closed or open and fixed |
| SKIN TONE | Variable | Rosy hue, despite skin color (blood flows to skin) | Less rosy hue, despite skin color (blood flows to skin) | Pale hue, despite skin color (blood flow to muscles) | May be pale and/or flushed | Noticeably pale |
| HUMIDITY — Skin | Dry | Dry | Increased sweat | Increased sweat, may be cold | Cold sweat | Cold sweat |
| HUMIDITY — Mouth | Variable | Moist | Less moist | Dry | Dry | Dry |
| HANDS & FEET (TEMPERATURE) | May be warm or cool | Warm | Cool | Cold | Extremes of cold & hot | Cold |
| DIGESTION | Variable | Increase | Decrease | Stops | Evacuate bowel & bladder | Stopped |
| EMOTIONS (LIKELY) | Grief, sadness, shame, disgust | Calm, pleasure, love, sexual arousal | Anger, shame, disgust, anxiety, excitement, sexual climax | Rage, fear | Terror, may be dissociation | May be too dissociated to feel anything |
| CONTACT WITH SELF & OTHERS | Withdrawn | Probable | Possible | Limited | Not likely | Impossible |
| FRONTAL CORTEX | May or may not be accessible | Should be accessible | Should be accessible | May or may not be accessible | Likely inaccessible | Inaccessible |
| INTEGRATION | Not likely | Likely | Likely | Not likely | Impossible | Impossible |
| RECOMMENDED INTERVENTION | Activate, Gently Increase Energy | Continue Therapy Direction | Continue Therapy Direction | Put on Brakes | Slam on Brakes | Medical Emergency CALL PARAMEDICS |

*Observe client states: To modulate arousal with brakes. Adjust in yourself: To think clearly & prevent vicarious trauma & compassion fatigue.

FIGURE 3.2 Autonomic Nervous System: Precision Regulation *Source: 2000, 2014, 2017 Babette Rothschild and multiple medical and physiology texts (Levine, 2010; Porges, 2011).*

that enables a more precise monitoring of ANS arousal while also providing the details of those features that are important to identify for making precision regulation possible. With regard to your self-care, self-observation will be your means to precise monitoring; that is where mindful self-awareness comes in. Then, once you make your observation, interpreting what it means is the next task, and last, identifying when you need to intervene to bring your arousal to a level that maximizes calm as well as your ability to think clearly. Below you will learn how to read the table and apply that knowledge to what you self-observe.

Please note that I am avoiding the use of the term *relaxed* when describing lack of stress. That is because relaxation implies a nonactivation of muscles, sometimes even flaccid muscles. For the purposes of reducing arousal, it is more precise to refer to the arousal state that is better described as *calm*. Moreover, it is often the case, as is discussed in Chapter 3, that having more toned, even somewhat tense, muscles makes possible a greater level of ANS calm.

Now take a look at the table. The six columns are meant to represent a continuum of ANS arousal, gradually increasing levels of stress from activation that is genuinely too low to arousal that is so high it might cause a life-threatening emergency. The color progression is also intended to reflect that increasing intensity. Though I have drawn the columns with lines separating them, the rainbow effect at the top is meant to illustrate that the borders between the columns are not rigid, that the defined arousal states can overlap or flow one into the other. In all likelihood there could be many more columns to describe further nuanced differences between them. For example, at a particular moment in time your own arousal might fall more on the cusp between one state and another. However, trying to account for additional distinct states would make this table, as well as understanding the

ANS as a whole, just too overwhelming. Therefore I limited the number of columns to six.

Across the top of the table are the titles for each column, using a behavioral term for each state: *lethargic, calm, active/alert, flight/fight, hyper freeze, hypo freeze.*

Each column is also assigned a corresponding role in the traditionally

| LETHARGIC | CALM | ACTIVE/ALERT | FLIGHT/FIGHT | HYPER FREEZE | HYPO FREEZE |

understood branches of the ANS: *parasympathetic I, II, or III,* and *sympathetic I, II, or III.* There is also indication of vagal nerve activity per Steven Porges's (2011) polyvagal theory. What I am calling the calm state is, I believe, akin to Porges's description of activation of the ventral branch of the vagus nerve, and my hypo freeze state is akin to his description of the collapse activated by the dorsal branch of the vagus nerve.

Below the titles, each column has a description of its primary state and a prediction of the level of arousal that goes with each. At the bottom of each column is a recommendation for interventions with clients during therapy; however, those may be somewhat different for our purposes of your self-care here. I will adapt those for you below.

Also at the top are two horizontal arrows that reach across multiple columns. To the left is a turquoise arrow with the label *normal life*; to the right is a pink one that reads *threat to life.*

I added those arrows to quickly identify the most usual and desirable states of arousal—calm and active/alert—and to distinguish them from the states associated with threat to life that are neither usual nor desirable.

It is very important for me to correct an important and common misconception. These categories of arousal are not diagnoses. This or that type of person or particular psychological problem is not represented on this table at all. What is represented is objectively observable (e.g., skin tone) and reportable (e.g., emotion) characteristics that coincide with various states of ANS arousal.

ANS arousal levels fluctuate continually as you tackle your day, rising and lowering in response to external circumstances (e.g., listening to soothing classical music) and internal dialogue (e.g., "Oh no! How am I going to meet that deadline!?"). There may be trends or patterns, but they are ever changing from moment to moment. Even if you are clinically depressed, suffer an anxiety disorder, or even PTSD, your arousal levels will fluctuate through the day. The goal is to monitor arousal in the present moment, and then, eventually, to be able to intervene when necessary to alter a state to improve your safety, clarity, and calm.

On the far left of the table is a column that lists multiple characteristics from top to bottom.

| PRIMARY STATE | | | | | |
|---|---|---|---|---|---|
| AROUSAL | | | | | |
| MUSCLES | | | | | |
| RESPIRATION | Shallow | Easy, often into belly | Increasing rate | Fast, often in upper chest | Hyperventilation |
| HEART RATE | | | | | |
| BLOOD PRESSURE | | | | | |
| PUPILS, EYES, EYE LIDS | | | | | |
| SKIN TONE | | | | | |
| HUMIDITY | | | | | |
| HANDS & FEET (TEMPERATURE) | | | | | |
| DIGESTION | | | | | |
| EMOTIONS (LIKEYL) | | | | | |
| CONTACT WITH SELF & OTHERS | | | | | |
| FRONTAL CORTEX | | | | | |
| INTEGRATION | | | | | |
| RECOMMENDED INTERVENTION | | | | | |

If you follow each characteristic across its own line from left to right, you will see how that characteristic likely changes as arousal increases. For example, respiration is very slow in the lethargic state and gradually quickens in frequency and speed in sync with rising arousal.

Notice that physical characteristics are on a buff-colored background and emotional and psychological characteristics are on a gray background.

Reading down a column, you should get a fairly good idea of what you might look and feel like when in that state of arousal. Just remember to allow for variations, that the arousal could be more toward the lower or higher end of that state. In addition, do not expect every feature in that column to be exactly correct. The idea is to look for the basic trend in that column. Bodies and minds have similarities in how they react to specific situations, so there should be commonality. But there are also individual differences, which means you will rarely, if ever, see a 100% match. You may have noticed, for instance, that some people cry when they are angry or breathe shallowly despite being very calm. Others may blush no matter what they are feeling or their level of arousal. In using this table, you will get to know your own individual traits, what is usual for you. Once you do, the table will become even more useful to you.

With regard to visually observable traits, you can look in the mirror to get a measure of your own state. Look at your skin tone or pupil dilation, for example. You might also notice your skin tone through your body awareness, as skin gets more warm when blood flows to it and more cool when blood flows away from it. That is why you might know when you are blushing if you feel heat on your neck or face. In that case, you will not need any visual confirmation.

Make sure to account for any environmental variables that might skew your observations. For example, right now my city is experiencing a heat wave and humidity is quite high; I do not have air conditioning in my office. As a result, today my hands and much of the rest of my body are warm, moist, and sticky through the day. Though it is not particularly comfortable, it has nothing to do with ANS arousal. Likewise, if the weather were cold and my heater broken, I might feel chilled, but it would not necessarily be because I was anxious or otherwise stressed.

## HOW TO USE THE TABLE

For our purposes here, your self-care, this table is best used in conjunction with your own skills of mindful self-awareness. Body awareness as well as awareness of your emotions and thoughts will all play a part in gaining a complete picture of your arousal level at any point in time. To begin with, periodically check in with yourself throughout the day; maybe start with once and then increase gradually to several times a day. It will be additionally helpful if you jot down your observations. If you keep a record, you will be able to look back to identify patterns and changes. Those of you who have the ANS table as a laminated card can write on it with a dry (not permanent) marker to track your arousal through a day or week, and then erase to start over (I would not suggest you write on the foldout in this book, though). When you check, pay particular attention to your heart rate, respiration, temperature of your hands and feet, and whether or not you are thinking clearly. In addition, note any other features that are useful to you. You will eventually discover which indicators give you the most reliable information. Once you have zeroed in on which aspects are most telling, you will be able to take one or more stress snapshots through the day.

When your stress is low (but you are not lethargic), and you are feeling calm and clear-headed, simply carry on with what you are doing. However, if you find your stress high, or creeping up, and you already are or are nearing danger of losing your ability to think clearly, it is time for intervention. Of course, it is better to catch rising stress before it gets into a danger zone where you lose your ability to be rational. However, you need to expect that, at least in the beginning, you will likely misjudge periodically until you get familiar with where your personal stress limits lie. Please be kind and compassionate with yourself when you misjudge; this process involves a very human learning curve.

Once you become adept at identifying your fluctuating arousal levels, you can start experimenting with strategies to see which ones help to calm you when needed or energize you when that is needed. Please note that no one strategy will work for everyone, and just about any strategy will work for someone. The idea is to identify and apply what works for you, a tailor-made tool kit. A selection of strategies follows after the discussion of low arousal.

## THE SPECIAL, RECENTLY IDENTIFIED, STATE
## OF LETHARGIC LOW AROUSAL

Understanding the lethargic state (yellow on my ANS table) may be important for your own self-care, particularly during times of extreme stress. It is for this reason that I want to make this section especially relevant for you, but first a little background might help.

As mentioned above, much of the literature on trauma treatment, inspired by Porges and Siegel, classifies what I have identified here as two different types of low arousal (Lethargic, yellow column; Hypo Freeze, purple column) as the same, that is, they recognize only one type of hypoarousal. The usual recommendation for intervention when hypoarousal is identified involves activating and increasing arousal through movement and activity. I honestly do not understand how so many do not see what seems to me obvious, the difference between a low arousal that routinely lacks energy

**FIGURE 3.3A**   Yellow PNS I column, lethargic = deflated.

**FIGURE 3.3B**   Purple PNS III column, hypo freeze = overinflated to bursting, collapsing.

(lethargic) and a systemwide collapse that is the result of extreme stress when one is pushed beyond all limits (hypo freeze). To follow my seemingly unconventional point of view, it may help to think of lethargic as similar to a balloon that is underinflated or deflated, and the collapse that is typical of hypo freeze as being like a balloon that becomes so overinflated or injured (by bullet, arrow, and such) that it bursts (Figure 3.3A and 3.3B).

With a couple of notable exceptions, both in your professional work and in your personal daily life, you will not likely observe in others or experience in yourself a true hypo freeze. That is an extreme response to ultraextreme stress. Those who are most likely to witness hypo freeze are emergency room hospital personnel and first responders including police, firefighters, and EMTs. That is because hypo freeze is most akin to medical shock. As you can see from the purple PNS III column on the ANS table, that state includes traits such as extremely low respiration and dangerously slow heart rate, which can be life-threatening. Usually such extreme reactions are the result of life-threatening violence such as being involved in or witness to shootings, explosions, rape, car accidents, and the like. It can also be the result of receiving terrifying news (such as someone who faints upon hearing of the sudden death of a loved one). As such, it is a rare occurrence in the psychotherapy office. That is not to say it can never happen there, but it is not usual. Hypo freeze in therapy is most likely to occur if the client is arriving just after experiencing or witnessing an event as described above or remembering such an event before having the stability to process the memory in a safe way. Of course, note that someone's arousal can lie on a cusp, for example, between hyper and hypo freeze, which could be a severe state, but not life-threatening. However, no matter which level of hypo freeze is present, I believe it must be distinguished from the lethargic state. Not to do so can potentially have unfortunate consequences. Interventions for the lethargic state should involve slowly increasing tolerance for activity and arousal (Brantbjerg, 2012, 2020). On the other hand, for hypo freeze, a state that is already overactivated and overwhelmed, we must necessarily include interventions that reduce arousal, threat, or provocation.

If you find yourself in shock in reaction to terrible news or witnessing violence, you should follow common advice for treating shock and for preventing and treating fainting spells. However, if you have these symptoms in the absence of acute threat, you would be advised to seek medical advice as there could be an underlying health issue.

The lethargic state is more likely to be familiar to many of you. In reaction to community and world crises, more people than ever are experiencing varying levels of depression, from mild to severe. Often when someone is depressed, if they check in with their ANS state, they will periodically find their traits fall into the yellow, lethargic category. As I said before, that does not constitute a diagnosis. The state can fluctuate, and it is certainly known that someone who is depressed can also experience high arousal, for instance with anxiety. But if you know you are clinically depressed, there can be a trend to often finding yourself in this state, especially if in addition to normal life, one or more crises (family, community, world) threaten your hope for the present or future. Even when the realities do not change, there are definitely things you can do to raise your energy level . . . slowly. Each intervention must be undertaken with care and patience. No rushing! See below for strategies to shift arousal levels. In 8 *Keys to Safe Trauma Recovery* (Rothschild, 2010), I suggest taking small steps. Merete Holm Brantbjerg uses the term *dosing*. The intention is similar, to approach raising available energy in manageable bits rather than trying to raise it all at once.

## IDENTIFYING ANS AROUSAL—BOTH SNS AND PNS

In *The Body Remembers* (Rothschild, 2000), I promoted the use of body awareness to help trauma therapy clients learn to identify and track their own states of ANS arousal. Learning these basics helps clients toward greater control over their arousal states. The same idea is relevant to and highly recommended for psychotherapists as well. Forester (2001) compared therapists who regularly practiced body awareness during clinical encounters with those who did not. She found that the frequency of attention to body awareness was a significant variable. In those clinicians who indicated lower incidence of vicarious traumatization, body awareness was the key. In addition, a preliminary investigation by Rothschild, Shiffrar, and Turner (2005) indicated that body awareness is critical for mediating the risks of vicarious trauma and burnout (see the appendix for a more detailed description of this project). Again, common sense: The more adept you become at recognizing, tracking, and evaluating the level of arousal in your own body, the better you will be able to regulate your arousal and mediate your own risks for compassion fatigue, vicarious trauma, and burnout.

The first step is to become familiar with the features of the various states of arousal as outlined in the accompanying ANS table. For some, first focusing on your own responses may come easier. Other individuals will learn this most easily by first observing arousal changes in others—clients, family, and friends—just to get attuned to observing it. Discover how you learn best. Once your observation skills are developed, they can be turned inward. Sometimes the intricacies of ANS arousal are most easily grasped in groups. Some readers may find it useful to get together with one or more colleagues and learn this together. If working with peers, take turns with the exercises in the next section. Observe each other one at a time and discuss what you see. Then the person who is being observed can give feedback on their own body awareness—a chance to develop skills of observation and self-awareness simultaneously. A major potential for preventing and healing compassion fatigue and vicarious trauma is tied to your ability to recognize the sensations that signal hyperarousal in you.

Using breathing as an example, what might distinguish breathing driven by a calm state from that which is driven by a hyperaroused state?

Calm, PNS breathing tends to be slow, long breaths, which go deep into the lungs, causing them to expand downward and the belly to puff out. In PNS breathing, the emphasis is on the exhale, sometimes even a sigh. Hyperaroused SNS breathing, on the other hand, tends to come in quicker gasps with an emphasis on the inhale, usually restricted to the upper chest.

Now, of course, I have described two extremes. Normal breathing for most people lies somewhere between those extremes. The idea, though, is to learn your own pattern of calm, resting breathing, and to identify how that is different from your breathing when you are mildly stressed and when you are highly stressed. That way you will have indicators of when you might be at risk. Then you will be in a position to intercede.

## IN SYNC WITH OUR CLIENTS

Many studies have looked at ANS synchrony between people. In fact, Levenson and Ruef (1997) devoted 10 full pages to a review of that literature in their book chapter, "Physiological Aspects of Emotional Knowledge and Rapport." Even synchronized heart rates between therapists and clients have been studied (Coleman et al., 1956; DiMascio et al., 1955; Stanek et al., 1973). Especially interesting is DiMascio and colleagues' 1957 study. They identified a direct concordance between the heart rates of therapists and those of their clients as the tension level of the therapy sessions fluctuated. However, they also found that heart rates were inversely related when the client was feeling antagonistic toward the therapist—somatic empathy versus somatic antipathy, so to speak. Levenson and Ruef went on to question the results of the aforementioned studies. Nonetheless, many therapists will recognize this kind of ANS synchrony in their own experience with clients. Sometimes the therapist's first hint that a client is becoming anxious is a quickening of the therapist's own heartbeat or breathing. Many psychotherapists already know that one way to calm a client's panic attack is to breathe slowly themselves. Panicked clients will often, unconsciously, synchronize their breathing to their therapist's, slowing it and becoming calmer in the process.

Autonomic synchrony is one of the core components of somatic empathy. As such, it is critical to be able to recognize it in yourself. Sometimes you will want to be in autonomic sync with your clients; it might help you know them on a deeper level. However, more often it could threaten your own well-being. The first step to controlling this synchrony is to become aware of its nuances and to evaluate for yourself when it is productive and when it could be risky for you. Exercises toward that goal follow below.

## Skill Building

### Arousal Awareness

Simple mindful body awareness is the single most useful tool for identifying levels of arousal—those that are beneficial and those that threaten good functioning. It is at least as, if not more, important for therapists than it is for their clients. Refer back to Figure 3.2. All six levels of ANS arousal will be useful for you to become familiar with, or even to memorize, so you will be able to identify what is happening in your own body.

Simple body and arousal awareness is a useful skill in itself. As mentioned before, Forester (2001) found that practicing body awareness alone could lower the incidence of vicarious traumatization. It can also serve as a baseline for evaluating the effectiveness of other skills. You can check what is happening in your body before and after you try an intervention and then compare. That way you can determine more precisely how and whether any particular skill or tool works for you.

--------------- EXERCISE 1: SIMPLE BODY AWARENESS ---------------

In a quiet room at a peaceful time, try this exercise: Sit comfortably and take notice of what you become most aware of in your body. Identify the temperature and humidity on the surface of your skin. Is it warm and dry, cool and moist, or something in between? Notice that there are differences depending on where your skin is clothed or bare. There will also be differences depending on how your blood is circulating at the moment. Remember, for instance, that some people naturally tend toward cold feet or hands.

Next, notice where your muscles are tense and where they are relaxed. Look for nuances of difference throughout your body (upper body versus lower body, right to left, etc.). What about your breathing? Is it deep or shallow, high in your chest or low into your belly? Also, notice how the expression on your face feels from the inside. What is the position and expression of your mouth, eyes, forehead? Can you feel your heartbeat? Is it fast, slow, or medium?

Take a look at the ANS table and the information you have gathered to guide you to identify your arousal level and estimate if it is optimal for you. You will find that some areas of your body are easier to be aware of than others. Discover the somatic cues that are most available to you and exercise the ones that are more difficult to notice.

Next, remember something pleasant from your life. Notice any changes in skin, muscles, face, breathing, and heartbeat. Just take note of the changes. You might write them down if that will help you to keep track and compare later. Then, remember something slightly unpleasant from the last 24 hours, or think about something you are anticipating with mild anxiety or irritation. Again, note changes in the areas mentioned above.

Finally, vacillate back and forth between pleasant and mildly unpleasant memories or anticipations, a few seconds with each, tracking the fluctuations. This will help to sharpen your awareness of changes in your body systems and ANS arousal. In this way, when you are not under any pressure, you can develop your skill in body and arousal awareness. The more you practice, the greater the chance that this knowledge will be available to you in actual stressful situations.

───────── **EXERCISE 2: PRACTICING BODY AWARENESS** ─────────
**DURING THERAPY SESSIONS**

Once you have a feel for what it means to be aware of your body, you can take that into the therapy session. Begin to practice awareness of your own body while working with a client who is less challenging to work with. Since learning any new skill takes some degree of focus, it would not be wise to begin with your most demanding client. Once you feel comfortable attending to your body sensations during a session with one or two easier clients, you will be able to begin using the same skills with more difficult ones.

When therapy sessions are engaging, it is sometimes difficult to remember to pay attention to your own body. It can be helpful to place something within your usual line of sight that can remind you to check in with your body from time to time. It can be a symbol or a word. Often a file card does the trick. It really does not matter as long as you recognize its meaning. Once that reminder is in place, during a session with your chosen client, once every 15 to 20 minutes tune in to your own body and assess for the distribution of temperature and tension differences, your breathing pattern, facial expression, position of your limbs, and so on per Exercise 1 above. Notice if and how some of these elements change throughout the session. At this point, put aside your interest in what the changes might mean. This step is solely for developing awareness. The additional exercises in this chapter and following chapters will build upon that base.

If the instructions above seem too much to tackle at this point in time, set your goal to a smaller step. In that case you can simply decide on a single area of awareness to check into once or twice during a session. Just check only the temperature of your hands, or just the depth or pace of your breathing. Sometimes what may seem like a ridiculously small step may be the perfect starting point. Aim for a step you are sure you can be successful with, and then gradually increase your skill one step at a time.

## EXERCISE 3: TRACKING AROUSAL

The better you are able to gauge your own levels of ANS arousal, the better you will be able to care for yourself during—and following—therapy sessions. Arousal awareness is a skill. Like any skill, it takes practice. It will be made easier by mastering the basics of body awareness, as in Exercises 1 and 2.

The ANS is not your only possible gauge. It may also be useful to notice what else is happening to your body: sleeping patterns, digestion, changes in vision or hearing, and so forth. Changes in those habits may be indicative of chronic changes in ANS arousal and are worthwhile to track for their own sake. For example, Bonnita Wirth (see above) may have benefited from such attention to her sleep pattern, noticing how that changed when she went into private practice. Had she done so, she may have noticed sooner that her body was not optimally managing the stress of her work. Monitoring your ANS will be your most direct tool for judging when you are managing things well and when you are not, both from moment to moment and over time.

As has been said, though, it takes practice and patience. First you need to become familiar with the signs of arousal as described in the previous section. Memorize them if you can or keep the ANS table where you can easily refer to it. Then, during a normal day, check in with yourself from time to time and pay particular attention to your heart rate, respiration, skin humidity, and temperature. Learn what is normal for you when you are calm or not particularly under stress. You can also learn what is normal for you under conditions of moderate stress. Once you know your own tendencies, it will be possible to differentiate your safety zone from your danger zone.

## EXERCISE 4: TRACKING YOUR AROUSAL LEVEL DURING SESSIONS

This exercise will guide you in tracking your level of ANS arousal during a therapy session with a client. Paying attention to your arousal level will help you know how your own system is managing whatever is going on in the session. For a multitude of reasons, a client's therapy session can adversely affect the therapist. All too often, when that happens the therapist does not know about it until after the session, if at all. Sometimes the aftereffects can be debilitating. By tracking your ANS, warnings of a possible difficulty can be identified during the session, enabling immediate intervention. That way, you will have more choices for managing your client work with fewer ill effects.

Tracking your arousal during a therapy session follows from what you learned in Exercise 2. Arousal awareness is just one, albeit specialized, form of body awareness. Again, it is advisable to begin your practice with a less-demanding client. It is possible that with such a client shifts in your arousal may be less dramatic, but tracking them will still help you get used to the process and get you in the habit.

As with the exercise for simple body awareness, post a file card or some other object within your line of sight to help remind you to pay attention to your arousal level. (When I was learning this, I wrote "ANS" in red on a white card and pinned it to the wall behind my client chair.) You could also leave the color ANS table on your desk or somewhere you can see it. Doing that carries a minor caveat, though. Some clients might be interested in it and want to learn what it means or how to use it. Personally, I have never had an objection to this as I like to share as much of my knowledge with my clients as they can usefully digest. However, I learned that there can be a risk. A few clients would actually monitor my ANS state, sometimes asking how I was feeling if they noticed me getting pale or breathing more quickly. Actually, I never minded and found it a refreshing part of the partnership of therapy. I learned ways to respond honestly to their observations without disclosing personal information that would not have been appropriate or helpful. But if this is something you would not feel comfortable with, then keep your copy of the chart out of sight.

For the first few sessions, it will be more than enough to scan your arousal level two to three times during a session. Rather than general body awareness, you will be specifically focusing on skin temperature and humidity, particularly in your hands and feet, along with heart rate, respiration rate, and how wet or dry your mouth is. Further, it is a good idea to notice just how much in contact you are with your body, your surroundings, and your client. Losing a sense of yourself or the room you are in can be a sign of dissociation, which is not advisable. You may not be able to identify dissociation once you are in it, but it is possible to learn to read the signs that you are on your way there (as some with epilepsy will learn to predict a seizure).

Once you gain confidence in tracking your arousal with a less challenging client, you will be ready to try the same with a client who is more emotionally demanding for you. The same principles apply: Several times during a session, check in with your body and gauge your arousal. An opportune time for this is when you are encouraging the same from your clients. When you ask them about their body awareness or arousal level, you can check yours at the same time.

Now that you can track your arousal level, the next task is gaining tools for regulating it. In the next section, strategies for lowering arousal are applied to the needs of the distressed therapist during psychotherapy sessions with clients. Conveniently, many of the same strategies will also work for your clients, but the focus here is on you.

### Maintaining Balance and Strength

BALANCE

This section is particularly relevant for those of you who live and work in countries or communities with additional stressors: natural disasters, war, coups, and so on, and for the rest of us around the world, during and following the COVID-19 pandemic. Maintaining mental and emotional balance has become a rarer commodity during the last few years—for everyone.

Stress, even when it is expected, can throw anyone off balance. Expected life challenges such as job changes, moving away, marrying or divorcing, saying goodbye to elderly loved ones, elective surgery, and so on, carry with them plenty of stress themselves. However, unexpected stress, whether personal or in reaction to community or world events, as well as trauma, can knock anybody completely out of balance. Achieving and maintaining the many aspects of balance is central to managing extraordinarily difficult, stressful, and traumatic times, also, perhaps especially, for therapists.

There are several categories of balance, including physical, emotional, mental, spiritual, work/free time, and so on. Actually, physical balance may be the best foundation for emotional, mental, and spiritual balance—they are all interconnected and interdependent. The greater the emotional and mental stress, the more likelihood that your physical balance will be affected. In fact, the vestibular sense, which is located in the middle ear, is at the center of physical balance. The vestibular sense is often affected by stress and trauma. That is why it is common for those with PTSD and chronic anxiety or panic to also contend with vertigo, a disturbance of the vestibular sense that causes bouts of intense, even debilitating, dizziness. Many do not know (or may not understand) that actual, literal, physical balance—as, for example, keeping yourself upright while standing on one foot—has a relationship to overall balance in your mind, body, and emotions. When you are off-kilter in one of those areas, you can more easily become off-kilter in others. The good news is that if you shore up your balance skills in one area, it will likely help to steady others.

Have you ever noticed that when you (or others) are emotionally upset, you (they) are more likely to stub a toe, break a glass, fly off the handle at a child or spouse, have more difficulty balancing the checkbook or finishing a work task, trip over a crack in the sidewalk? I guess it is possible I am the only one, but I have more experience like this than I care to admit. I can say honestly for myself, being wobbly in one area of my being can definitely overflow into others—among other mishaps, I have had many sprained ankles, bruises, and kitchen messes to prove it.

If you can relate, the road to greater steadiness is fairly easy and absolutely free: increase your facility for physical balance. For one, improving your physical balance will, over time, have a positive influence on your emotional and mental stability. In addition, since practicing balance requires one's full attention in the present moment, it is also a useful practice for taking a mindful mental break from upsets and worries. However, how you go about improving your balance, like everything else, must be individually tailored to your own abilities, needs, tastes, and time.

## QUICK REVIEW OF THE NEUROPHYSIOLOGY OF BALANCE

Physical balance is achieved through a rather complex interaction of the two sensory systems in your brain and body. As discussed in Chapter 2, the exteroceptors are the five senses you are likely most familiar with, including hearing, sight, taste, touch, and smell. Exteroceptors take in information from the environment external to your body. For example, it is the sense of touch that helps you know if you need to put on a sweater, that is, whether your skin is warm or cold. The touch nerves in the sole of your foot tell you that your foot has reached the floor.

Interoceptors include proprioception and the vestibular sense. The vestibular sense, centered in the middle ear, is the central mechanism for your sense of balance. But additional interoceptive nerves also play a role in balance. Interoceptors are at work telling you the bend in your joints and the degree of tension in your muscles. They also communicate information about your body status and location in space. When you are mindfully paying attention to your breathing, heart rate, stomach sensations, balance, and so on, you are focusing on interoceptors.

Balance requires both exteroceptors and interoceptors. Proprioceptive nerves in your muscles and joints communicate information about your body position. Vestibular nerves evaluate your relationship to gravity and tell you which way is up. At the same time, your visual sense helps you orient your body position in relationship to your surroundings. And the sense of touch on the soles of your feet (or, depending on your position, also your hands or buttocks) is necessary to feel your contact with the support beneath your body (floor, chair, mattress, and so on).

Have you ever visited one of many tourist attractions with names like Gravity House, Mystery Hill, or some such? Typically the signage or a guide will tell you that the forces of gravity in that place defy the normal rules. When you enter the attraction's building, you may all of a sudden find that you cannot keep your balance.

The secret is (warning: spoiler alert) that the building (or room) is constructed on a slant that will disorient your sense of balance. The trick is highly successful, thus the popularity of these attractions. In lighted surroundings, most people depend on their sense of sight rather than their vestibular sense to tell them which way is upright. If, while you are inside these attractions, you close your eyes, your vestibular sense will kick in and you will know accurately which way is up. However, when you open your eyes, you will see your body is at odds with the visual cues. Unless you know this trick, it is very disorienting. However, such attractions provide insight into the interplay of interoceptors and exteroceptors in our ability to keep our physical balance.

The mystery is revealed by how such a house is built (Tabler, 2017).

There are many factors (besides houses built to fool you) that can disrupt the vestibular sense, including stress and trauma. So it is not unusual that in stressful times many people find themselves more clumsy or even having bouts of vertigo (a dizzying disturbance of the vestibular balance system).

It is for these reasons that including portions of physical balance practice and training can be helpful in reducing risks of falling and such, and also can help you to feel more balanced emotionally. Yoga, for one, is terrific for improving balance. Many yoga positions depend on or involve balance. One of the better known positions in that category would be the tree pose. You stand on one foot with the other resting on the calf or thigh of the supporting leg, with your hands reaching for the sky. For some that is an easy position; for others it will feel quite advanced and challenging. Basically, it is a good example of the interplay of interoceptors and exteroceptors. If you need proof of that, try keeping that pose (or any other way of balancing on just one foot) with your eyes closed. Unless you are a very advanced practitioner, it will not be possible. For more basic balance training, see the next section.

## BALANCE TRAINING PROGRESSION

For those of you who gain your balance training through yoga practice, this section may be repetitious or feel too elementary. However, I want to include it for those who (like me) prefer to start with the basics and train up slowly. What follows is one example of progressive balance training. These exercises are standard practice and are taught in all sorts of exercise classes. Please note: Begin each exercise in a modified form, for example, a wider stance or shorter time period. Then build up skill slowly.

1. Narrow stance, random reach: Stand with both feet on the floor close together and reach with your arms in different directions, in random patterns.
2. Narrow stance, rotational reaches: Stand with both feet on the floor close together, then rotate hips and look in the direction of each random reach with your arms.
3. Balance on one leg for 10–20 seconds. Then switch to the other leg. Variations: Try with one leg and then the other with random reaches or rotational reaches as above.
4. Balance on one leg, slowly swinging the other leg to the side, to the front, to the back.

5. Single leg raises. Try in different directions: side leg raise five times, front leg raise five times, rear leg kick five times, high knee raise.

6. Walk slowly forward, then backward with a very narrow stance (nearly, but not quite, like walking a balance beam). Start with feet slightly apart and gradually reduce the distance until setting feet down along the same straight line (as on a balance beam).

7. Balance on one leg while the toes of the opposite foot mark a clock on the floor, tapping a circle around the balancing foot. Switch to the other leg.

8. You can increase the challenge of each of the exercises above by standing on an uneven surface such as a thick bath towel or squishy yoga mat. When you get good at one or the other, you can add additional challenge by closing your eyes once in a while. Just do not try that before you are confident with your eyes open.

## STRENGTH

Getting and staying calm while your family, community, or the world is in crisis can be a major challenge. Nearly every day it seems as though someone is telling me to "just relax." Whether it is a friend, television commercial, book, podcast, TED Talk, whatever, it seems that everyone recommends relaxation as the soothing salve of choice. True, much of the time it is good for many people to relax. However, some of you might notice that generally, or particularly in times of stress, relaxation does not appear to be the good friend you have been told it should be. It is a complaint I have heard often, more so in the last few extremely stressful years.

Did you know that a good many people actually get more anxious when they try to relax or do stretching, say, per yoga? Actually, they have a name for it: relaxation-induced anxiety (Heide & Borkovec, 1983; Mental Health Daily, 2015). If you are one of those who have experienced this conundrum, you are in good company, including me. Even though it goes against just about everything we have ever heard about managing stress, it is true: Some people just do not get benefit from simple relaxation or relaxing practices. In fact, those of us who fall in to this cohort get the opposite: We can actually suffer from relaxation—not just the anxiety it induces, but also due to feeling odd, embarrassed, or even a little crazy that what (seemingly) helps everyone else does not help us.

No worries, though. For those of us who do not gain calm through relaxation, there are alternatives, no matter how counterintuitive they might seem. Here is the secret: If you become more anxious or unglued from relaxation, do the opposite; that is, boost muscle tone, gain muscle strength, and, yes, even increase tension, to become more calm.

However, to be successful, increasing muscle tone, tension, or strength for the purpose of calming must be done with a few caveats. First of all, the strengthening must be practiced in a nonaerobic state, that is, contracting the muscles without strain that would unnecessarily increase heartbeat and respiration. This is because increases in stress usually involve both. So keeping breathing and heart rate slow supports the goal of becoming more calm. Of course, aerobic exercise can also have a place in managing stress, just not for this application.

It is best to begin small and slow, picking one or two muscles or muscle groups to strengthen. For example, push-ups may be chosen to increase strength in arms, back, and chest, or wall sits to strengthen thighs and stomach muscles. Begin with a low-challenge position. For some, that may even mean starting with wall push-ups. Whatever is chosen, just do a few. Stop when your muscles just begin to tire. When the goal is calming, it will be counterproductive to do repetitions until the muscle burns or becomes exhausted. That is what you do if your goal is big muscles. When your goal is toning to increase calm, pushing an exercise to exhaustion could actually increase anxiety instead. Instead, each day gradually increase repetitions, always stopping at the start of tiredness. It is also a good idea to keep track of your progression and stress level pre- and post-exercise as well as through an average day. That way it will be possible to evaluate if a particular area of strength training is useful to help you be more calm.

Take note that it is possible that strengthening one set of muscles might induce calm, but doing the same with other muscles might induce anxiety. That is because no body is built the same as another. The distribution each of us has of more and less strong and toned muscles throughout our bodies will be very different from one person to another. Therefore, which muscles facilitate calm or anxiety will also be different. As always, it is an individual thing. Below are a few sample exercises to get you started. Note that the same principles can be applied to different muscles and muscle groups.

## RELAXED VERSUS CALM

The goal is to become calmer so that you can think clearly. (This concept is expanded on in Chapter 4.) Calm and relaxed are not necessarily the same thing. Relaxation involves loose muscles; calm is indicated by low ANS arousal. Therefore, increasing relaxation may be contraindicated for on-the-job stress that requires a high level of functioning. Consider that some muscle tension might actually be "friendly tension," helping you to better manage the demands of your personal and professional lives.

Increasing muscle tone is easy enough. Most forms of exercise will enhance tone. It is a good idea to combine body awareness with exercise (or any other of these skills, for that matter) to be able to discover precisely which exercises will be most useful for your own stress management. Get into a regular exercise program: Use the machines at the gym or free weights at home, walk, swim, bicycle, or something else. Discover where additional muscle tone might shore you up emotionally. As above, when increasing muscle tone for this purpose, it can be important to stop exercise short of muscular exhaustion. Sometimes at my gym I notice people exercising until they are nauseated or nearly passing out. Their bodies are signaling that they have gone too far, but they are not listening; the slogan "Do it till it burns" echoes in their ears. Follow the wisdom of your body and stop when you begin to be tired, while the exercise still feels good. That way you will look forward to, rather than dread, the next time.

In the Danish Bodynamic training program (which I attended in Copenhagen, 1988–1992), I learned their theory about a relationship between specific muscle strength and managing stress and assertiveness. Though there is no research on their hypothesis, you can try for yourself to see if strengthening specific muscles helps you out. For example, when you find yourself under stress, do you lack "backbone"? Is it hard for you to stand up for yourself? If so, you might try to strengthening the long muscles of your back and neck, so that it is easier to hold your torso and head upright. Lying flat on your stomach and slowly lifting your head can help to increase tone in the muscles along your spine and neck. Sitting up straight will also strengthen those muscles.

Are you prone to "go weak in the knees" when you are surprised, frightened, or stressed? Adding strength to your thighs may help. Knee bends or skiing exercises can help develop stronger knees.

Have you noticed having trouble "standing on your own two feet," not able to make decisions or do things on your own? Strengthening the muscles in your lower legs may help. Try exercises that flex the ankle, working the muscles on the backs of your calves.

Is it difficult to be assertive, to say "no" or "stop"? Doing push-ups to add strength to your arms' triceps may prove useful.

Is it difficult to "hold yourself together" when stressed? Increasing tone along the outsides of your thighs may help. Side leg lifts are particularly useful for this.

It may also be handy to be able to increase muscle tone in the face of immediate stress, to put on the brakes. For that purpose, exercises from Rothschild (2000) are reproduced here. They can be used as described or to inspire you to find other muscles to tense that will benefit you in a pinch.

- INCREASING MUSCLE TONE IN PERIPHERAL MUSCLES
  It is important to note that any exercises to increase tone should be done only until the muscle feels slightly tired. Releasing the tension must be done slowly. This is not progressive muscle relaxation. The idea here is to try to maintain a little of the contraction or tension. Try one exercise and evaluate it with body awareness before going on to the next. If tensing causes any adverse reaction (nausea, spaciness, anxiety, etc.), you can usually neutralize that reaction by gently stretching the same muscle—making an opposite movement.

- SIDES OF LEGS
  Stand with feet a little less than shoulder width apart, knees relaxed (neither locked nor bent). Press knees out directly to the side so that you can

feel tension along the sides of the legs (if you are wearing slacks, along the seam) from knee to hip.

- LEFT ARM

  Sit or stand with arms crossed right over left. The right hand should be covering the left elbow. The right hand provides resistance as the left arm lifts directly away from the body. You should feel tension in the forward-directed part of the upper arm from shoulder to elbow. The right hand provides resistance to the back of the elbow as the left arm pushes directly to the left. You should feel tension in the left-directed part of the upper arm from shoulder to elbow (Robyn Bohen, personal communication, April 1991).

- RIGHT ARM

  Sit or stand with arms crossed left over right. The left hand should be covering the right elbow. The left hand provides resistance as the right arm lifts directly away from the body. You should feel tension in the forward-directed part of the upper arm from shoulder to elbow. The left hand provides resistance to the back of the elbow as the right arm pushes directly to the right. You should feel tension in the right-directed part of the upper arm from shoulder to elbow (Robyn Bohen, personal communication, April 1991).

- THIGH TENSING

  Sitting in a chair, place both feet flat on the floor. Press weight onto your feet just until you feel tension build in your thighs.

There should be no risk to experimenting with the different muscle-toning exercises as long as you use your mindful awareness to determine which exercises are okay for you to use (the ones that increase calm and clear thinking) and which you should bypass (the ones that result in anxiety, spaciness, and cloudy thinking).

### Applying Brakes for the Therapist

The idea of putting on the brakes for managing the rigors of trauma therapy was introduced in *The Body Remembers: The Psychophysiology of Trauma and Trauma Treatment* (Rothschild, 2000). There the theory and strategies were geared to enhancing the client's control over the debilitating symptoms of PTSD (and other types of distress) and for keeping trauma therapy at a digestible pace for each client.

Actually, for psychotherapists, brakes are also useful, particularly for reducing or preventing in-session hyperarousal and protecting against the direct impact of client material. Paying attention to your levels of arousal and putting on the brakes will help you monitor and manage your own vulnerability to compassion fatigue, vicarious traumatization, and burnout on a day-to-day, session-to-session basis.

To use brakes effectively, it is suggested that you first become familiar with the theory of ANS arousal and attain a degree of arousal awareness, as described earlier in this chapter. The idea is to be able to identify ANS arousal in yourself and then to be able to apply the brakes to keep your arousal within the calm (green) and active alert (blue) ranges. That means that you can lower arousal when it becomes too high and also that you can allow it to rise a bit when that enhances your drive, assertiveness, follow-through, and so on, staying in the range identified by the turquoise arrow, normal life.

The following case illustration will give you an idea of what putting on the brakes may look like when applied to the needs of the therapist. Instruction in specific braking skills follows.

Elena is a clinical social worker in a family service agency. She sees a wide variety of clients of various sexual orientations, ages, and types of presenting problems. One of her long-term clients, a 63-year-old man, was facing the loss of his wife of 30 years; she was terminally ill. For the last few months, as her client's grief rose to the surface, Elena was having symptoms of anxiety during and following their sessions. Elena knew the basis of her countertransference: Her own mother died two years before—at nearly the same age as her client's wife—after a long ill-ness. Elena was still feeling the loss. She wasn't suffering posttraumatic stress, simply normal grief. The fact that her grief was being exacer-bated by her client's is rather typical of uncontained countertransfer-ence, as defined in Chapter 1. However, that knowledge alone was not adequate to reduce the heart palpitations and shortness of breath that were triggered as she helped her client with his grief. Though Elena attended grief counseling and was making headway, she needed a stop-gap measure to help in the interim. She wanted to continue working with her client, but without increasing her own discomfort.

During a regularly scheduled meeting, the agency supervisor asked Elena to describe, with as much detail as she could, what happened to her during sessions with her client.

She said, "For the first few weeks, I would become anxious during the sessions. Now, actually, my anxiety begins before the session in anticipa-tion. As I am walking to the waiting room to get him, my heart races and my hands and feet go cold. This has really become a bad pattern. Gen-erally, I'm at least somewhat anxious the whole session. After he leaves, I'm a bit shaky for a few minutes, but writing up session notes helps me to calm down."

The supervisor particularly noted that last comment. It was relevant that Elena already had at least one tool for bringing down her arousal before she saw her next client. Logically, since that tool worked, it was likely that others would also.

The supervisor and Elena spent the next half hour experimenting with a few tools for putting on the brakes (muscle toning, as above, and distance boundaries and body armor, discussed below). They discovered several that looked promising to help Elena, and she agreed to try one or more before and during the next session with her client.

The following week, prior to meeting her client, Elena felt the usual anxiety. Her heartbeat accelerated, and the temperature of her hands decreased. Per the supervisor's assignment, this time Elena spent a couple of minutes increasing muscle tone in her arms (one of the tech-niques she and the supervisor found to be most helpful). She realized it was working as she noticed her hands warming up and her heartbeat slowing a bit. When she brought her client back to her office, Elena made a point of moving her own chair back about a foot more than usual—preoccupied by his grief, the client appeared not to notice. During the session, Elena continued to monitor her arousal and anxiety (as discussed a few pages back). About halfway through the session, her heartbeat began to quicken. Again Elena increased tension in her arms (as shown in the previous exercises), and then wrote a few sentences on her notepad and left it on her lap. The notepad provided something for her hands to hold onto and also a small barrier between her and the client. As a result, Elena's anxiety lowered, and she was able to complete the session effectively. Following the session, she had some mild anxiety, but nothing like the high levels following previous sessions.

Simple tools helped Elena to reduce anxiety and continue working with her client. Sometimes it is just that simple. However, each practitioner will have to discover which tools work best and under which conditions. Several are introduced in the next section.

## USING BRAKES

The author of this relevant email has given me permission to include it here and also to identify her:

*Dear Babette,*
*I recently started working as a counselor at a rehab for recovering addicts. The suffering there is unlike any I have come across before. I found myself overwhelmed. This was in conflict with my ideals to resonate with another's pain. I recently realized that I wasn't feeling compassion, or even empathy by resonating. I was feeling what in Buddhism is called "horrified anxiety." So this started me thinking about how I can "put on the brakes."*
*Sharon Collins, Norfolk, England*

The discussion and skills that follow should help to address Sharon's concern over how to put on the brakes. This section focuses on skills that are specifically geared to lowering ANS arousal and putting on the brakes in the moment. By now you may have realized that you already do things that effectively put on brakes for you. If you have not already, it would be a good idea to write them down so you will have a better chance to remember and use them when you are under stress. In addition, when those tools are not adequate (or do not work for you), one of these that follow may help.

The question of when to put on the brakes is individual and best answered using the guidelines in the earlier description of ANS states. The commonsense questions are: Where do you function best? Are you at your most competent when your system is calm (green)? Do you function better when you are more in the active alert range (blue)? It is doubtful that any psychotherapist functions well when arousal has reached the level of fight/flight. In general, you will probably find that your arousal levels vary from day to day, client to client, and topic to topic. How often you use a tool for applying the brakes will depend on how effectively a tool works for you and how often you check in with yourself to evaluate your arousal level. For instance, on a day when you are feeling well and calm to begin with, you might monitor your arousal only once or twice in a session. But on a day when you are agitated, or when challenged by personal, work, community, or world stress, or even particularly distressing client material, it might be a good idea to take stock several times in a session. If you have difficulty keeping a dual focus (you and your client at the same time), you might use the time to evaluate your own state when you ask your clients to evaluate theirs.

When under stress, you may find that just focusing on your body (as you did in the Arousal Awareness section), becoming aware of your heart rate, breathing, skin, muscles, and face, will be enough to reduce anxiety and maintain an optimal level of arousal. Simple body awareness alone often makes arousal more manageable. When simple body awareness is not adequate, you may find some of the skills that follow to be useful additions to your toolbox.

INTERVENTION: MINDFUL BREAK FOR THERAPIST AND CLIENT ALIKE

One of my favorite interventions is just a simple timed break for both therapist and client to reboot. It is easy enough to do, and most clients will appreciate the opportunity to reset their nervous system as much as you do. Simply go to your phone's timer app and choose a time interval and peaceful tone. On my phone I choose the one called meditation bell, but there are others you and your client might like better. I usually set it for 15–20 minutes. When it goes off, both client and therapist stop whatever they are doing or talking about and take two or three slow, deep breaths. That is all there is to it. Then they resume where they left off. I like to take this timed break two or three times per session, but you and your client can decide what is optimal for you both.

Caveat: Of course it is important to discuss and negotiate this with your clients beforehand; do not just spring it on them.

--------------------- EXERCISE: FINDING SENSORY ANCHORS ---------------------

Choose a memory of something pleasant, preferably of a place or person that gives you a feeling of calm and safety. Do not look for a perfect memory; instead, seek a "good-enough" memory. For example, if your grandmother was usually very kind, but a few times lost her temper, restrict your memory to the times (or a time) when she was not angry. If your favorite place in nature is now a housing development, remember it as it was. However, if tragedy is associated with a person or place (violence or disaster), it would be best to pick something or someone less potentially provoking.

Next, awaken the sensory memory (any combination of visual, auditory, tactile, smells, or tastes) associated with that person or place. Using the example of a grandmother, she might be remembered in the kitchen with her apron on baking cookies, humming as she works. There might be a memory of warmth and the smell of cinnamon or fresh bread. Once you have elicited one or more sensory memories, notice what happens in your body, particularly in your ANS: What is happening in your heart rate, breathing, body temperature, and level of tension? If for any reason you get an unpleasant reaction (heart pounds, hands or feet get cold, etc.), let that memory go and choose another one. Once you have an image that gives you pleasant body sensations and an increased feeling of calm, you will know that is a potentially useful and safe anchor for you.

To test it, remember a mildly uncomfortable situation (far from the worst) from your work: An irritated client, an incident of feeling inept, a single mild trigger from a client's material. Switch to the calming image of your anchor as soon as your body begins to feel uncomfortable. Bring in as many of the sensory memories as necessary to help your system calm down. There is an added bonus for sensory anchors that include pleasant smells or tastes. You might bring something to work that actually recalls that memory: a bottle of cinnamon or piece of chocolate. If the visual memory is particularly powerful, put a photo on your phone to refer to for strengthening your sensory memory.

Over time, practice in switching between memories of distressing situations and your sensory anchors will help you to become adept at rapidly turning uncomfortable, stressed body states into calm. Below are two examples of the effective use of sensory anchors. Faith actually discovers her anchor at the source of her distress, and Robert learns to distill the motion of his favorite sport to a small movement he can use even during his work hours.

## ACCENTUATE THE POSITIVE

Faith is a clinical social worker for children who have cancer. She loves the children and her work, though she periodically succumbs to the stresses of knowing some of them will die. Faith was very clever in her choice of anchor. Her strategy will not be useful to everyone, but it is worth mentioning. When a strategy like hers works, it is a very valuable adaptation of the technique of sensory anchors.

Faith's major stress was managing her feelings when one of the children died. She usually suffered many days of depression and ruminated on rethinking her career choice. Then she would get irritated with herself and get back on track. Generally, she continued to cope, but it was a little more difficult to bounce back from each subsequent episode. She was becoming fearful of burning out.

With a little help from a consultant, Faith found her strength in the flip side of the source of her depression. For her, the most uplifting events of her life were the periodic (if too few) declarations of a cure. When a child was discharged well and healthy, she celebrated! Elation was the best word she had to describe the feeling. In her body she felt an excited buzz, and her lungs expanded so she could take full, deep breaths. Those highs could last several days and recharge her batteries to carry on. So, for Faith, her calming anchor was the same as the source of her stress: her patients—as long as she restricted her focus to the ones who got well.

Together with the consultant, Faith developed a plan: The next time one of the children died, she would mediate her grief with vivid memories of those children who were cured. She would remember what they look like, the sound of their laughter, the shared tears of joy. She practiced evoking each of them one at a time. She found that doing this conscientiously helped her to alleviate the depression and questioning when a child died. It was a delicate balance. Faith had to learn how to permit her own grief at the loss, as well as remember the elation of the successes. Over time she was able to find her rhythm in the most trying times.

## SUBTLE MOVES

If your sensory anchor is an activity (e.g., dancing), accessing it in times of stress can be particularly powerful but not always practical. Robert's situation demonstrates how an anchor that involves movement can be refined for use anywhere.

Robert is a prison counselor in a medium-sized facility. He sees and hears about trauma daily. He describes the whole compound as "vibrating with primordial strain." One of the ways he manages his own stress is by playing handball with friends two days a week. He loves it and knows that his spirits are best on the days he plays. During a period of time when Robert was particularly bothered by job stress, he received help from a local consultant. Together they reviewed—in both image and movement—how Robert feels playing handball. He loved it all, but his favorite play, the one that made him feel most powerful, involved a particular foot position, torso twist, and arm movement. When Robert demonstrated the movement for the consultant, he reported feeling happy, strong, and hopeful. The consultant encouraged Robert to actually rehearse the movement repeatedly, gradually narrowing the range of motion—broad movements becoming smaller and smaller until Robert could feel his favorite play in his body without the consultant seeing any action. Eventually, just the impulses of muscular movement would provoke the positive feelings. This took a bit of practice, but eventually Robert could just imagine the play and feel the movement in his body even though he wasn't actually moving. (If you can, right now, imagine yourself taking a pleasant walk. If you can feel a little of the effect without actually moving, you will have the basic idea.) Robert found this to be a powerful tool. On days when he didn't have a game, he could still call up the feeling of it to mediate his stress. A few times he was also able to call up the body memory of playing handball when he became overly distressed while working with one of the inmates. With the client none the wiser, Robert could imagine a few handball moves. As he felt the power and strength in his body, his hyperarousal drained, and he was able to keep his full attention on his client.

The technique used with Robert distills an anchor to its smallest elements, so that it can be used at will, under almost any circumstance. If you have a resourceful activity, experiment and practice to refine it in your imagination. This kind of sensory anchor can be very powerful in combating vicarious trauma and other in-session stressors.

### How Close Is Too Close?

The term *boundary* is commonly used in psychotherapy jargon to describe several phenomena. Psychotherapists usually think of their professional boundaries as restricted to defining the ethical and sexual limitations of the therapeutic relationship. This section focuses on two additional aspects of boundaries relevant for therapists: those that involve physical distance, your comfort zone, and those which help you to feel adequately protected inside your own skin, "body armor."

## COMFORT ZONE

Your comfort zone is your personal space. Most psychotherapists are familiar with the idea with regard to interpersonal relationships. We often teach our clients about paying attention to distance boundaries, helping them to feel comfortable in interactions with partners, children, coworkers, and friends. But we often neglect our own need for the same during sessions with our clients. Actually, though, boundaries between therapist and client can be vitally important. For the goal of your own self-care in particular, paying attention to the physical space between you and your client can be important. Very simple adjustments will aid you in maintaining a professional distance—a sense of yourself as separate from your clients.

For many of you, taking care of your personal space during therapy sessions will mean having to override what you were told in college or professional training programs. And that applies whether you are working in person or an online platform such as Zoom. Most psychotherapists were and are taught to work with clients in close proximity, face-to-face and always looking at each other, even though sitting closely and having constant eye contact is not always welcomed or good for either therapist or client.

Recognizing an optimal space between you and a client—whether the physical space in a room where you are sitting together or the distance you are from your computer screen and camera—is usually rather easy. All that is required is the simple use of body awareness. You can use the basic skills described earlier in this chapter, noticing your autonomic arousal and other sensations to gauge at which distances you are and are not comfortable. It is important to keep in mind that what is optimal for you will change from day to day, client to client, and session to session. Closeness with a particular client one day does not ensure that closeness will be comfortable the next time (for either of you). Ultimately, finding a distance that is comfortable for both therapist and client is ideal, though that may not always be possible. In those instances, some negotiation and experimentation will help. An example from my own practice may be useful. In this situation we were both in the therapy room.

My client, Saul, was rather controlling. He liked me to sit within a foot of him and always kept eye contact. Over the first few sessions, I became more and more uncomfortable sitting so close to him; my shoulders would get tense, and I often had a headache by the end of the hour. I found that I was beginning to dread seeing him. Discussing his issues of control did nothing to loosen his need to keep me close. Though he insisted he liked the proximity, I nonetheless wondered. Sometimes it felt as if there was a cushion of air, like the surface of a clear balloon, pushing at me. That sensation made it hard for me to breathe sometimes. During our fourth session, however, I saw something that had evaded me before (sometimes when I am sitting too close, I cannot see or think as well as I'd like): Saul's chest was held very high, as if he was holding his breath.

That observation emboldened me to suggest an experiment. I asked Saul if it would be okay for me to move my chair back a couple of feet. I promised him I would return to my original position when he wanted me to, but encouraged him to try the experiment. He skeptically agreed. When I backed up, he immediately exhaled (as I had suspected he might). Pointing out what I just observed, I asked, "What happened?" Saul replied that he must have been holding his breath. When I helped him to tune in to his breathing, he reported breathing easily. When I asked if I should return to the closer proximity, he just said, "No, that's okay. I'm comfortable with you there." After that session he no longer insisted on us sitting so close, and I became much more comfortable working with him.

Saul was not ready to acknowledge that he also had been uncomfortable with my sitting that close, but the experiment still worked to give us both more breathing room.

## ROOM TO WORK

Of course it is an advantage if your office is large. Then you can experiment with furniture placement and greater and smaller distances between seats. But if your office is small, there are still many options.

Rosalyn worked in a family service agency as a psychologist. New to the agency, she was assigned one of the smaller offices, only about 100 square feet: room for a desk, two chairs, and a few books. She often felt that clients were nearly sitting in her lap. It was hard for her to feel any separateness, and sometimes she felt overheated and headachy. The arrangement was also not comfortable for many of her clients; the most fragile ones would startle nearly every time she moved. Inspired by a training course on therapist self-care, Rosalyn took a look at her floor plan. She had originally arranged her desk against the far corner, under the window, to maximize the available floor space. That made it possible for her to sit with her back to the desk, directly opposite her clients, as she had been taught to do. But since she was uncomfortable so much of the time, she decided to experiment with changing things around. Turning her desk to face the side wall gave Rosalyn more length in the room. That made it possible for her to sit a little further away when she or her client felt the need for more space. Also, her desk had a writing extension that pulled out like a cutting board. When she was feeling most vulnerable, or with the most fragile clients, she pulled the extension out and wrote her notes on it, creating an actual (if narrow) barrier between herself and her client.

That minimal intervention gave Rosalyn and her clients more options for negotiating their proximity in the therapy room. Paying attention to body sensations gave Rosalyn the motivation to experiment and find a more optimal furniture arrangement.

## KEEPING BOUNDARIES WHEN WORKING ONLINE

The COVID-19 pandemic changed the setting in which many therapists work with clients. Suddenly the majority of therapy was conducted by phone or online via Zoom, Skype, FaceTime, or other online platforms. For some it was a temporary shift; for others it became a permanent switch in how they conduct therapy. Today, of course, many therapists continue in a combination, seeing some clients in person and others online or by phone.

When you are talking with clients online, boundaries are different but nonetheless still important—for them, and also for your own self-care. There seems to be a tendency for most everyone to sit at their computer with their face close to the camera so their image fills the other person's screen. As a result, I hear lots of complaints of headaches and *screen fatigue* (a new term coined during the time of COVID-19). I always suggest that the therapist (and likewise the client) experiment with their physical distance to the screen. There really is no reason to sit so close; you would not be up in each other's faces like that if you were together in the same room. And, as with everything else, what is optimal is very individual: for therapist, for client, and for the two of them together.

## GET YOUR COMPUTER OUT OF YOUR BEDROOM!

Though this section is mostly devoted to physical boundaries, another type of boundary is worth mentioning while discussing working with clients online. To be honest, I am rather shocked by how many therapists are working from their bedrooms with their beds and other personal objects fully in view to their clients. There are multiple disadvantages to that kind of arrangement.

First of all, for many clients that will be way too much exposure to the therapist's personal life. In addition, it could make it difficult for the therapist to keep other kinds of boundaries when their private space is in view. However, even more important is your self-care. If you are working with clients from your bedroom, there is genuine risk that you will take your resonance with them to bed with you. When you are working from home, whether in person or online, making a separation between work time and free, personal time is extremely important for your well-being.

If possible, move your computer to another room: If that is not possible, use one of the background choices available on your videoconferencing platform, or blur your background so the client cannot see it. And then, at the end of each work day, create some kind of ritual that turns your bedroom into 100% bedroom once again. At the least, put your laptop away or fully cover your desktop computer. It would also be a good idea for you to track if doing this makes any differences for you. But I would wager a fair amount that you will sleep better.

## COMFORT ZONE EXERCISES

First, if you are unfamiliar with what it feels like in your body to be in proximity (at varying distances) to another, you might practice with a colleague, friend, or family member. You can try a common boundary exercise, either in person or with both of you on computer screens. You and a partner begin by standing or sitting at a distance (10 to 15 feet for in-person, a few feet if on computers). First, each of you take stock of your body sensations and for a baseline. Then one of you approaches the other slowly. Look for the reactions in your body to the changes in distance, stopping or saying "stop" when you notice a shift. Any nuance counts.

Second, beginning with a single client, pay attention to your body sensations, particularly your arousal level, during the session. Experiment with positioning to maintain an optimum level of arousal in yourself. You can move your chair or lean your body forward or back. You can also turn your chair so more of your side is turned toward your client or the screen, rather than facing head-on. You can write notes or not. If you do write notes, try different styles: Write on your lap, on a lap desk or book, at your desk, and so on. The idea is to experiment with many different possibilities to increase your options. Once you get the idea, you can try the same experiments with as many clients as you like.

Third, when working in-person, look at the layout of your office. Is there any way to move the furniture to your advantage, as Rosalyn did? Feel free to try different arrangements, or to add items that might increase your comfort:

a small table, a knickknack or stone, a plant, and so forth. When working online, try different computer angles and positions.

## BODY ARMOR

When dealing with volatile client emotions, feeling a sense of protection on a body level can be a big advantage. Of course, you still want to be able to connect with your client, but sometimes feeling safe and comfortable will make that more possible. For some it is very difficult to grasp the concept that feeling vulnerable does not necessarily increase availability and connection. Sometimes it actually provokes the opposite: withdrawal and restriction. For those of you who will find it beneficial, strategies for increasing body armor follow. (Increasing body armor is a concept I learned in a 4-year professional training course with Bodynamic Institute in Copenhagen, Denmark, 1988–1992.) Use your ANS as a gauge to tell you which interventions are most effective in helping you to become more calm and clear thinking, along with the additional pointers mentioned.

## JILL'S VULNERABLE CHEST

After 12 years as a counselor for survivors of incest, Jill was afraid she might need to switch careers, or at least clientele. While in the past she was able to maintain a professional distance in her work, for the last couple of years she had been feeling increasingly affected by the situations and states of her clients. Her agency agreed to pay for outside consultation with me, hoping to hold on to one of their best therapists.

> **Jill:** I just can't do it anymore! Their stories didn't used to get to me, but now I am thinking about my clients all the time, and I wake from dreams and nightmares of the scenes they have described.
>
> **Babette:** Is this different than it used to be?
>
> **Jill:** Yes. For many years I had no difficulties. I didn't take my clients home with me, and they didn't invade my sleep. This is really getting to me!
>
> **Babette:** What do you think changed?

Because Jill had no problems with her work for many years, something must now be different. I wanted to see if we could track it down. If we could identify a trigger, helping her would be easier. But if not, other interventions were still available.

> **Jill:** I don't know. I just feel more vulnerable, I guess.
>
> **Babette:** Can you identify when you started becoming more vulnerable to your clients?
>
> **Jill:** I'm not sure. But certainly I've been more distressed in the last two years or so.

Was there something relevant in her personal life, either in the last two years or in her past? If so, I might not be able to help her with the particulars, but could refer her to someone else for therapy. This kind of supervision can sometimes get tricky. It is always advisable to maintain a clear delineation between consultation and therapy. Supervision that crosses that line can contaminate the usefulness of the sessions and confuse the relationship between the therapist and the consultant.

> **Babette:** Did anything change in your life shortly before or during that time?
>
> **Jill:** Nothing of significance. No births, deaths, illnesses, moves, etc., just more job stress.
>
> **Babette:** And what about incest or some similar issue in your own background?
>
> **Jill:** No, nothing of the sort. I am sure my distress is not from my past. I know what it is like to have one of my own issues triggered by a client issue; that has a different feeling, like anxiety. What I am feeling now is more heavy, depressed, stressed—burdened.
>
> **Babette:** Can you tell me how you experience that in your body—both in session and in your daily life?

At the least, identifying the effect on her body could lead us to tools that could give her support, shore her up, so to speak.

**Jill:** Day to day, like I said: heavy. I feel like I am dragging around. In session I often feel tired and sometimes sad.

**Babette:** Remember being with one of your clients right now, just one. What happens?

**Jill:** Suddenly I feel very tired.

**Babette:** Where?

**Jill:** All over. I feel like I want to crawl into bed.

**Babette:** Is the feeling you have now anything like what you experience during a session?

**Jill:** Yes, exactly.

**Babette:** And when you come back to focus on me and this room?

**Jill:** Less tired. I feel fairly normal.

**Babette:** Then shift your awareness back and forth between the memory of your client and the here and now in this room. As you do that, see if you can identify where in your body the tiredness starts from and lifts from. I want to help you find out where, in a way, this client gets to you, where inside you, so to speak, your vulnerable spot.

When there is such a clear difference in response, it can be useful to shuttle awareness between one and the other, tracking somatic sensations as they change. Jill shifted her awareness several times before she realized what was happening.

**Jill:** [With a small startle reaction] That's interesting. My attention keeps coming to my chest, here [points to the upper part of the breastbone]. I don't know if that is the answer to your question, but that's what happened.

**Babette:** What happens there as you shift your attention?

**Jill:** It seems that's where, as you asked, the tiredness starts and lifts. When I imagine my client, I get tired starting there [points to chest]. Then it sort of radiates out to the rest of my body. When I bring my attention to this room, that's where I first start feeling better. So, what does that mean?

**Babette:** I don't know yet. First, I'd like to help you to increase your muscle tone there, help you develop a "thicker skin," so to speak. Then we can see if that has any impact on how you are feeling in session and day to day. No guarantees, but I think it's worth a try. Are you game?

**Jill:** I guess I'm at the point of being willing to try almost anything. What should I do?

**Babette:** Since it is your chest where you first feel the tiredness, I'd like to see what happens when you increase the muscle tone of your chest. Actually, I'll direct you to increase the tension in the pectoral muscles that cover the ribs and breastbone. First, try putting the palms of your hands together at about the height of your chest where you pointed before. Then push the palms together until you feel tension under your breasts. That's the pec- torals—you might remember doing an exercise like this when you were a teenager.

**Jill:** [Smiling] Yes, with my girlfriends. We thought it would increase our bust size.

**Babette:** It can do that by increasing the muscle mass underneath the breasts. But that is not the point here. What I am aiming for is seeing if increasing muscle tone changes anything for you. Right now the idea is to press your hands together and hold the tension until the chest muscles just begin to feel tired, and then release very, very slowly. That way you can gradually build up tone. If it is useful and you want to, you can use push-ups for a similar effect. Go ahead and do that three times with a rest between each. [Jill slowly tenses and releases three times.] What do you feel?

**Jill:** I feel a bit stronger there. Maybe my mood lifted slightly, but I'm not sure.

**Babette:** That's fine. Next I want you to imagine being with that same client again. Notice what happens, how you feel, and if there is any difference, neutral, positive, or negative. It is extremely important when evaluating any exercise to be completely open to whatever the result. Especially when working with muscle tone, the result is unpredictable.

**Jill:** Well, I didn't get that same jolt of tiredness. I'm curious to see if it changes anything with an actual client. But how can I do that tensing in an actual session?

**Babette:** First, it may be most useful to be increasing the tone in those muscles on a regular basis. That can give you a feeling of thicker skin. To do that, you can use the exercise we tried here or push-ups. Just remember to ease off at the beginning of tiredness in the muscles. If you exhaust them, you may lose the protective potential. For use in the session, let's design a technique for you. Try pushing your palms together again and see if you can isolate where you feel the tension build in your chest. [Jill uses her thumbs to point to a spot just about halfway between her waist and her collarbone.] Then release that slowly. Now place your arms in a more normal in-session position. [Jill's hands meet in her lap.] From that position, see if you can cause tension in the same spot.

**Jill:** I can't do it if my arms stay relaxed. But if I press the heels of my hands together slightly, then I can feel it.

**Babette:** So keep trying it, gradually decreasing the observable movement.

**Jill:** I think I am doing that. Can you see it?

**Babette:** Yes, but only because I am looking carefully and know what to look for. I doubt most clients would notice—maybe one who is an athlete or personal trainer, but not others. You could try it a few times during a session. Maybe add a mental note like, "I am keeping my client's feelings out of my chest." Something like that. What would fit?

**Jill:** Perhaps, "If I don't let this client get to me, I'll be better able to help her."

**Babette:** Fine. You might write that down so you remember it. Try both the tensing movement and that phrase over the next two weeks. Pay attention to how you feel before, during, and after sessions and at the end of the day. Feel free to edit your mental phrase if you find something better. I'll also be interested to hear what happens with your dreams. Don't worry if this doesn't help, as there are more strategies to try. It is important to evaluate honestly so I'll know where to help you next time. Keeping a log would be useful so we can identify any visible patterns.

Jill returned to supervision two weeks later much encouraged. She still had a few client dreams, but no nightmares. Her day-to-day energy and mood were much improved. The increased muscle tone appeared to be working to give Jill a more protective, thicker skin protecting her chest. Encouraged, I recommended that Jill also get into a regular exercise program, something she used to do and had stopped—curiously enough—about two years before. Over the next couple of months, as Jill became more physically fit, she also became more fit to continue her very demanding job. There is no way to really know, but it is possible that the timing of the onset of Jill's symptoms and her reduction in exercise may be linked. Nonetheless, it now seems clear that increasing muscle tone in her chest and adding regular exercise were important skills for Jill's self-care repertoire.

────────────── **EXERCISE: THICKENING YOUR SKIN** ──────────────

Having a thick skin is always useful for reducing feelings of vulnerability and permeability. If you feel like your clients are getting to you in ways that are not healthy for you—or helpful for them—then thickening your skin might be called for. Start with one client who seems to get to you in a way that you do not like. As Jill did, remember being together with that person, including your distance and position in relation to them. Pay attention to your body as you remember being with this client. If you cannot get a sense of the client through your memory, you can try this first step when you are actually with the client. But then follow the next steps by yourself (or with a colleague or supervisor).

Notice where in your body you feel vulnerable to this client. Where, physically, does this client or the client's material get to you, or get under your skin? Is it in your chest? Your arms? Your stomach? Your forehead? Your groin? Somewhere else? In the place where you feel vulnerable, tense up the muscles of that area. For example, if the vulnerability is in your stomach, you can tense up stomach muscles by doing a sit-up or partial sit-up—on the floor or even in a chair. Just bring your head and knees a little closer in a crunch if you are lying down, or raise your feet slightly off the floor if you are sitting in a chair. You can also try to suck in your gut. You will know you are being effective when you feel the muscles across your belly tense up. For vulnerability in your back, you can try pulling your shoulder blades together or pushing your elbows into a wall (standing) or the back of your chair (sitting). For the forehead, furrow or raise your eyebrows. To increase tension in the groin, you can raise or tighten the pelvic floor; the commonly used Kegel exercises are good for this purpose. If you cannot find the right way to tense up in your spot of vulnerability, feel free to send me a brief email (babette@trauma.cc). Mention that you are reading this book and name the area where you would like to feel a thicker skin. I will be happy to suggest how you can achieve that.

Once you find the correct spot and tensing movement, hold the tension only until the muscles begin to be tired, and then release the tension very slowly. That should leave a little added tension when you are done. Next, remember being with your client again and see if there is any difference: Do you feel worse, better, the same? If you feel less vulnerable when you imagine the client, then you might work to distill the tensing movement down to a small one you can do actively in the session (as I did with Jill). For stomach tensing, you cannot drop to the floor to do a sit-up in the middle of a session, so you would need to try to get some of that same tension while sitting still in your chair. To distill a movement for increasing stomach tension, for example, you could lift your thighs slightly, together or one at a time. This requires stomach muscles, and the movement can be nearly imperceptible to an observer. In addition or alternatively, you can do the same tensing as a muscle-toning exercise on a regular basis and see if that helps increase your feeling of thickened skin with that client. Remember that this is an experiment and you may need to try or adapt several exercises or muscle areas before one works for you. Do not worry, though. If this type of exercise is not effective for you, there are more to try.

## FASHION AND BLING

How you dress can enhance or diminish your feeling of separation or boundary with your client. You may already be paying attention to how you dress with clients, either consciously or instinctively. Which items in your wardrobe give you a greater feeling of security or stability? Are there certain clothes you wear on days when you feel more fragile or on days when you feel more masterful? Are you dressing in a particular fashion with certain clients? In general, paying attention to your workday attire can be used to advantage in taking better care of yourself.

Specifically, it can be a useful strategy to designate an item of clothing (one you already have, or one you purchase) as a "bulletproof vest." You can wear this item on days when you feel especially vulnerable, or with the clients who get to you most easily. Sometimes items of jewelry can also serve this purpose. Remember Wonder Woman? She had bracelets that deflected bullets and such. In a similar vein, you can imbue your own medallions or bracelets with "protective power" to deflect feelings that are not yours. After reading this, you may even now realize that you wear a certain pendant because it exactly covers an especially vulnerable spot or makes you feel strong. If not, find (or assign) one that will.

Stephanie is an experienced psychologist. In the past year she changed jobs and is now working for an eating disorders clinic. She has sought consultation because she is already on the verge of burnout. She often feels exhausted and edgy and complains that she is constantly hungry—previously not a usual state for her. Stephanie is fairly confident that this is the result of projective identification, that her clients are projecting their exhaustion and hunger into her. She wants to learn how to get them to stop.

The following consultation excerpt begins about 15 minutes into the session. We had already discussed a couple of Stephanie's clients as well as her understanding of projective identification. I suggested that she might not need to get her clients to change for her to feel better, that she might be able to bar their access to her system. At this point she was skeptical but interested. In my own mind, I was already speculating where the difficulty might stem from. Sometimes it is multiple sources, sometimes a single major one. I had several things in mind to explore with her. Spatial boundaries were the first on my list.

**Babette:** Tell me about how you and your clients typically sit together.

**Stephanie:** To some extent, it depends on the client. Usually I sit in a chair, and my client sits on a couch. Typically we're rather close, our knees a foot or so apart. Most of my clients are hungry for contact as well as for food.

**Babette:** So how is it for you to sit so closely?

**Stephanie:** To be honest, it took some getting used to. At my previous job—an HMO—I had a much bigger office; I was used to three or so feet between. But I've adjusted and seem to manage from session to session.

**Babette:** Would it be okay to experiment here and see what happens in you if we were to sit that close? [Currently we were sitting across the distance of my consultation room, about 5 feet from each other.]

**Stephanie:** Okay. Already I feel a little nervous, but that is probably just performance anxiety.

**Babette:** You are probably right, but it could be something else or a combination. Let's pay attention to your initial response before we move at all. How do you experience that nervousness? What are the sensations in your body that are signals to you that you are nervous? Are you shaking? Cold? Feeling your heart beat fast?

**Stephanie:** None of those. It's more like mild butterflies in my stomach.

Based on that report and my own observation, I summarized that her sympathetic nervous system was not highly activated, in the blue active alert column, SNS 1 (see Table 3.2). But I wanted to take care when we sat closer. This was consultation, not therapy, and I did not want to provoke an unhelpful response.

**Babette:** So would it be okay to try to sit closer?

**Stephanie:** Yes. Now I'm curious.

**Babette:** So, you decide: Which of us do you want to move?

**Stephanie:** I think I will.

**Babette:** Then you move closer a bit—not the full distance. I want you to pay attention to what happens to those butterflies, and any other sensations you notice in your body. [Stephanie moves forward about a foot and a half.] What happens?

**Stephanie:** Nothing in particular. I feel the same. Can I move closer now? [I nod. She moves forward an additional foot.] Now something changes. I feel a little tense and I'm starting to get a headache.

As I had a mild headache myself, I wanted to see if we could determine if she was picking up on mine, if I was picking up on hers, or if it was just a coincidence that we both had slightly achy heads.

**Babette:** Where do you feel the headache? [She identifies the exact location of my headache.] This may surprise you, but you have perfectly described the headache I came in with today. Are you generally prone to feel what others feel?

**Stephanie:** I guess so. . . . Do you think this has a bearing on my exhaustion?

**Babette:** It may, and also on your hunger. Many people find it difficult to distinguish their own feelings from another's, and also sensations, when in very close proximity—think of the couples you've worked with who can't maintain separate feelings.

**Stephanie:** Well, it is true that I often tune in to my children and husband. My kids know they can't fake a stomachache to get out of school because I can tell when it's not true. All I have to do is give them a hug. But if you are right, why should my clients' hunger or exhaustion continue to dog me between sessions? That doesn't happen with my children's ills or hurts.

**Babette:** It sounds as though you are very aware of your intuition with your children; you know that you can feel their pain. Awareness can make a big difference. You can certainly try that with your clients. Just being aware of the possibility that you are tuning in to their hunger and tiredness may be enough to free you between sessions. However, if that is not adequate, you may need to experiment with changing your seating arrangement.

**Stephanie:** But I can't change the physical distance with my clients; my supervisor insists they need the closeness. What else can I do?

This was tricky. As an outside consultant, I had to be careful. It would not help Stephanie for me to put her in conflict with the policies of her workplace, no matter how strong my opinions.

**Babette:** I'm thinking of a couple of things. First of all, you may want to talk with your supervisor about working with boundaries for the benefit of your clients. That is certainly an issue for many of those with eating disorders. If you are having discomfort sitting that close, there is a good chance some of your clients may be too. The only way to know is to experiment and ask. Helping clients to find the balance between comfortable boundaries and comfortable closeness can be fruitful work. However, if your supervisor won't budge, then there are clandestine ways you can increase the boundary for yourself, even sitting a foot away.

**Stephanie:** Well, I want to leave here feeling hopeful, like I have a couple of things I can actually do to take care of myself even if nothing changes at work. I like the idea of increasing my awareness; it would be neat if that did the trick. And it would be good to also have a concrete tool to use if being mindful is not enough. I like the idea of clandestine boundaries. Does that mean I could increase distance from my client without anyone catching on?

**Babette:** It has that potential anyway. Remember, this is just an experiment. That means I want you to try one thing for a day or two, at most a week, and evaluate how it affects you, both for better and for worse. That way you can find which, if any, strategies actually work for you.

**Stephanie:** Okay. I'll make notations after each session.

**Babette:** Yes, and at the end of each day. You might keep a separate journal for this, so that you can keep your experiments private. How do you usually feel when you leave work, and in the evening?

**Stephanie:** Exhausted and ravenous. That's where we started.

**Babette:** Good. That gives us a great gauge to use. Measure each evening on a scale of 1 to 10 your level of exhaustion and also hunger, 10 being the worst. Looking back, can you guesstimate your average?

**Stephanie:** Certainly some days have been 10s. But probably I average around 7. So, what can I do if I can't move my chair and awareness is not enough?

**Babette:** In general, have you ever noticed feeling differently, depending on how you dress?

**Stephanie:** Well, on weekends I usually wear denim jeans and sometimes a denim jacket. I like to call them my tough clothes because I feel a bit more masculine, less vulnerable than when I wear a dress or thin slacks and light sweaters.

**Babette:** With your clients, you can use the same idea. Think about your wardrobe, what you usually wear to work. Are there any outfits or items that you could put on to feel more thickness—space or distance—between you and your clients?

**Stephanie:** Since it's winter, I could try a bulky sweater. I also have a leather vest that I like; it's soft, but thicker than cloth. I could try those.

**Babette:** Sounds like they have good potential. What about jewelry? Do you remember Wonder Woman?

**Stephanie:** [Laughing] You mean like her deflector bracelets? Could I deflect the projective identifications?

**Babette:** [Laughing, too] Exactly! Of course your bracelets wouldn't

have that actual power. You have to imagine that they do. Worth
a try. Then, I think you will have enough things to experiment with
in the next two weeks.

When Stephanie returned two weeks later for her next consultation, she
reported that several things had worked. First, her increased awareness that
her clients might be getting to her on a body level had made her more alert.
That simple insight managed to reduce her hunger following sessions. She
continued to feel hungry during the session but afterward was able to let it
go. However, awareness alone was not enough to protect her from exhaustion. She experimented with clothing and found that her bulky sweater
worked particularly well. On the three days she had worn it, she rated her
tiredness level as only 3. The leather vest did not work at all. She was still
intrigued by the idea of deflectors, and we explored what pendant she might
have or buy to use for that purpose. All in all, most significant for Stephanie
was the discovery that she could actually do something herself to disrupt
a projective identification, as she continued to call it. She no longer felt it
to be inevitable nor so powerful now that she had some tools to intervene.

## PUSHING AWAY WITH THE EYES

Some people are particularly vulnerable when in eye contact with others.
Those with soft, open, and inviting eyes are the most likely to engender
openness and trust. As those traits figure strongly in the qualities that attract
clients to us, many therapists fall into this category. However, sometimes
that kind of openness in the eyes can also make the boundary between
therapist and client foggy. When that happens, the therapist can take in
too much or feel too exposed. If these concepts feel personally familiar to
you, it might be of use for you to learn how to have more choice about eye
contact with your clients. You can also learn to have more control over how
eye contact affects you, and the impact what you actually see has on you.

Most simply, Hodges and Wegner (1997) remind us that the mere action
of averting your gaze—even for a few seconds—from emotionally expressive
clients can often be enough to help you better regulate your own responses.
Such a commonsensical proposal becomes even more useful with the added

understanding of mirror neurons (see Chapter 2). For these to activate, an action must be seen. That is why "when we carefully attend to others performing a series of manual activities, we find our own muscles 'helping them out'" (Hatfield et al., 1994, p. 32). Not only will looking away from your client periodically be a relief for you, it will also be a relief for many, if not most, of your clients. And some clients will likely prefer that you never look at them at all.

Pushing away with your eyes is another way to manage unpleasant responses to eye contact. In learning this skill, as with the others offered in this book, it is not meant that you should change your normal way of looking at people or being in visual contact all the time. This skill is meant to add an additional tool to your repertoire, to use or not use as appropriate. Experiment with it first. Only if it is useful to you should you add it to your tool kit.

Somatic psychotherapists trained in the theories of Wilhelm Reich call this idea of pushing away with the eyes *creating an ocular defense*. It is meant to enhance your sense of distance between you and your client, to create a boundary or separation between your own and your client's eyes. It can be helpful when increased separation would feel protective or calming for you. It can also be indicated when it would give you a better feeling of professional distance and clear thinking for helping your client. And it is particularly useful when the possibility of physical distance is limited or when you are working with clients online.

It is best to practice this skill with another person (partner, colleague, friend, etc.). In the absence of such assistance, you can try it with an animal (cats work well). First, though, it may be good to try it looking in the mirror at yourself.

Tune in to body awareness, particularly around your eyes and face. However, also notice other aspects of your body per previous instructions (see Chapter 2), including sensations in your gut. Then notice (but do not judge) how your eyes and the area around them look: soft, hard, inviting, rejecting, smooth, wrinkled?

Next, tense up the muscles of and around your eyes, so that they look less inviting when you look at yourself, and they feel harder on a physical level, more defended. If you do it correctly, you will feel tension in and around your eyes, and the scope of your vision will narrow and may become sharper.

Take it easy at first so that you do not give yourself a headache. If you do, just ease off and it will subside. You can practice this (or any other new skill) in small portions or steps rather than all at once. Try shifting between relaxing your eyes and tensing them. Gradually reduce the tension around your eyes while maintaining the tension of your eyes themselves. Using the mirror will help with this. The goal is to be able to maintain maximum eye tension without that tension being easily observed and without pain or exhaustion.

When you develop some confidence, you can try it with a family member (children are great because they are often sensitive to nuances of expression). You can also try it on the street or in a store. Experiment with changing your eye tension and see if that affects how people treat you and approach or avoid you in public.

Once you gain some confidence, take your new skill into your office. When a client begins to talk about something that distresses you, try tensing your eyes and pushing away. You may want to add a mental note, something like, "It is okay to not take in my client's distress." Find your own words that best suit your own situation. Notice how you feel, including your level of arousal, before and after you apply the method.

As a side note, you can apply the same strategy if unwanted strangers often approach you on the street. Hardening the eyes can change an inadvertent message of invitation to a purposeful rebuff.

## KEEPING YOUR EDGES

Your skin is your most obvious and concrete boundary: your edge. It is the material that holds all of you in, and holds everything and everyone else out. Solid as the skin is, though, it is something that is easy to lose contact with. When a sense of the body's edge is lost, separation between the self and another may become more difficult. Good skin awareness can help you stay in optimal self-contact and aid in differentiating your own states from those of your client.

During a session, the easiest way to get a sense of your body edges is to feel your skin inside your clothes. You can try one or more of these: Move your feet a little inside your shoes and feel the insole of the shoe against the skin of the bottom of your foot. If you are wearing socks or stockings, you may want to feel the material against your foot. What sensations are you aware of? What kind of inner surfaces are you contacting? Rough, smooth, soft, scratchy, or something else? Slightly shift your weight in your chair so that you can feel the seat of the chair against your buttocks. Again, you might want to focus on the seat or on your clothes—whatever works best for you. Feel your legs inside your trousers or skirt. Slight movement will help to slide the material against your skin and will help you to feel that edge more clearly.

For areas that are unclothed, such as your hands and face, you can achieve the same effect by focusing on the difference between your skin temperature and the air temperature. Of course, if the temperatures are quite close, that might not be so easy. You can also rub your hands together or rub your hand on your arm and feel the friction of each against the other.

Between sessions, splashing cool water on your hands and arms or on your face will help to highlight those edges.

If feeling your edges is difficult for you, training this awareness when you are not with a client might be helpful. When you take a bath or shower, use a slightly rough cloth or sponge or a cool spray of water to help you feel your skin—only do this if it is comfortable for you. You can use your awareness of your autonomic arousal to gauge if this is useful for you or not. If you become nervous or dissociated doing these or any other exercises, stop and use others that calm you down and help you be present.

### Notes for Somatic Psychotherapists and Body Workers

Those of you who work by touching your clients may already know how easy it is to take on client states (physical and emotional) simply through the physical contact between your hands and their skin, even when you are working with them fully clothed. It is quite common for therapists who touch to have little or no sense of boundary between the surface of their hands and the bodies of their clients. This is something I also know about personally as I started my career as a massage therapist before becoming a somatic psychotherapist (body psychotherapist in those days). I was also a client for many years in therapy models that involved touch. Though it has been several decades since I have worked with touch, I still remember what it was like. So from both sides, therapist and client, I strongly recommend that you develop and keep a boundary between yourself and your client at the surface of your hands. This will help you to keep your client's material from entering your system, yours from entering theirs, and will allow your client to "be in their own space."

To accomplish this, practice feeling the difference in temperature between the skin of your hand and the surface of the body you are touching. I have sometimes helped therapists learn this boundary by placing a piece of paper between their hand and the client's body. Doing that makes the feeling of boundary more concrete. Also, moving your hands often will help as the longer you stay in one place, the easier it is to lose the ability to differentiate your surface and theirs. It takes practice and focused awareness to develop this skill, but it will develop with practice.

### Strategies for Shifting Arousal Levels

First of all, it is important to distinguish your own stress level as separate from the stress you may feel in resonance with another. Chapter 2, "Managing the Ties That Bind," is helpful for identifying and reducing that risk. Strategies, below, will help you manage your own stress. As you experiment with or apply one or more, please make sure you individualize to your needs and tastes. That is, make use of those interventions that help you feel more calm, more toward the PNS 2 or blue SNS 1 columns on the ANS table (Figure 3.2). Attempt only one activity at a time and carefully evaluate before repeating or moving to another. No matter if you are lowering arousal or raising energy, always aim to do less rather than more, particularly at the start. And no matter which strategy or exercise you are trying—suggestions from this book, those you already know, or something you have learned from others—always stop after each trial to evaluate the effect before moving on to the next. Ask yourself, observe, and refer to the ANS table:

- Am I feeling more present or more spaced out?
- Am I calmer or more distressed?
- Are my ANS indicators moving more toward or away from the green, calm, column?
- Is my energy level moving in the preferred direction (less for those who are hyperaroused, more for those who are feeling lethargic)?

Make sure to stop, and never repeat, any intervention that pushes your arousal into the orange, red, or purple. And remember: No matter how terrific an activity is for someone else, if it does not help you, it is not your friend.

## QUICKLY LOWER HIGH AROUSAL

Likely you are already familiar with a slew of strategies that you have used for yourself or applied with those you help. Below I list some you may already know and perhaps some you do not. Notably, however, I leave out interventions to calm respiration. I know that directing someone to slow or deepen their breathing is a common calming strategy. However, I rarely use it, either for myself or for others. The reason is that, per the ANS table, variation of respiration is a major indicator of the level of ANS arousal. When someone is told to change their breathing, using respiration as a reliable measure of arousal is lost. My personal and professional preference is to use respiratory fluctuations as one of my gauges for evaluating how the ANS is being affected—for clients and for myself. Of course, it is not wrong to instruct yourself or someone else to change their breathing, but you do risk losing a handy ANS measurement tool. Below are some additional strategies:

- Apply mindfulness
- Track your body awareness
- Look, listen, feel your surroundings
- Pay attention to your exteroceptive senses
- Access and remember resources
- Tap your feet
- Sit back in your seat
- Feel the seat under your buttocks
- Pet your cat or dog
- Imagine walking along a balance beam
- Call a friend
- Listen to a piece of music that calms you
- Remember your favorite person

Obviously, this is not an exhaustive list, but some ideas to get you started. Add to it as you apply strategies you know and learn others.

## SLOWLY RAISE LETHARGIC ENERGY

If you find your ANS level spends a good amount of time in the yellow, Lethargic column, it may be useful to learn to slowly raise your energy level. I learned this most important principle of somatic work from Merete Holm Brantbjerg (2012, 2020), as I discussed in Chapter 2. She calls it *dosing*. Dosing is a similar idea to my concept of *taking smaller steps* (Rothschild, 2010), however applied most specifically to building up energy capacity in the body. Careful dosing is the key to raising lethargic energy in a tolerable and lasting way. If you try to do too much at once or too often, you are more than likely to find it difficult to maintain and continue. Admittedly, this area of somatic psychology is much more vast than there is space for in this book. For a more in-depth look at Brantbjerg's theories and approach, see her website and articles.[10] For our purposes here, an introduction.

When engaging in activity to raise your lethargic energy, you must pay attention to:

- Scheduling. When you engage in raising your energy level may be relevant. Consider and experiment with if, for you, it is more helpful to attempt earlier or later in the day, before or after meals, and so on.
- Frequency. How often is beneficial or optimal for you? It could be one or more times daily or one, two, or three times a week. Try out variations and see what works best for you.
- Amount. This is one area where the slogan less is more most aptly applies. Better to do a tiny, successful amount than try for more than you are able and feel as though you have failed.

---

[10] Moaiku Relational Trauma Therapy (http://www.moaiku.com/).

## SAMPLE ROUTINE FOR SMALL-DOSE BUILDUP
## TO WALKING AROUND THE BLOCK

This might not apply to you, but perhaps you can use these principles to tailor something for yourself that is just right for you. This example combines both Brantbjerg's dosing and my smaller steps and is inspired by Sam, whose depression became so severe that he would just lie around all day. He knew it would be good for him to take a walk, at least around the block, but he just could not do it. When he tried, it just all felt so overwhelming. I helped him to break down the goal of walking around the block into smaller steps, some of them very tiny. He identified these:

1. Sit in chair rather than lying down.
2. Wiggle toes.
3. Grip chair arms.
4. Tense thighs.
5. Imagine getting up.
6. Actually stand up.
7. Walk to door.
8. Open door.
9. Stand on porch.
10. Walk from porch to sidewalk.
11. Walk from porch, down sidewalk to corner.
12. Walk around a quarter of the block.
13. Walk around half of the block.
14. Walk the entire block.

Literally, step by step, it took two full weeks for Sam to accomplish his goal of walking around the block. But the point is that he did accomplish it, in his own way and with his own timing. After the first round-the-block walk, he continued to do the same, gradually increasing frequency and distance. After months of being unsuccessful at "just" going for a walk, he plotted his own, slow, course to success.

You can do the same. Identify one (and only one) task or exercise that you have been unsuccessful in gathering your energy for. Then consider the steps that might be involved toward accomplishing that goal. Once you have your list, simply attempt one at a time. And, of course, evaluate along the way, celebrating each successful step. If, however, you are not making headway, consider if all or some of the steps you have identified might be too big. If that is the case, break them down into even smaller steps.

# CHAPTER 4

# Thinking Clearly

This chapter builds on the theory and tools from previous chapters. The Neurophysiology of Clear Thinking is the feature of the theory section of this chapter. Following that, the skill-building section will help you to maintain or get back to your own clear thinking with tools that include: "knowing thyself," strengthening your inner observer, controlling internal self-talk, and bolstering your internal frameworks that aid clear thinking. Additional sections on nurturing your work space and a proposed structure for some aspects of your self-care will guide you to strengthen external, environmental, and personal life frameworks that can enhance your ability to think clearly.

## Theory

### The Neurophysiology of Clear Thinking

Most people have difficulty thinking clearly when agitated or highly stressed. There is good reason for this. The explanation is found in understanding how the brain and body function under stress. The key to maintaining clear thinking is to, as the British say, *keep calm*—even when challenged to the maximum by a demanding client or boss, or crises in your family, community, country, or the world.

Now, well into the 21st century, it is easy to think that brain study is an old science. Actually, however, it is still in its infancy. In fact it is an ever-evolving area of science with new discoveries emerging even as I write. As with the development of any branch of science, hypotheses come and go. However, in each area, there are always some theories that continue to hold up under scrutiny. One of the most useful, especially for the purposes of this chapter, is Paul MacLean's (1973) mid-20th-century concept of the *triune brain*.

According to MacLean's now widely accepted schema, the human brain consists of three regions or levels. Each has its own specific areas of control and responsibility though all are, of course, connected. The lowest level, what he calls the *reptilian brain*, is the region that includes the brain stem and cerebellum. In the main, the reptilian brain preserves body function and basic life support, including stabilizing temperature and respiration. It is neither rational nor emotional; it just continues to do its essential job. Even when there is a total loss of higher brain performance, the brain stem is often able to continue to function.

MacLean named the middle brain region the *limbic system*, a term commonly used today. It includes the thalamus, hypothalamus, amygdala, and hippocampus. As the old medical school joke goes, the limbic system is responsible for the "four Fs of survival": fight, flight, feeding, and sexual reproduction. The limbic system is known to be the emotional center of the brain. It furthers survival of the individual and of the species by provoking body systems into action to avoid danger and pain, and to seek safety and pleasure.

With regard to evolution, the *neocortex* is the most recently developed of the brain's regions. Its higher functions are what separate the primates, particularly humans, from animals lower on the evolutionary scale. The neocortex takes survival in humans to a higher level. For example, the ability to construct shelters where they are advantageous, rather than having to seek shelter only where nature provides it (e.g., a cave), is one of the evolutionary upward steps facilitated by the neocortex. The neocortex also makes planning, judgment, and rational thought possible. Creativity, art, music, and such are the result of the interplay between cortical and limbic regions.

Germane to this chapter, a balance between the functions of the neocortex and the limbic system is necessary for therapists to be able to maintain clear thinking despite family, world, and work pressures, as well as client distress.

## AUTOMATIC RESPONSE VERSUS RATIONAL THINKING

There is an ongoing disagreement in psychology as to which comes first, thought or feeling. Those with a cognitive–behavioral bent see thought as the precursor (Wolpe, 1969). And we all know our thoughts do, at least sometimes, affect our feelings. On the other side are those with a more emotional or body-oriented influence who believe that feeling precedes thought. The argument dates at least from the late 1800s when followers of James (1884) and Cannon (1929) argued for their views. Joseph LeDoux (1996) has an excellent discussion of those arguments in *The Emotional Brain*. The truth probably is somewhere in between: Sometimes thought is the precursor, sometimes feeling is. The focus of this chapter illuminates Cannon's view (as well as Damasio's, as discussed earlier) by looking to the body for the underlying source of feeling: the sensory nervous system and the amygdala, one of the structures in the limbic system.

## THE EARLY WARNING SYSTEM

The amygdala acts as a kind of early warning system. It processes emotion before feelings become conscious in the cortex. Smiling when hearing the voice of someone you love before you have had any thoughts is an example of the amygdala's communication speed. It works like this (you may want to refer back to the nervous system chart featured in Figure 2.1): The sound of the loved one's voice is communicated to the amygdala via exteroceptive auditory nerves in the sensory nervous system. The amygdala then generates an emotional response to that information (likely pleasure or happiness in this example) by releasing hormones that stimulate the visceral muscles of the ANS and which can be felt as pleasant sensations in the stomach and elsewhere. Last, the amygdala sets in motion an accompanying somatic nervous system (skeletal muscle) response, in this case, tensing muscles at the sides of the mouth into a smile.

A similar process occurs with unpleasant types of stimuli, including trauma. When someone is threatened, the amygdala perceives danger through the exteroceptive senses (sight, hearing, touch, taste, and smell) and sets in motion the series of hormone releases and other somatic reactions that quickly lead to the defensive responses of fight, flight, and hyper or hypo freeze. Epinephrine arouses the SNS, stopping digestive processes (hence dry mouth). At the same time, it raises heart rate and respiration to quickly increase oxygenation in the muscles to meet the demands of self-preservation (flight and freeze) and self-defense (fight). For a review of ANS function, see Chapter 3.

It appears that the amygdala is immune to the effect of stress hormones and may even continue to sound an alarm inappropriately. That could be said to be the core of PTSD—the amygdala continuing an alarm even after the actual danger has ceased. Unimpeded, the amygdala stimulates the same hormonal release as during actual threat, leading to the same responses: preparation for (or actual) fight, flight, or freeze. The war veteran who dives for cover at the sound of a car backfiring is an example of the amygdala's power to re-provoke the body's emergency response in the absence of actual danger.

Why does the amygdala continue to perceive danger when there is none? For the purposes of therapist self-care, how could the activity of the amygdala impede a therapist's clear thinking?

## THE RATIONAL SYSTEM

The hippocampus helps to process information on its way to the prefrontal cortex and lends time and spatial context to memories of events. How well it functions determines the difference between normal and dysfunctional responses to stress and trauma and normal versus traumatic memory. An example will help to explain and may further clarify the James–Cannon controversy.

In his book, *The Emotional Brain*, LeDoux (1996) described the survival response involved when, while taking a walk, you encounter an object that looks like a snake. Naturally, the amygdala signals a subcortical alarm message—"It's a snake!"—which sets in motion a series of reactions that culminates in your foot halting in midair. The amygdala's nonverbal message travels at lightning speed. Meanwhile, a second communication pathway occurs that, though quick, takes longer, eventually getting the message around to the cortex, where rational and verbal thought takes place. When the alarm reaches the cortex along with the visual image of the object, it is then possible to evaluate the correctness of the amygdala's perception and put this evaluation into words. If the alarm was accurate and it is a snake, you will freeze until the danger has passed, that is, the snake slithers away. If, however, there is a discrepancy—what was thought to be a snake is discerned by the cortex to be a fallen, bent tree branch—the cortex then sends a new message (often verbal) to the amygdala ("Hey, it's only a stick") to stop the alarm immediately. The hippocampus, along with the thalamus, assists the transfer of the initial information—the image of stick or snake—to the cortex, where it is then possible to make sense of the situation. This is the normal way information is communicated, as long as the hippocampus is able to function.

## HOW STRESS CAN COMPROMISE RATIONAL THOUGHT

The hippocampus, however, appears to be highly vulnerable to stress hormones, particularly epinephrine and norepinephrine, released by the amygdala's alarm. When those hormones reach a high level, they suppress the activity of the hippocampus; it loses its ability to function properly. Information that could make it possible to discern the difference between a snake and a stick never reaches the prefrontal cortex, and a rational evaluation of the situation is not possible.

The hippocampus is also a key structure in facilitating resolution and integration of highly stressful and traumatic incidents and traumatic memory. It inscribes a time context on events, giving each of them a beginning, middle, and—most important with regard to traumatic memory—an end. When stress hormone levels are reduced through gaining control over hyperarousal, the hippocampus can function properly again, making it possible for the cortex to recognize when a traumatic event is over, perhaps even long past. Then it can instruct the amygdala to stop sounding an alarm. For the hippocampus to continue to function, arousal levels must be kept low, in the calm (green) and active alert (blue) ranges. This means that for you to be able to think clearly, your hippocampus must be able to function. Putting on the brakes as discussed in Chapter 3 will help to keep your arousal low enough to ensure continued clear thinking.

## SOMATIC MARKERS AND CLEAR THINKING

Usually people believe that emotion interferes with rational thought, that it clouds one's ability to think clearly. However, neurologist Antonio Damasio (1994) found that this is not the case. Actually, he proposed the opposite to be true: Emotion is necessary to rational thought. Damasio describes an emotion as a conglomerate of sensations that are experienced in differing degrees, positive and negative. They make up the somatic markers, which help guide decision making. That is, body sensations that underlie emotions are the basis for weighing consequences, deciding direction, and identifying preferences.

The function of somatic markers is most recognizable in the kinds of choices people make every day based on gut feelings. Damasio has worked with and studied individuals with damage to regions of the brain having to do with feeling emotion. He discovered that those whose brain damage eliminated or greatly diminished access to their feelings were no longer able to make good decisions. He concluded that feeling emotions is necessary to rational thought and decision making. Further, he found that it is body sensations (emotions) that cue awareness of feelings. Therefore, to be able to make a rational decision, one must be able to feel the consequences of that decision in one's body. According to Damasio, just projecting a cognitive judgment is not enough; it is the feel of it that counts.

Regulating your arousal to maintain clear thinking necessitates mindfulness and some experimentation. The following case will illustrate.

Toby has been a licensed clinical social worker in private practice for six years. This consultation was one in a series of regular biweekly consultation sessions.

**Toby:** I came today expecting to ask for strategies to help me work with a client who has been arrested twice for shoplifting. But actually, what I need is ways to manage the helplessness I feel with this client. It's not normal for me to feel this way. I don't know that I can help her. In the sessions I lose my train of thought and have trouble staying focused. I feel ready to give up on her.

**Babette:** There are a couple of ways to go with this. Your helplessness with this client could have roots in your own history. However, since this is not a usual reaction for you, I would suspect that the origin lies elsewhere. At this point, I'd suggest we look at what is happening in your body as you work with this client to assess if the helplessness stems from something in your interaction.

**Toby:** Okay, I'll agree to that.

**Babette:** Then let's begin with where you are right now. First, get a sense of your current somatic state. What are you aware of in your body and your feelings? I want to establish a baseline to compare with as we explore your countertransference—the feeling of helplessness—you brought up. Paying attention to your body will help to identify what could be somatic countertransference, that is, countertransference on a body level: body sensations or feelings that are provoked within the therapeutic encounter. Somatic countertransference may or may not have connection to something in your current or earlier life. What do you notice?

**Toby:** I'm a little nervous here [puts hand on chest]. Also, I'm excited to get help with this!

**Babette:** How about temperature? What do you notice in your hands and feet?

**Toby:** They feel normal temperature.

So his arousal was likely in the green, calm, perhaps moving toward blue, active alert. We'll keep an eye on it as his sense of nervousness is still there.

**Babette:** Okay, now shift your awareness. Can you remember the last session with that client? You can do it with eyes open or closed. That's up to you. You might visualize her if you are good at that kind of imagery. But it's okay if you don't see her; the idea is to just have a sense of what it was like to be with her last time.

**Toby:** [Closes eyes] It's good you said that. I'm not good at visual imagery and was afraid I couldn't do it. But I can definitely get the feel of being with her.

**Babette:** Great. Take a minute or so and then tell me what happens in your body as you remember her.

**Toby:** The nervousness increases in my chest, and my hands and feet have gotten cool.

That meant his ANS was becoming more aroused, moving into the blue, active alert. Remember, if the arousal becomes too high, hippocampal functioning can be lost. That might be what was happening with Toby, why he was losing his focus.

**Babette:** Continue to imagine being with your client and notice what's going on in your head. What kind of things are you saying to yourself?

**Toby:** Actually, my mind is sort of blank. It is not always easy for me to think with this client. I get drawn into what she's saying and then I can't think.

**Babette:** Has anything changed in your body?

**Toby:** Well, actually, I can't feel it as much.

**Babette:** What is the temperature of your hands and feet?

**Toby:** I think they are cold, but I can't feel them as distinctly now.

Toby is describing a mild dissociative state, not too severe as he can still hear me and answer my questions. But that means his arousal is moving toward the orange flight/fight. If he becomes this hyperaroused just by imagining being with this client, he is likely becoming at least this hyperaroused when actually with his client.

**Babette:** Sounds like you lost a degree of contact with yourself. Stop imagining your client for now and talk with me. [Toby shifts pos-

ture, and his eyes clear.] Is that typical when you are with this
client, that you don't pay attention to yourself?

**Toby:** Yes, I think so. I get sort of numb.

**Babette:** Do you think that could have a relationship to your feeling of
helplessness with her?

**Toby:** Maybe. Once I'm feeling helpless it just builds. And after the
session I feel badly that I've not been able to help her more. I
believe I have some tools that might help her, but I lose track of
what to do.

**Babette:** Based on what happens in your body here when you merely
remember being with her—the nervousness in your chest, your
cold hands and feet, loss of contact with yourself—I suspect your
ANS arousal is high enough that you are losing the benefit of your
hippocampus and its communication with your cortex. If I am correct, then that might be why you stop thinking clearly.

**Toby:** That's a little scary. Can I change that?

**Babette:** Yes, of course. The key is to keep your arousal lowered when
you are with her. Then your hippocampus will continue to function normally, and it will be possible for you to think clearly. Let's
try some things and see what might work. Based on what you
said before, helping you to stay in touch with yourself will probably be important.

Sharing the theory should help Toby two ways: first to conceptualize what
was happening within himself, and second to help his clients, who might
also lose clarity due to hyperarousal. Now that he understood what was
going on, it was time to see if he could intervene and get back his ability to
think clearly with his client.

**Toby:** That sounds good. What should I do?

**Babette:** Again, remember being with your client and see what happens in your body.

**Toby:** Whew! The anxiety comes back very strongly and my feet and
hands go cold again.

The arousal was triggered very quickly. That made me wonder what he might be doing to make himself more vulnerable. Taking a good look at his posture, I thought I might have a clue.

> **Babette:** I notice that you are sitting with one of your legs tucked under you. I wonder what would happen if you put both feet on the floor. Try that and see if anything changes for better or worse.

I must always be open to the possibility that an intervention will hurt rather than help. Everybody is different, so you never really can know until you try. Asking in this way reduced the chance that Toby would feel led to a particular answer. I really wanted to know what would happen to him. If the result was good, we could build on it. If the result was bad, it could point us toward something else.

> **Toby:** Well, first thing I notice, I can breathe easier. I hadn't realized I wasn't breathing much, but now I can. Should I still be remembering being with the client?
>
> **Babette:** Yes. That way we can pretest some things that might work when you are actually with her. You won't know, though, until you actually try them at that time. Experimenting in this way can help you choose some things to do that will likely help. I'm glad that getting both feet on the floor was useful. Think of it as getting both of your feet on the ground—a more stable base. We can try taking that a step further. With your feet on the floor, put some pressure on them so you tense up a little in your thighs. [Toby complies.] How's that?
>
> **Toby:** Dunno. I feel a little spacey.

When the result is increased arousal, spaciness, and so on, then it is important to stop and go back to the intervention that was useful.

> **Babette:** Then stop doing that, and just feel your feet on the floor.
>
> **Toby:** Okay, that's better. What happened?

**Babette:** The only way to find out what helps you is to experiment. When you get an adverse response like spacing out or getting more anxious, you should stop doing it and cross it off your list. Then go back to something that gave a helpful response to get settled again before you try another. What do you do with your hands when you see this client?

**Toby:** Nothing in particular.

I was wondering if doing something with his hands might help anchor his attention. Also, having objects in his hands, like a notepad and pen, might also provide some physical separation between him and his client.

**Babette:** Do you ever take notes?

**Toby:** I usually write up sessions after clients have gone. Some of my clients don't like it when I take notes during the session. Do you think I should?

**Babette:** Remember, the idea is to find what works for you. Taking notes might be something to test out. You can assess for yourself if it is useful. And if it is, we can discuss how you might negotiate with a client so that you can do that during a session.

**Toby:** When I imagine doing that now, the notepad feels like it is a sort of barrier between us. And my hands and feet have warmed up a lot.

**Babette:** Actually, that's a good response. The warmth in your hands and feet means your arousal is lowering. That's good news for your hippocampus. I think that will be plenty for you to try out with your client until our next consult: feet on the floor and taking notes. One last thing: Before you see her, check in with what is going on in your body so you have a baseline to compare with. Then during the session, do the same a couple of times. How will you remember?

**Toby:** I think I'm just going to start out with my notepad on my lap and feet on the floor. I'll write a note to myself at the top of the page.

**Babette:** Next time I see you, I'll be curious about how it went.

Over the next few consultation sessions, Toby built on what was begun here. He continued to keep his feet on the floor and take notes. Next he added a couple of muscle-toning exercises to thicken his skin. The combination of interventions worked to bring down his arousal with this difficult client. Once he was able to maintain clear thinking while working with her, his feelings of helplessness disappeared.

## Skill Building

### Know Thyself

It will come as no surprise that it is a good idea for every psychotherapist to be familiar with their own life history. The better you know yourself, the greater the chance you will be able to maintain clear thinking when you are provoked by a client or a client's material. All therapists come face-to-face with their own personal issues at times during work with clients. Sometimes a therapist's own experience can be used to enhance the client's therapy—a beneficial use of countertransference. At other times it can interfere—as with unmanageable countertransference. The only way to ensure your ability to tell the difference is to know yourself—present and past—as well as possible. Accomplishing that may involve private soul-searching or it may mean seeking your own therapy. Most psychotherapy educational programs now require a certain amount of personal therapy as part of their curriculum.

Being intimately familiar with your past will make it more likely that you will maintain clear thinking and easily distinguish your feelings and issues from your client's. Of course, having the opportunity to resolve problems that linger from your past can also be a bonus for your daily life. At the least, awareness of issues and problems not yet resolved will help to keep your thinking clear when your feelings become provoked in sensitive areas.

——————————— **EXERCISE: TAKING A SELF-HISTORY** ———————————

You may already have had many hours of psychotherapy or in other ways have gotten to know yourself well. This section is written for those who have not yet delved into their past or would like guidance in deepening their self-knowledge.

One way to become familiar with your past is to write up your own history, asking yourself the same questions as you would a new client. It can be useful to write it down, but it is not necessary. The point is to know yourself at least as well as you know your clients, preferably better. Below are some suggested areas to include, though this is not a complete survey. Feel free to bypass any questions, or add others.

CURRENT STATUS
* What is your current living situation and marital or nonmarried relationship status?
* Are you satisfied or not?
* List any children and their ages.
* Briefly comment on relationships between the family members as well as the family as a whole. Note the physical and mental health of each family member.
* Do you have any animals? If so, what role do they play in your life and in your family structure?

HEALTH
* How is your own physical and mental health?
* Review your health history.
* Have you been hospitalized? Had surgery? Major injuries?
* Are there any serious concerns in either area that add to your daily stress?
* Know your drug (legal and illegal) and alcohol history, and your current usage.
* Also pay attention to how much caffeine and sugar you consume.
* Write down all medications you are currently taking, psychotropic

and medical—include homeopathic remedies, vitamins, and other supplements.

- If you have or have had bouts of depression or bipolar episodes, look for patterns. Include planning, attempts, or gestures of suicide.

## RELATIONSHIPS

- List close friends and extended family members.
- How are these relationships individually?
- On the whole, do you feel adequately supported in your life?
- Are you burdened by responsibilities for family and friends?
- What gives you pleasure with the people in your life?
- What gives you pain?

## WORK

- Describe your job(s) and your workplace(s).
- Which aspects do you most and least enjoy?
- Are there coworkers or responsibilities that give you significant stress?
- If you are in private practice, do you have adequate collegial support?
- If you work in an agency, do you feel supported there?
- Are you satisfied with your chosen career?
- Do you wish for a different type of work or workplace?
- Do you look forward to retirement or not?
- Consider your financial situation.
- Do you have adequate income, or is this an area of stress for you?

## FAMILY OF ORIGIN

- Detail your family-of-origin constellation.
- Go back at least two generations, including grandparents.
- If it is complicated, draw a chart or genogram to see the relationships.
- Indicate who is alive and who is not.
- For deceased family members, include how old they were at the time of death and what they died of.

SIGNIFICANT LIFE EVENTS
* List any life events with significant emotional charge: happy, sad, exciting, frightening, enraging, disgusting.
* List any life-threatening events not covered above.
* List any events of physical or sexual violence not covered above.
* Include a review of your sexual history: how you learned about sex, how you managed puberty, first sexual experience, and so on, and your current sexuality.

SPIRITUALITY
* What are your spiritual beliefs, if any, whether or not they are part of an organized system?
* Also, note your relationship to nature.
* Add anything else possibly missed by the previous questions.

Once you have all of your personal information put together, in your mind or on paper, consider which issues or areas enhance your professional competence and which might compromise it. Also make note of areas that parallel issues any of your clients have, whether or not they are currently working on them. Look for common themes that might give you difficulties and also those that could give you advantages.

Next consider your religious, political, and moral values. Are any of your values in conflict with those of your clients? If so, how are you handling that, or how will you handle it when it comes up?

Finally, when you discover you are having difficulty with a client, you can refer back to what you know about yourself to see if any parallels or triggers are causing you difficulty (as Ruth does in Chapter 6). When they are, sometimes just that knowledge will be enough to separate your issues from your client's. If that is the case, your thinking will clear quickly, and work with that client will be less difficult. However, if awareness is not enough, talking with your supervisor or a psychotherapist may be indicated.

### Strengthening the Observer

Psychoanalysis calls it the *observing ego*; transactional analysis calls it the *adult ego state*; van der Kolk called it the *observing self* (van der Kolk et al., 1996). Buddhists call it the *witness*, and other disciplines have names unknown to this author. Here it will simply be called the observer. No matter what name you give it, though, this is an integral part of the self and crucial to clear thinking. The observer is able to view and simultaneously evaluate both external and internal reality. Adequate functioning of the observer is vital to emotional health—for psychotherapists, their clients, and everyone else. Without a strong observer, it can be all too easy for therapists to confuse the stresses, feelings, and states of their clients with their own.

## DUAL AWARENESS

Dual awareness is a core function of the observer. Having dual awareness means being able to simultaneously attend to and reconcile both external (from exteroceptors) and internal (from interoceptors) sensory information (you can review these systems in Chapter 2). It is an important ability to maintain in life in general and under stress in particular—for anyone, but especially for a psychotherapist. Without dual awareness, clear thinking is not possible. It is a skill made possible by the effective functioning of the hippocampus and prefrontal cortex, and is facilitated by keeping arousal within the calm (green) and active alert (blue) ranges. When these brain regions can do their jobs, you will be better able to do yours.

Normally, dual awareness functions automatically in the background, unconsciously. We do not usually notice it. Basically, dual awareness reconciles all of the information we are taking in through our sensory nervous system: both the exteroceptors (what I see, hear, etc.) and the interoceptors (balance, position, internal sensations, etc.). The exteroceptors register information from the external environment, and the interoceptors gather information from our internal systems. When all goes well, your internal state is in sync with your awareness of your surroundings; your internal reality jives with your external reality. A few examples follow.

You are walking in your favorite place in nature on a beautiful day. Your exteroceptors are picking up on the light, warmth, bird sounds, brush crunching under your feet; the whole scene is peaceful. At the same time, your interoceptors register the calm state of your gut, your deep breaths, your steady balance and pace. All is well on the inside and the outside.

Sitting in a room with friends, you notice that your heart rate has increased and your chest has become tight (interoceptor). You wonder why. You turn your awareness to your external environment and notice the smell (exteroceptor) of cigarette smoke and locate by sight (exteroceptor) the source as a cigarette held by someone sitting near you. You remember that you are allergic to cigarette smoke and move to the other side of the room. The exteroceptive perception (someone smoking) reconciles with your internal sense of tight chest and elevated heart rate (both triggered by secondhand smoke).

Later with the same friends, your chest becomes tight and your heart rate increases once again. What is it this time? You turn your awareness outward but do not smell anything aversive or see anyone smoking. What else could it be? You pay closer attention to the conversation and hear (exteroceptor) that the current topic is workplace deadlines. You remember that your boss has been after you to turn in a report and you realize you are anxious since you have not yet done it.

In all of these examples, the exteroceptive information reconciles with the interoceptive, as is usual. But this is not always the case, particularly when dealing with those plagued by PTSD as well as anxiety and panic disorders. And for therapists: When your empathy dial is turned up, maintaining simultaneous attention to internal and external cues may become difficult, raising your risk for vicarious trauma, compassion fatigue, or burnout.

PTSD is the poster child for the failure of dual awareness. When the capacity for simultaneous attention to the internal and external is lost, dual awareness is no longer possible. Rothschild (2000, 2003) has described failures of dual awareness in individuals with PTSD. In those cases, a bias is developed toward the internal cues of fear. When that happens, restriction in the lives of those with PTSD is partially the result of a reliance on internal (interoceptive) cues to define external reality. These individuals lose touch with the value of their exteroceptors. In extreme cases, victims of PTSD conclude that their surroundings are dangerous because they feel scared all the time. They lose the ability to use exteroceptors to accurately evaluate the external environment by what they see, hear, and so on. Because of that, their fear regenerates and regenerates. They are unable to use exteroceptors to recognize when they are actually safe. Certainly, therapists can fall into that same pattern, especially those who already have PTSD or vicarious trauma.

Failure of dual awareness in psychotherapists is best illustrated by situations where a therapist jumps to conclusions: "I'm feeling scared, so my client must be doing something dangerous (or threatening)"; or "I'm feeling irritated, so my client must be doing something provocative (or wrong)." In such cases the issue is not the client's behavior, but the therapist's possible misinterpretation of internal sensations. (Remember the example of how the amygdala reacted to a stick as if it was a snake.) Often the consequence is inappropriate confrontation of the client, resulting in confusion and frustration for both client and therapist. While such loops in logic are not terribly common, they occur often enough. You may have taken on new clients who had recently discharged a therapist after being unable to resolve such a situation. Or you may have experienced this yourself in your own therapy. Most of us have gotten at least a few new clients in this way.

There is an additional way that failure of dual awareness can manifest that practitioners should be alert for. The opposite can occur. That is, psychotherapists can become overly reliant on the external environment to dictate what they should be doing. Psychotherapists, like most helping professionals, are caretakers by nature. Many of us have cared for our families beginning in early childhood, or are the primary caretaker in our current family. We are, for the most part, in the habit of putting others first. This tendency is definitely a resource as it helps us to have interest, energy, and focus for dealing with difficult client material. It gives us endurance and an ability to ignore or put aside our interoceptive sensations of tiredness or stress when we believe another's needs must come first. But it can also be a deficit if we allow that tendency to override our own needs for rest, debriefing, emotional expression, diversion, and so on. The story of Bonnita Wirth (see Chapter 3) is a good example of an exteroceptive bias. She lost contact with her body and the interoceptive signs that could have alerted her to the fact that she was not sleeping well. Luckily, she made a cognitive decision to change paths before she actually succumbed to burnout.

When a therapist is biased in favor of the external environment, there can be a serious loss of contact with the internal self and the gauges of self-regulation that are also centered there. If contact with the interoceptors has been weakened, for example, a therapist might not pay attention to signs of stress, tiredness, or overload. In fact, exteroceptive bias in therapists might just be a major risk factor in burnout. In addition, when internal emotional states such as fear or anxiety do not come into awareness or are ignored, practitioners could put themselves in dangerous situations (e.g., accepting violent clients without adequate protection).

It is important to keep in mind that feelings are an aggregate of interoceptive sensations and states (somatic markers) and that they are survival mechanisms. Fear alerts us to danger; anger tells us that we are being pushed too far, and so on. Acknowledging our feelings is crucial for keeping us safe and otherwise able to care for ourselves. Turning off one system in favor of another is risky.

Thus, for therapist self-care, dual awareness—being able to take into account information from all systems inside and out—will contribute to decreased professional risks for compassion fatigue, vicarious trauma, and burnout, not to mention increasing overall safety.

---

### EXERCISE: DUAL AWARENESS IN THE SESSION

This technique is very useful for quickly putting on the brakes when high arousal is threatening hippocampal function (or has already hampered it). It can also be useful when you find it difficult to keep your concentration or attention focused. As for most of the other skills described in this book, having a baseline gauge of body awareness before you start a session can be very helpful. Then, during a session, be mindful so you can be alert to identify the pull of your interoceptors—rising arousal, anxiety, feeling uncomfortably drawn into what your client is working on, floundering attention, and so on—so you can shift your attention to dual awareness. Turning on your exteroceptors will help to remind you where you actually are in the moment and what is currently happening. Such action can restore clear thinking quite rapidly. This is one instance where working in a noisy office can have advantages. You can use the (often) irritating distraction as an exteroceptive ally to connect you to the here and now.

For those who have a quiet office or want additional tools, it can be useful to designate one or more items in your office to be your in-session reminder. You can choose a picture, a knickknack, your computer—anything. A successful reminder of this type will keep you in or bring you back to clear thinking when you lose touch with yourself, or if you become triggered into distress. It is called a reminder because, by turning on one or more exteroceptors, it reminds you of the here and now. Examples follow.

Sometimes it is useful to choose a reminder that is active, a procedure like counting the panes in a window or lights in the ceiling. The idea is to have a kind of "power object" or activity that can help you to remain rooted in the now, in yourself, and in your office rather than slipping into your or your client's future worries, past trauma, or current distress. While it can facilitate your client's therapy for you to have a sense of something being triggered in your past or a feeling for the issue your client is working with, becoming immersed in it will be detrimental for both you and your client. As the therapist, you always need to maintain awareness of where you are—dual awareness—so that you will be able to continue to think clearly. A commonsense rule of thumb for therapist self-care: Make sure that one person in the therapy room is thinking clearly at all times. Because you cannot expect your client to be that person, you had best ensure that it is you.

The more you get accustomed to using your dual awareness reminder, the more useful it will be for you during stressful times with clients. A successful reminder will both calm you and clear your thinking. To practice, first think of something slightly distressing and notice how that distress feels in your body. Next, make contact with your reminder and evaluate if sensations of distress weaken or disappear. If they do, you have chosen a reminder that works well for you. You will know if you need to choose a different reminder if there is no change or your distress increases. If using a visual reminder is not effective for you, try a tactile one: your pencil, a stone in your pocket, the texture of your clothing, or your chair's upholstery, for example.

——————— **EXERCISE: CONTAINER CONSTRUCTION** ———————

Clients bring us upsetting material on a regular basis. One of the most common functions of the psychotherapist is to "hold" what the client cannot. Usually this happens in an abstract way when clients tell us their troubles or describe the painful or horrific things they have experienced. However, many therapists—both consciously and unconsciously—continue to carry around client material throughout their workday and on into their private lives. If thoughts of clients, their problems, or history intrude into your free time, you may be holding too much or too many of your clients in your mind-body system. Some therapists believe that this is what they are supposed to do, not noticing whether doing so causes any ill effects. Though the effect of carrying around client material is sometimes benign, thinking or worrying about your clients between sessions may indicate a possible problem. If you discover that your sleep is being regularly disturbed by dreams of clients or you are having nightmares similar to your client's (symptoms of vicarious trauma), you are certainly carrying around too much. A strategy for containing and then putting aside client material was inspired by one of my own clients.

Roger was sexually abused repeatedly as a young child by a neighbor. He felt very ashamed and never told anyone until he entered therapy as an adult. He had managed to wall off that part of himself and went on to have a fairly successful life. When his own son became a toddler, however, Roger began to have anxiety attacks and episodes in which feelings of shame—being dirty and repulsive—would overwhelm him.

One weekend, Roger helped his son with finger paints; together they made pictures. That day, his son was only interested in the brown colors, many shades of brown. Roger enjoyed painting with his son and went on to paint his own picture in browns. He really got into it, realizing he was putting all of his self-loathing into the painting. The next week he brought it to me, completely crunched up in a plastic bag. "Here," he said. "Keep this for me. I don't want these feelings anymore!" Together we decided I would keep the bag in the back of my file cabinet. He never asked for it

> back. Actually, I even forgot about it for several years until I came across
> it while cleaning out my files.

That experience gave me an idea that has proved useful for myself and for some of the therapists I supervise and teach: Put distressing client material in a container and leave it in the file cabinet (or somewhere else secure) between sessions, at the end of the day, over weekends, and during vacations. Don't carry it with you.

Many psychotherapists already use the idea of creating a container with their clients, helping them to put aside and manage distressing memories or thoughts on a daily basis or between sessions. But we do not usually think of using the same strategy for our own benefit when clients leave their distressing feelings and memories with us—that is, when we find ourselves overly preoccupied by a client following or between sessions, or even after discharge. Creating a container can be useful for us, too.

The potential container can be a real physical container, like Roger's bag. It can be something sturdier: a box, a safe, or a file drawer. You might also create a container in your imagination, so long as the imagined container feels real enough to you and does the trick, effectively holding what you want it to. You will recognize an adequate container by using your body awareness to gauge your arousal, and by checking to see if your thinking remains clear.

I will use myself for one of the case examples, along with two of my trainees, to describe instances in which this skill has proved effective. However, please take note that the success of creating a container largely depends on your own creativity in creating it and belief in its adequacy, so resist any urge to just copy from these examples. Create your own container that is personally suited to you.

Usually my file cabinet does the trick. In it I have a folder for each client. It is also where I store my notepad overnight and on weekends. So any and all information about my clients is kept there. Of course it has a lock for general security. That lock is also an added benefit when I use the file cabinet as my container. After a particularly demanding day, or when I have a client who is preoccupying my mind, I make a minor ceremony out of putting away my files and notes and turning my key in the lock. Sometimes just the physical act of storing the material and locking up is enough. When that is not adequate, I will add an action or some words. Once I brushed my hair and left the brush in the drawer; I felt as if I was clearing the cobwebs from my mind and leaving them locked up for the night. The next morning when I found the brush, some of the concerns about a particular client that had been unresolved fell into place. Another time a particularly clingy client gave me a small gift. Usually I will leave such a thing on display on a shelf. But this object kept dragging my attention back to that client. It was inconvenient. I decided to keep the object in the file cabinet and only brought it out when the client came for a session. It was a good compromise; the client was not offended and I was no longer bothered.

A psychologist who attended one of my training courses asked for help with ruminations about one of his clients. For at least a full day following sessions with the client in question, the psychologist would continue thinking about him during session breaks and in the evening. Sometimes thoughts of this client would keep the therapist awake the night after a session. We developed a twofold strategy that proved useful. First the therapist agreed to arrange to debrief with a colleague shortly after each of these sessions (so the colleague became a container). Second, the psychologist constructed an especially sturdy file folder for that client's papers. He broke down a packing box and used the flat sides, cutting and taping to make a 9 × 12 × 3-inch container with a flap. After talking with the colleague, he would take the client's file and any additional notes and put them in the cardboard file, wrap it with sturdy string, and lock it in his office closet. He would leave it there until shortly before the next session, when he would take it out and review his notes. After doing this religiously for a few weeks, one evening he was rushed and forgot to pack up thoroughly. The next day he realized that he was free of client ruminations even without using the cardboard container, and he laid it aside. He continued, however, to debrief with his colleague and utilize supervision until the underlying countertransference issues were resolved.

One of the clinical social workers attending a training program discussed a strategy she uses on a regular basis following sessions with trauma clients. She often hears horrendous incidents of rape, physical and sexual abuse, and torture. For too many years she would suffer anxiety and some-times nightmares after hearing the details of such incidents. On the advice of a colleague, she bought a beautiful box with a volume of about two cubic feet. She found it at a yard sale and was told it was jewelry box (evidently for someone with a lot of jewels), which is why it had a lock and key. The social worker located the box in a corner of her office and placed a small cactus on it. After sessions in which terrible stories were told, she would move the cactus and open the box. She imagined all the horrible things she had heard being sucked into the box, embellishing her fantasy with visual and auditory effects. Sometimes she would make motions to sweep those things into the box as well. When she felt satisfied that the distressing material was fully loaded, she would close the lid, lock the box with the key, replace the cactus, and put the key in the bottom drawer of her locking file cabinet. She knew when she had effectively packed all of the distress into the box as it no longer dogged her throughout her day or night.

Obviously an element of belief in the ritual is necessary for the effective use of this kind of container strategy. For those who find this kind of tool appealing, it can be very useful. However, do not be daunted if this one is not for you.

## PHYSICAL EXERCISE

Those in professions involving high emotional and physical stress, particu-larly police, firefighters, and the like, know that physical exercise (working out, sports, etc.) helps them to reduce stress and maintain clear thinking. Psychotherapists can also benefit from a regular schedule of exercise or sports. Any way you can use your body to let off steam, increase muscle strength, promote endurance, and so on will help you to clear your head and better manage the stresses of your work. The key is to find something that is pleasant for you to do on a regular basis: walking, running, swimming, play-ing tennis, digging in the garden, working out, yoga, tai chi—anything that works for you. Sometimes it is difficult to get started with regular exercise, but once you get in the habit, it quickly becomes self-rewarding. Starting with small goals and gradually increasing duration and frequency will likely help. If you can interest a colleague, friend, or your partner in joining you, then the benefit multiplies with the camaraderie.

### Editing Self-Talk

Paying attention to how clients speak to themselves inside their heads, specifically what they say, is a common intervention in psychotherapy. This practice originated as a cognitive–behavioral strategy. Most of you will have used such an intervention with one or more clients. Usually we do this to help clients understand that how and what they think can affect how they feel (one side of the James–Cannon debate). Of course, the same applies to the psychotherapist: How you regard your clients, what you hear from your clients, if you identify with your client, and how you judge your own competency will all have a significant bearing on how your work affects you. Basically, this is common sense. For example, if you think of yourself as competent in your work, you will have a better feeling about it than if you judge yourself as often or largely falling short. Likewise, when you use language that increases your identification with your client, it will be harder to find a comfortable separation.

## REDUCING IDENTIFICATION

Sometimes the simplest intervention is the most powerful. When in doubt, it is almost always worth trying. However, the simplest solution might not be obvious unless you are using your common sense. When your internal dialogue is phrased to increase identification with your clients, it can also simultaneously put you at risk, turning up your empathy dial. The only way to know if what you tell yourself is having a negative impact on you is to experiment, trying identification-oriented dialogue with some clients and separation-oriented dialogue with others.

Rich is a gay psychotherapist with a general practice that includes a range of LGBTQ+ clients. He often finds his gay clients more emotionally demanding to work with. The days that include a majority of gay clients are usually more stressful and exhausting for Rich. He noticed the pattern himself, and it bothered him a great deal. Having much in common with those clients should, he thought, be an asset, not a handicap. He judged himself to be overly sensitive and worried that he was ill suited to work with a gay population.

During a consultation session, we took a look at why Rich was having so much difficulty. He confided that his own sexual coming of age had been difficult; most of his family had difficulty accepting him after he came out. Though that was some years ago, he still had emotional scars that stung. Rich felt especially close to his gay clients but was beginning to worry that such closeness actually hampered his ability to help them. At the least, he knew it had a cost for his own well-being.

Could a simple intervention help Rich? Based on how he talked about his clients and his own competence, I became suspicious that his internal dialogue could be compounding his problems. Rich confirmed that he mentally used phrases in silent response to his clients' reports that increased his identification with them: "like what happened to me," "like I sometimes feel," and so on.

It is often expedient to start with the simplest thing, and that is what I suggested to Rich. I proposed that he try a different internal mantra during sessions with one or two of his gay clients in the next week. We discussed various possibilities and eventually agreed on: "I have experienced things like this client has, but he is not me. His problems are his and not mine, and right now it is his turn to get help."

Admittedly, Rich was suspicious of my simple idea, but he agreed to try it. At the next consultation, he reported that he was somewhat less stressed. He thought that the mantra might be helping but wasn't sure. Seeing as he was feeling a bit better, though, he decided to keep using it. Rich suggested adding another mantra: "I may not be able to help [my client], but that doesn't mean I am incompetent," which also led us to a discussion about his feelings of responsibility for his clients' welfare, what was reasonable, and what was not.

Over the next few weeks, Rich became adept at finding different ways to think about his clients and his work with them during the sessions and in between. His stress eased to a large extent and his thinking cleared.

This minimal intervention worked well for Rich, but it will not for everyone. However, in my experience, it is useful often enough to keep on the list of possible interventions to experiment with.

## SELF-CRITICISM

Chronic self-criticism can be as debilitating for a psychotherapist as for anyone. At the least, it hampers effectiveness and clear thinking. Sometimes simple tools will not be enough to stem the internal onslaught, and other interventions will be necessary.

Mason had recently received an MA in counseling. He was hired by a local agency to provide psychotherapy to a general population. Mason's training had all been top-notch, and he had received both good grades and good evaluations in graduate school. While his tendency toward self-deprecation had kept him working hard in school, it was now becoming debilitating as his internal critic escalated. No longer preoccupied with homework in the evenings and on weekends, Mason found he was spending inordinate amounts of time reviewing client sessions and finding fault with himself. The internal dialogue seemed unstoppable. Mason was becoming more and more troubled. His insightful supervisor was familiar with Mason's tendency to self-criticism. Usually he didn't think much about it, as it appeared Mason was doing a fairly good job with his clients. But when the supervisor noticed a change in Mason's demeanor, he asked about it.

Frankly, the supervisor was shocked to discover just how severe and active Mason's inner critic was. They discussed the situation and agreed that adequate intervention was beyond the scope of the supervisory relationship and that Mason could probably benefit from some personal psychotherapy. Likely, it would not be a short-term course, as the roots reached back to his childhood and family of origin. But Mason felt encouraged to be supported in taking this step.

## STORIES OF TRAUMA

Sometimes client stories provoke arousal and upset even when there is no shared history between therapist and client. Especially when working with trauma, the stories clients tell can be particularly disturbing.

Aris is a psychologist in a center for tortured and traumatized refugees. Daily, she hears recountings of terrible acts that were done to her clients. Highly committed to her clientele, there are times when Aris feels guilty that her life has been so easy in comparison. She has never experienced anything even remotely so awful. Sometimes she fears that she can't relate enough to what has happened to her clients to really be able to help them. At those times, she often finds herself describing to herself in detail what it would be like if some of those things happened to her. As a result, Aris is prone to nightmares about captivity and torture that are starting to encroach on her ability to function in her daily life. Actually, she is beginning to suffer from vicarious trauma.

Her supervisor, who had been doing the same work twice as long as Aris, gently suggested that Aris stop attempting to identify with her clients. In the supervisor's experience, that kind of descriptive identification was much more hurtful than helpful. They discussed the pros and cons of sharing client experiences. Aris was helped to see that her less traumatic life history gave her a stability and positive life view that potentially could be useful to her clients. The supervisor also recommended that Aris remind herself often that those horrible experiences were her clients', not her own, to consciously make that separation and turn down her empathy dial.

That simple intervention stopped Aris's nightmares. But it took several more months of discussions with her supervisor to fully make peace with the differences in her and her clients' backgrounds.

—————————————— **EXERCISE: SELF-TALK** ——————————————

1. Identify one client with whom you feel stressed during or following sessions. Write down at least three phrases that describe how you feel about yourself when you are working with this client.

2. During your next session with this client, pay attention to the thoughts that go through your mind, what you say to yourself about yourself, your client, your work. Write them down. It may help to keep a piece of paper separate from your client notes for this purpose. It is important to record the phrases so that you can later look at them concretely and objectively.

Take a look at both sets of phrases (1 and 2 above). One at a time, determine if a particular phrase has an enabling or disabling effect on you.

Read a phrase aloud or just say it in your mind and feel the impact it has on your body and your feelings: Do you become more or less calm? More tense or less? Does your mood lighten or darken?

If you feel a pleasant effect, make a note of that and move on to the next phrase.

When you find a phrase that has an uncomfortable effect, rewrite it. Change the phrase to something that makes you feel neutral or better rather than worse. You can use the example of Rich, above, who changed his feeling of incompetence by recognizing that he would not be able to help everyone.

Take one or two of your rewritten phrases into the next session with your client. During the session, use that phrase in your mind and see if and how it affects you. Do you respond differently than you did to the original phrase? Does the new phrase help or hinder your professional competence? Does it help or hinder your clear thinking?

If you like the result, continue to use the new phrase. If you do not like the result, do not use it. Try this with at least two phrases for each of three clients before you decide whether this type of skill is useful for you or not.

---
### EXERCISE: INTERNAL SUPERVISION
---

List the three most disabling things you have ever heard from a supervisor. Do you say any of them to yourself? If so, why? List the three most enabling things you have heard from a supervisor. Do you say any of them to yourself? If not, why not? Make a list of helpful internal supervisor feedback you can regularly give to yourself.

### *Nurturing Your Work Space*

Look around your work space, home or office. What do you need to change, add, or remove to make it a more nurturing space for you? Most of us spend approximately one-third of our lives in our workplace. What are you usually looking at? How does the furniture you usually sit on feel to your body? What about clutter? Are there areas that need cleaning up? Or, the opposite, is your space too sterile? Do you need to add clutter or cozy touches? Do you like greenery or flowers? If so, how about adding some to your space? Or tropical fish? Are your window coverings adequate—enough light and enough privacy?

A couple of years ago, frustrated in a new office, I realized I needed an electric kettle so I did not need to go down the hall to make tea. Just having that within my reach helped me to feel much more cozy and cared for in my office. It was a simple, inexpensive change that made a big difference.

For those of you who work in different spaces throughout a day or week, what can you take with you that will add to your feeling of being cared for and nurtured? For instance, some clinicians carry favorite pictures, stones, or other talismans with them to enhance their feeling of continuity from place to place. Whatever it is, take the time and budget the money necessary to feel cared about in the place where you work. The more comfortable you feel in your work space, the clearer your thinking will be.

### *Structured Self-Care*

Structure and planning ahead can be allies when it comes to taking adequate care of yourself. Remember, adequate self-care ensures greater calm and clear thinking—a bonus for both you and your clients.

For the following exercise, use a new sheet of paper so you will be able to keep your responses in a place where you will see them. This will help you remember to do the things you planned. At the end of each task is a list of hints to inspire your own list. These are only meant for inspiration and by no means include all of the possible things that you might do for yourself. You are welcome to send me an email with your own ideas and strategies to pass on to others. These plans can relate to your work with clients, your work with supervisees, or your interactions with colleagues. The term *session* is meant to refer to any of these situations. If it is relevant for you, make separate lists for the first two categories as they apply to different situations. And make sure not to overload yourself with expectations to do all of it at once. Perhaps tackling one of the areas at a time would be a better pace for you. Small steps.

Below are the categories, with possibilities from me as well as others who have done this exercise. The suggestions are only to give you an idea of what kinds of things might be important. As with anything else, to be useful, your goals and interventions must be tailored to your needs and tastes.

List three or more things that you will pay attention to during each session:
- Position
- Facial expression
- Breathing pattern
- Body sensations
- Arousal level
- Areas that need more muscle tone
- Self-talk

Assess for each new client or those with whom you have difficulty: What do I need when I am with this client?
- A thicker skin
- Increased muscle tone

- To feel my edges
- To feel my feet
- Remind myself that she is not me
- Remind myself that his story is not my story

List three or more things that you will do between each session:

- Write some notes
- Open a window
- Get a (warm) drink
- Go to the restroom
- Wash hands
- Stretch
- Tone up muscles
- Do a cleansing ritual
- Listen or dance to music
- Eat a snack

List three or more things that you will do at the end of each day or each evening:

- Put client and/or colleague material in a secure container
- Take a shower
- Say evening prayers
- Yell out the car window
- Call or talk to a friend
- Exercise
- Read the paper
- Watch some television
- Read a good book
- Change clothes

List three or more things that you will do (at least) one time each week:

- Get exercise
- Have sex
- See a movie

- Visit with friends or family
- Do volunteer work not related to my employment
- Get out in nature
- Do something artistic
- Have the weekend free to do fun or nurturing things

List three or more things that you will do (at least) biweekly or monthly:
- See my own therapist
- Talk with a supervisor or consultant
- Take a mini vacation
- Have or attend a party

Now, decide two things:
- Who you will discuss these plans with (partner, friend, colleague, therapist, supervisor)?
- Where you will post your list (or parts of it) so that you will see it and be reminded to follow your plan?

## FUTURE TEMPLATE

Imagine yourself on your job in the future. One at a time, imagine problems that might arise and make plans for how you would tackle each. Write down your strategies and make note of where you might need more information or more practice.

## NEW CLIENT SELF-CARE ASSESSMENT

With each new client, as part of your normal assessment, ask yourself, "What do I need to look after myself with this client? What are the issues that this client might trigger in me? Which characteristics or styles does this client have that I need to be prepared for?" Consider all of the things you have learned from this book (self-talk, muscle tone, mirroring, etc.) as well as tools you already have or ones you may want to seek out in the future.

## CLEANSING RITUALS

I have heard reports from many practitioners that following sessions with particular clients, it seems as if the clients are still sticking to their skin. For that and similar feelings, when it seems a client is still hanging around, cleansing rituals can be helpful.

Washing hands is the most obvious and most common cleansing ritual (used consciously and unconsciously). Many therapists routinely visit the restroom between sessions, sometimes only to wash their hands. Others prefer to cleanse the room's atmosphere by opening a window or door and airing it out. When that is not possible or preferable, spraying scents or burning a candle, incense, or dried herbs (sage is often used for this purpose) may be an option—of course for any of these you need to be respectful of fire safety, office rules, and coworker and client allergies. And since many have been working online, sometimes rebooting the computer can feel like a cleansing.

For some, imagined cleansing—of the room or their person—is useful. I have been told about several images:

- A gentle wind that cleans the air and lingering distress from the room
- A shower of water or energy that rinses off all traces of the client and session from the skin
- Going for a walk or run somewhere in nature
- Swimming in cool water

This list is by no means complete. I have included it only as inspiration for you to find your own. As with many sorts of rituals, the success of a cleansing ritual relies on belief. You have to choose or create one that makes sense to you and suits the needs of your body and mind. Try several before you settle on one or two.

## HOME FREE: END-OF-THE-DAY RITUALS FOR LEAVING WORK AT WORK

Do you practice any kind of ritual at the end of the day to mark the end of work and the beginning of leisure? This is important if you work in an office any distance from your home, but it is especially important if you are working at home.

It can be a good idea to be aware of what you might already be doing or to create a new ritual for yourself. The goal is for you to really leave your work and clients at your workplace (even if that is your computer on your desk at home), so that your free time is really free. That includes evenings, weekends, and vacations. Many practitioners need something concrete to do to make the transition from work to free time. Some of the things they do include taking a shower, having a glass of wine or cup of tea, changing shoes, changing clothes, listening to music, saying evening prayers, locking client files in a drawer or file cabinet, talking to a friend, partner, or colleague about their day, and so on. Do some experimenting to find what works for you.

Note that this section, as well as this entire book, has focused on the impact of practicing psychotherapy on the psychotherapist. Both theory and skill-building interventions are aimed at maximizing your self-care in relationship to your work. Of course, other aspects of a therapist's life are also relevant to overall well-being and self-care. Family issues, financial problems, illness (personal or a loved one's), just to name a few, can all deeply affect any individual, including a psychotherapist. Addressing aspects of the professional's personal life, however, is beyond the scope of this book.

CHAPTER 5

# Self-Care During Shared Community/World Crises

Needless to say, the COVID-19 pandemic that began in the winter of 2020—along with several accompanying and compounding emergencies including world and national political instability, upheaval due to extreme disparities of race, gender, financial means, and so on—changed much of the way psychotherapists conduct therapy as well as adding an additional layer of challenge to managing their own self-care. It is likely that you were affected as well to a lesser or greater degree. For one, most therapists were forced to shift from seeing clients in-person to managing therapy sessions on the phone or various videoconferencing platforms. You may also have had to adjust to receiving professional training and supervision via online formats. Many of these changes have become permanent. As if that were not enough to adjust to, each and every one of you has had the added challenge of caring for highly distressed and sometimes traumatized clients who are suffering from many of the very same distressing situations that you are as well. These may include, but are certainly not limited to, dire health concerns, drastic changes in family and social circumstances and interactions, financial instability, worries about the future of your community, country, and the world.

It is therefore that this chapter is aimed toward helping you to juggle these additional challenges while maintaining good (enough) self-care. I will begin with a personal story that I hope gives some historical perspective.

## Perspective

I have been lucky in my life. At least since I became an adult, I have never taken for granted the privilege of my European ancestry and growing up and living in relative peace and freedom. In the United States, I have lived in Los Angeles, California, and St. Louis, Missouri, and for nine years I lived in Copenhagen, Denmark. I have also been lucky to give professional trainings in the United States, Canada, most western European countries, Australia, New Zealand, and Singapore. Currently, thanks to the technology of Zoom webinars, I am expanding my training programs into Taiwan, Romania, Czech Republic, Brazil, and more. I have also been hired and have volunteered to give trainings and supervision to mental health team members in various war- and strife-torn countries through the International Red Cross and Red Crescent as well as Médecins sans Frontières (Doctors Without Borders). As a result, I continue a growing exposure to diverse cultures and various governments. As a resident, I have witnessed firsthand how liberal and conservative communities, as well as capitalistic democracy and constitutional socialism, work during times of peace. Every government and culture has advantages and disadvantages as well as pleasures and challenges. Needless to say, no social or political system is perfect. Often, as I might complain or whine over this or that obstacle in my life, I have turned to observations of conditions in less fortunate parts of my current town, country, or the world at large for perspective. I am grateful and frequently give thanks for how relatively easy my life is and has been, despite a few episodes of trauma and periodic personal difficulties. Over the years, as I have watched and heard of war and other natural and manmade crises around the United States and the world, I have wondered what it must be like to have one's life suddenly and completely upended.

# September 11th

Prior to March 2020, the nearest I ever came to anything close to the shock and trauma of global chaos was on the morning of Tuesday, September 11, 2001. It is very clear in my memory—mind and body.

My building manager called me a little after 7 a.m., breathless and loud: "TURN ON YOUR TELEVISION. NOW! ANY CHANNEL." Then he hung up. My heart already racing (as it is now while I am remembering), I did as instructed. And just like nearly everyone else in the world, I reacted with shock and fear at what I saw and heard: the devastating aerial attacks on the World Trade Center in New York City.

The building manager had not awakened me; I was already up to get ready for work. My first client was at 9 a.m. Luckily, my office was nearby. Of course, I had never experienced anything like that before, and I did not know what to do. My mind raced. Had any of my clients heard the news yet? What about my first client? Was there time to reach her before she would be on her way? This was 2001; many did not have a cell phone. Would she and my other clients be coming in for their sessions? Should I just show up? Should I call them? Certainly everyone would be as shocked as I was! How was I to manage helping them cope when I, myself, might come unglued at any moment?

Luckily, in a moment of grace I got a grip: I commanded myself to make a cup of herbal tea and then to sit for a minute. I needed to catch my breath, and write down a list of what I should do next. It helped to make a structure. I took inventory, as mindfully as I could manage. Thankfully, in Los Angeles I was a long way from the most immediate disaster and threat (although at that hour no one knew if there would be more planes aimed at additional cities). I briefly called my closest family members to make sure everyone was okay. I dashed off an email to a dear colleague and friend in Finland to alert her daughter, who was due to fly that day to visit me; I hoped to catch her before she left for the Helsinki airport as I was fairly sure flights would be canceled and did not want her to get stuck somewhere.

Those priorities out of the way, I felt free to think about my clients. I checked my messages (telephone answering service in those days). Two of the six I was due to see that day had already canceled. However, I had not heard from my nine o'clock client. I called her. No answer. Honestly, I did not feel like going to my office to be "the therapist" for the day. I wanted to curl up in bed or be with family and friends. But then I remembered this client was from New York City and realized I did not want to take the chance that she had not yet heard the news, or that she had and was expecting that I would be there for her. I pulled myself together, got dressed, and drove to work.

Oh my gosh, it was the strangest workday, challenging on both professional and personal levels. Admittedly, I was hugely relieved that my first client had, indeed, heard the news. I had not wanted to be the one to tell her. And all of her family was okay. Whew. We spent her hour talking about the attacks, sharing our impressions and feelings; a time of mutual connection. Though it was not a usual therapy session—as a profession, we do not usually recommend that degree of therapist disclosure—I am not sure I could have done anything else that first hour, as I was still rather in shock myself. I was grateful she did not need more than my human presence in those moments.

The next hour was the most bizarre. My second client came in and just launched into her usual report of her week and her life, focused much on her dysfunctional relationship with her mother. For me it was surreal. At that point, no one knew the extent of the threat to the continental United States, including if attacks were aimed at the West Coast as well. For all we knew at that moment, it could be the start of a major war. And this client was either uninformed or indifferent. In my feelings I was shaken, and in my mind I was in debate. I wondered if I should check with her that she knew about the attacks. What was my primary professional obligation: to make sure she was informed in case her own safety could be at risk or to simply follow along with her stated psychotherapy goal to talk about her mother? Based on my belief that safety is always the first priority, I decided to interrupt her to at least check that she had heard that morning's news. She had, indeed, but seemed unperturbed and wished to spend no time on it at all. She immediately reverted to recounting her issues with her mother. Having satisfied my safety-first concern, I did my best to stay focused on her and her goals, but I would be lying if I said it was easy or that I was completely successful. However, I do not think that client noticed if my mind wandered a bit. Admittedly, I was much relieved when her session ended. But I was also a bit shocked, again, when I tuned back to that day's reality. Somehow I had managed to displace at least a portion of my feelings while focused on my client and her mother issues. I guess that was a kind of survival dissociation under those unique and unsettling circumstances.

The rest of that day was split between attending to clients, checking in with my loved ones, and minding my own emotions. I vacillated between feeling disconnected and then connected to myself depending on the demands of the moment. The best and most connected part of that day was in the evening when I was finally able to join loved ones at dinner.

I was a long way from New York City and the actual dangers and deaths of the September 11 attacks. Though it took a while, after the initial jolt, each subsequent day became calmer as we learned there would be no more attacks and the shock slowly dissipated from my system. However, I know that for those who were directly affected—including thousands who were injured and lost loved ones, homes, and jobs, including East Coast colleagues and the wealth of helping professionals and volunteers who sprang into action that day and in the days that followed—the duration and impact of dealing with those events lasted much, much longer.

Truth be told, one could question my decision on September 11th to discuss and even bring up that day's events when my client had not and, moreover, to share some of my own feelings. Therapists who are trained from various schools of thought will have different opinions, from the most conservative to the most liberal therapeutic viewpoints. But, to be honest, that day I was not considering theory or what my supervisor might tell me. In that initial moment of crisis, I mostly was present in much (though not quite all) of my humanness.

Come to think of it, I now remember being called by a couple of journalists that day who, having come across my first book, *The Body Remembers* (published the year before in 2000), while researching trauma in connection with that day's events, reached out to me as an expert on the topic. They wanted self-care recommendations for their readers and listeners.

How bizarre that was to me, because I was struggling with the same things, myself. Nonetheless I knew exactly what I needed that day: to be with my loved ones. Contact and support, as I have mentioned in the introduction to this revised edition, are the most important factors in mediating and healing trauma, also for the helpers. So that was the advice I gave to the journalists: Tell everyone to get together with others in their homes, churches, synagogues, mosques, neighborhood centers, and so on. I also advised people to check on and help anyone who was housebound, to share food and invite people in. That day and the days following, anything that would get people to gather together and mutually support each other was my most sound advice. . . . And, as mentioned, toward the end of my workday, that is exactly what I did myself.

## MARCH 2020: THE WORLD UPENDED

Since I was born after the end of World War II, until March 2020, the crisis of September 11 was the only (albeit brief) experience I had in my lifetime with being personally upended by global trauma. The events of 2020 beginning with, but not limited to, the consequences of COVID-19 were—and still are—many and ongoing (health, financial, politics, environment, and so on). The complications and consequences throughout the globe continue to mount on and on and on. Sometimes it seems like a taste of what I imagine it might be like living in a war-torn country because the future is so uncertain, with both known and unknown dangers lurking.

Many people are getting their first exposure to living for an extended period of time in a very traumatized environment that extends vastly to our neighborhoods, cities, states, countries, and world. The challenges— personal and professional—are numerous. I, and I know others, sometimes feel as though our world changed drastically, as if it turned over completely, unexpectedly, and within a matter of a few days or weeks. To me, it sometimes seems as though the world flipped upside down overnight. It has been (to say the least) extremely distressing and completely dizzying. And everyone, our families, our friends, and those we aid professionally all must get used to and deal with life in what is popularly termed "the new normal." I also regularly consult with mental health professionals who either give direct service or supervise those who are in the trenches in embattled countries around the world. I can tell you that they are equally unsettled by these current world crises and the impact they have on populations compounded by the stresses and challenges they were already dealing with: war, famine, and other devastation.

I am writing this in the middle of one particular siege. However, the impact and consequences of all of these seismic world changes will be with us for years to come. The impact of these shared traumas and catastrophes are likely very much front and center in your life and work. It is important to remember that even when trauma is shared with family, friends, colleagues, and clients, each person, family, and community is affected differently. Moreover, the degree of impact on any individual depends, in part, on how that individual experiences and perceives each aspect, and on which part of their history, deficits, resilience, and resources are activated. We each interpret and experience such shared events in our own individual, unique ways.

## Taking Control When Your World Feels Out of Control

What could be more human than feeling out of control when the world around you is in chaos, rocked by, for example, war, terrorism, pandemic, political coup or attempted coup, racial or religious oppression, and so on. Under such extremely disconcerting and often dangerous circumstances, many will feel out of control of their lives—at least to a large extent. At the time of this writing, that is how the world is now (war, terrorism, oppression in many places, COVID-19 everywhere). That is how I and most people I know feel right now. The feeling of being out of control is easy to succumb to, to feel overwhelmed by.

Under such extreme circumstances, it is easy to believe that there is nothing you can control. And therein lies a trap. *Do not fall for it* as doing so can lead to (or worsen) despair and depression. Therefore it is extremely important to pay attention to the areas of your life where you actually do have control, no matter how insignificant they may seem. The reality is that there is always something you can control, even though sometimes you have to look for it and may need to be creative, or even devious. If you read the memoirs and biographies of people who have survived war, slavery, imprisonment, apartheid, tyrannical parental control, and so on, you will find a common feature: Each of them found something they could control in their circumstances, their body, or their mind. One stellar example is Nelson Mandela. For him, one important tool was the poem "Invictus," written by William Ernest Henley in 1875, that helped him to remember where he could keep control despite his imprisonment:

> Out of the night that covers me,
> Black as the Pit from pole to pole,
> I thank whatever gods may be
> For my unconquerable soul.
> In the fell clutch of circumstance
> I have not winced nor cried aloud.
> Under the bludgeonings of chance
> My head is bloody, but unbowed.
> Beyond this place of wrath and tears
> Looms but the Horror of the shade,
> And yet the menace of the years
> Finds, and shall find, me unafraid.
> It matters not how strait the gate,
> How charged with punishments the scroll.
> I am the master of my fate:
> I am the captain of my soul.

Do you have similar examples of learning about the experiences of others: from the news, social media, books, films, or from your own family and friends? What tools, mechanisms, and tricks can you identify in the ways others managed to survive their experiences with catastrophes?

Then turn your thoughts to yourself: What are the ways in which you already know you keep control? Write them down—which is another way to keep control—so you can keep a record to refer to. And then consider:

In what other ways or areas would it be good for you to feel or have more control?

### Small Areas of Control Count

In *The Body Remembers* (Rothschild, 2000) I introduced a client of mine whom I called Arnold. He came to me at his wife's insistence as he was on the threshold of hospitalization. He had become so seriously disabled following a traumatic incident that he began to believe that he was totally hopeless and helpless. In our first meeting, Arnold recounted everything he had lost:

> "I can't work anymore. All of my friends have deserted me. The doctors have given up on me. I can't focus to do anything because I feel so afraid all of the time. I'm a wreck. I can't do anything for myself."
>
> I picked up on that last comment and observed, "You say you can't do anything for yourself. However, I see you are clean shaven. Who shaved you today?"
>
> "Why, I did!" he replied.
>
> "Who dressed you, then?" I asked further.
>
> "I dressed myself," he answered a bit suspiciously.
>
> I pressed on: "Who fed you your breakfast?"
>
> "I didn't eat much," he asserted.
>
> "That's okay," I answered, "but what you did eat, who fed you?"
>
> "Well, I fed myself, of course!"

To be honest, at that point he was starting to get angry with me, rather offended by the "stupid questions" I was asking him. But I did not mind a bit. Actually, I was encouraged. For one thing, he was feeling angry instead of afraid, anxious, and helpless. For another, he had just identified several areas where he was completely competent and in control—he just did not realize that as yet. Certainly I had to be careful and strategic in helping him to see this, but nonetheless I was encouraged.

Of course Arnold was my client and not a helping professional or therapist, but it is the principle of recognizing even the smallest areas where you have control of your life—personal and professional—that is important here. I have lost count of how many of my students, supervisees, colleagues, friends, and family members complained regularly about all of the areas where they felt they lost control during the COVID-19 pandemic. And the more any of them listed their perceived losses, the more they, like Arnold, felt helpless and hopeless. Where appropriate, I would turn the conversation to one of identifying areas where they still maintained control. Similarly, the more they recognized areas where they maintained or took control, the more hopeful they would feel.

### Routines

For myself, I realize that my morning and daily routines are one way I keep some sense of control as well as adding to my self-care. For example, in the morning I always start with a prayer meditation practice, then I make herbal tea, sort my vitamin supplements for the day, brush my teeth, and do some sort of exercise (hopefully for at least 30 minutes).

Since we started having pandemic lockdowns, my sleep/wake habits altered drastically. In the past I was very much a lark (an early morning person), but I have turned into an owl (late night person) instead. That threw me for a while, and I felt rather out of control, that is, until I was able to accept that my body and mind must have their own logic for the switch—even if I did not understand it right now. Once I stopped fighting it, I realized I might actually enjoy it. My work schedule (when I am not giving a webinar) has finally gelled in the last couple of months so that I find I am most satisfyingly productive when I stick to administrative tasks before lunch and writing after lunch. And that leaves me time some mornings as well as evenings to keep up and catch up with family and friends, as well as my latest Netflix binge series.

You might already know what your routines are or you might first identify them on reflection. It is also possible that you do not have any routines that help you to feel more in control. If not, is it time to establish one or more? Of course demands of family and work might require some negotiation so that you can keep or create helpful routines, but it might be worth some experimentation.

# Taking Time Off

Piet Hein, a prominent Danish mathematician and inventor, was beloved by his fellow Danes for (among other things) keeping up their spirits during the World War II German occupation of Denmark. Starting in 1940, he published little poems he called Gruks (translated into English as Grooks) that were laced with a Danish form of humor that was deeply ingrained in the culture, but easily missed by foreigners no matter how well they grasped the difficult language. So he was able to take digs at the Germans that were delightful to those in the know but missed by the targets of his humor even if they were fluent in Danish.[11] He was also a wise, keen-eyed, and sharp-penned observer of human nature and postwar continued to express his wisdom through his Gruks. One of my favorites, relevant for the topic of this chapter, concerns his admonition (translated by me from the original Danish),

WHAT GOOD IS ALL OF YOUR KNOWLEDGE AND WISDOM

IF YOU HAVE FORGOTTEN HOW TO WASTE TIME?

In both good and difficult times I have adopted that maxim as one of my most treasured mottoes and goals. I endeavor to waste time at least once a week, preferably for an entire day and sometimes more than one. And I regularly share Hein's wise words with students and colleagues, which is usually most appreciated. Everyone seems to agree with Hein's principle, though, I have found, few are actually able to put it into practice.

It can be difficult to schedule actual breaks even in the best of times. Coordinating with demands of work, family, and other obligations limits our choices. As a result, most therapists I know consider going away on a holiday or vacation to be the only way they can really get away and get actual R & R—rest and restoration. However, when there are family, community, national, or world crises happening, a proper holiday may not be

---

[11] For anyone wishing to learn more about Piet Hein or his Gruks, see Wikipedia (n.d.) and Piet Hein (https://piethein.com/).

possible. That is definitely what happened during the COVID-19 pandemic. Because therapists were restricted to staying at home during lockdowns, many just figured they would keep working and not take any kind of break. The result? Lots of compassion fatigue and burnout, often taking the individual by surprise.

In that vein, a new term has entered the English vocabulary, *staycation*. A staycation is basically a vacation that is spent at home, preferably not working. Some people use them as an opportunity to catch up with home upkeep or household chores. But more and more staycations are being used as substitute for restful travel holidays when travel is otherwise restricted or unaffordable. And when there are no other options, a staycation can give you a much-needed break that includes catching up on rest and relaxation. Because over the last 30 years or so I have traveled the world 3–5 months per year for my work giving lectures and trainings, staycations have been a part of my regular routine for a long time. When people have asked me where I am going for my vacation, I have often said, "I travel for my work—for my vacation I am staying home!" And then do so eagerly. However, I will admit that sometimes it takes some maneuvering to protect my staycation so it is actually a break from demands and being busy. I have even gone so far as to not tell most people that I have scheduled a staycation time off because sometimes that has left me vulnerable to their, "Oh! Well as long as you are home and not doing anything else, you can _____ for me." Fill in the blank with all sorts of tasks and favors that would not feel like a break or rest for me.

My dear colleague, Emma Radway-Bright, has gotten the hang of staycations. She posts regularly on Instagram under the name TherapyButton, advising clients, self-helpers, and fellow therapists on books, insights, managing therapy (from both perspectives), and self-care. Among other things, each week I look forward to photos of the fresh flowers she treats herself to regularly. Recently I was applauding her enthusiasm for a much-needed staycation. She had just the right idea of how to take time off in spite of COVID-19 travel restrictions. Her Instagram post included:

I had a fab holiday!
A week of lie-ins.

A week of good meals.

A week of meeting up with friends [within restrictions].

A week of reading. . .

What an amazing week of rest, indulgence, laughter, love, friend-ship, and cake!

Of course she planned for it, making dates with friends in person and online. She made sure she had the books she wanted to read, and she stopped setting her alarm clock those mornings. At the end of the time off, she really felt like she had gotten a much-needed break.

I know that for many of you it has been frustrating and disappointing not to be able to travel. But that does not mean you cannot have time off. It is actually imperative for you to do so if you want to be able to continue your work in a competent way and to stay healthy. What might your own staycation include?

## Time Management

A confession: Too often these days I find myself in a similar bind as I do today. It is after 5 p.m. already. And though I had planned to be working on this book all day, I am only now getting to it. Where did the day go?

Much of the world has been in turmoil for years, if not decades. Some of you have been in the thick of it for a long time; others had your first experience because of the onset of the COVID-19 pandemic. Whatever your point of entry, high stress and trauma are now everyday facts of life for most of us. Our resources are stretched to the max because every individual—clients, family, friends, neighbors, and ourselves—needs an exceptional amount of ongoing support. For some of you this is the usual; for others, these are exceptional times. No matter if you are familiar with this kind of turmoil or new to it, the fact of it poses unique and pressing challenges to therapists who, though they are accustomed to taking care of others, find their time even more in demand than ever. Crisis calls from clients, as well as friends and family, can impact one's usual or intended ordered life and time management. I know that is certainly true for me.

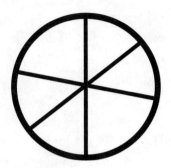

**FIGURE 5.1**  Example of Time Management Pie Chart

How much more time are you spending on the phone, FaceTime, Skype, WhatsApp, Zoom, and so on? My calendar is rocked nearly daily by unexpected needs from those in my sphere. In addition, all of the groups I attend for professional (supervision) as well as personal support (women's, spiritual, meditation) are all meeting more frequently. I have many more events (albeit online). Finding time for myself is definitely more difficult now. I cannot even begin to imagine what it is like for families, particularly those with small children. Nearly all of my family, friends, colleagues, and students complain of the same.

Whether pre-, peri-, or postpandemic or other crises, if you are wondering what has happened to your ability to manage your time, here is a simple exercise.

Draw a circle and assign pie sections to represent your current situation. Start with something like Figure 5.1 and then move the lines to better represent your own situation.

Think in terms of fractions or percentages. What portion of your day or week (draw separate circles for each if that would be helpful) is spent on or devoted to various interests and demands? Do not forget the personal ones such as eating, sleeping, hygiene, and so on. And, of course, include categories of work, relaxation, exercise, other self-care activities, and quality time with family and friends.

Remember, any exercise like this must be totally individual. Your circle will not look like anyone else's. Therefore, there is no wrong way to do this. Your time management circle is yours. Period. Feel free to adjust it as many times as needed until you feel satisfied that it represents your life currently. And, in fact, if a circle feels limiting for any reason, use another shape or model: a square, a percentage table, whatever is useful to you.

Once you have a drawing that feels reasonably representative of you now, take some time to just look at it. How do you feel? Do you notice any reactions in your body, emotions, ANS arousal, or thoughts? Which sections do you like? Which sections do you not like? What do you think of the portions? Is there anything you would like to change?

Next, draw a second figure to represent the time management proportions you would like to aspire to. Then take time to look at it and feel what it would be like to achieve that kind of command over your time. If this is what you would like to strive for, write down a plan for how you will get there. Remember to think in terms of changing your time allotments step by step. The best of plans for change can backfire if they are attempted too quickly or in too big chunks.

## We Are All Trauma Therapists Now

You might be surprised to see this section that focuses on work with clients, as this book is written with your self-care in mind. Actually, that is exactly why this section is here. Many of you are traversing uncharted territories with your clients due to the shape of the world or your community at this time. That can rock you if you are not prepared. So just in case, I want to address some basics of trauma-informed therapy for any of you who are not yet well versed in this growing area of practice.

Whether it was part of your formal education or postgraduate training, or the result of client, community, or global crises, to one degree or another, by now every therapist and helping professional around the world is dealing with traumatized patients and clients on a regular basis. They are also likely juggling their own traumas. What I endeavor to do here is to provide a brief trauma-informed primer to guide those both seasoned and those new to dealing with trauma. Guidelines for helping traumatized individuals and communities in traumatizing times are somewhat different than during normal times. Below are a few important rules of thumb.

- Remember and apply the basics of crisis intervention.

There are many models for crisis intervention, but they all have basic goals in common. Mainly the aim is support and to enhance the ability of the individual, family, and community to cope with whatever has occurred. For example, that means prioritizing the basics of survival: safety, shelter, food, and so on. Sometimes the temptation to process emotions will be strong, but often that will not be the best for stabilizing a situation and strengthening coping. Enhanced coping requires reinforcing and strengthening (rather than confronting) defense mechanisms of all sorts.

- Follow Pierre Janet's phased structure.

This is one of the best models of common sense for the treatment and management of trauma and PTSD. It is universally useful. You can apply the principles no matter what your training or treatment orientation or model may be. Janet recommended in the late 1800s to first establish reliable safety and stability in the client's daily life and psychological state (1887). This does not mean symptom free, but an ability to manage symptoms, to be in control of them rather than controlled by them. The second phase of Janet's structure involves reflecting on and making sense of the memories of past events. But since that can be destabilizing in itself, the foundations laid by the first phase, when strictly observed, make it possible to safely and sanely traverse traumatic territory. Phase three for Janet involves integration of the traumatic experience into one's personal narrative, utilizing what is learned to improve present and future life.

- Do not process past trauma when someone is living in trauma.

The logic of this axiom is supported by Janet's phased structure, as above. To be able to process trauma memories and emotions, a reasonable degree of stability and safety is required for those procedures to be safe and productive. If one is living in trauma, those prerequisites are not available.

Following the principles above means that, particularly during crisis times, processing trauma memories may need to be postponed or put aside to prioritize basic needs, including emotional and physical security.

### The Imperative Art of Interruption

The above guidelines sound easy, right? Well, actually, they're not. They are all valid, and it is a good idea to aspire to follow them. But what do you do when you have clients in front of you drowning in flashbacks from their past, triggered by current events, or intent on and hoping to purge memories from their minds by recounting their traumas, no matter how dissociated or dysregulated they become? How do you apply those basic principles when the client is already flooded by trauma past and trauma present?

My answer is simple to assert but not so easy to apply if you remember that your first priority is client safety: You must interrupt the overwhelmed, dysregulated client. When someone is freaking out, so to speak, you must assertively command their attention and insist on helping them to stabilize—no matter how strong their pull is into trauma, and no matter how much they protest being wrenched away from their memories (visual, auditory, kinesthetic). Whether the memories are from that morning or 50 years ago, a person in a state of decompensation (meaning their coping skills are not operable or available) will not be able to make sense of past or present or act in their own best interest. Yes, psychotherapy should be about what the client wants help with. However, remember this important rule of thumb:

THE THERAPIST IS RESPONSIBLE FOR THE CLIENT'S SAFETY,
PHYSICAL AND PSYCHOLOGICAL, DURING THE THERAPY SESSION.

So you must interrupt and stop them from becoming even more unstable, dissociated, or dysregulated.

I am aware that the idea of interrupting a client who is talking or emoting is antithetical to just about everything we are taught as psychotherapists and helping professionals. And, of course, there are situations when following the client wherever they go will be appropriate and safe. But not during times of upheaval or if they become dysregulated or dissociated by doing so. And definitely not when their family, community, or world is in chaos. Wait until those situations have settled down, that the situation of their life is also stable and safe. Then you can see if the client can manage to talk or express nonstop without disintegrating. But for those other times, please make peace with the skill and kindness of interruption.

### Tools for Instant Stabilization

Many of the tools from the previous chapters that were presented for your self-care may also be useful in helping to stabilize your clients (mindfulness, increasing strength and balance, taking control where possible, and so on). However, first and foremost, I would recommend drawing on your knowledge of the sensory nervous system and syncing that with your skills for mindful attention. One of the quickest routes to stabilization at any time is to use exteroceptive senses (hearing, sight, taste, touch, smell) to anchor in the now and identify the tone of the present situation (whatever that may be). When your client is having a flashback or emotionally uncontrolled episode, stop them (per The Imperative Art of Interruption, above) and insist they pay attention to their current environment. Remember, though it is difficult to interrupt, you are actually not helping anyone by letting them continue in states of dysregulation and flashback. When they cannot stop that them-selves, it is the therapist's job to help them stop. Ask your client to name objects, count lights, identify colors, or read the calendar or time on the clock, in the room they are in, whether that is with you or over the phone or an internet connection. Do not ask them "Where are you?" as such an unde-fined question risks a client in flashback replying they are at the site of the remembered trauma. Be specific: "Where are you *now* as you are talking with me, *today* during our session?" And then have them specify how they know where they are based on the exteroceptive senses: what they see, hear, and so on. When you want to help someone to stabilize, it is usually less helpful to attend to body sensations and emotions, as often those will wrench the client's awareness into the past. Keep their attention on the present using their five senses. And then use those same senses to help them to evaluate if their current environment is safe or not. It is important to tell the truth. If they are actually, presently, in danger, then the task is to help them out of that situation. But if, as is usually true during a session, they are in safe surroundings, using their eyes and ears, and so forth, will help them to actually know that. When someone is highly dysregulated, it may take several rounds of interruption and direction to exteroceptors before they are able to maintain awareness in the present. But your perseverance will be worth it.

### Partner With Your Client

As the client is always the best expert on themselves, asking and negotiating what they know will help them stabilize in the now is a worthwhile discussion to take up. I have had clients direct me to remind them to look at their phone, write their name, announce the date and the time, talk about their dog, pull out a picture of their spouse or best friend, order them to tap their hands on their knees or rub their hands together, and so on. Others have asked me to put up a hand and say "stop" or "not now." Often an individual will already know what helps them most to gain control.

### Careful Client Pacing Reduces Therapist Risks

As discussed above, Pierre Janet's model for pacing trauma therapy is good for clients. Likewise, it is good for therapists. Now that you have gained an understanding of how empathy and resonance can impact your own nervous system—body, emotions, and mind—it makes sense that helping your client to stabilize their nervous system and symptoms, and to pace how (or if) they remember their traumas, will also help you to reduce your risks for compassion fatigue and vicarious trauma. When clients are able to regulate their nervous systems, then the therapist is no longer in danger of resonating with dysregulation.

I can imagine that some of you will protest that pacing and regulating the client for the good of the therapist seems improper. If such a practice would put the client in more jeopardy, then I would agree with you. However, since helping clients to stabilize and self-regulate is (or should be) among the primary goals of safe trauma therapy, then it can only be a good thing that the therapist benefits as well.

# CHAPTER 6

# Concluding Reflections

This chapter wraps up and ties together the ideas laid out in the forgoing pages. The first section concludes the discussion on projective identification that was begun in Chapter 1. Next, an in-depth case study demonstrates one way in which the theories and skills covered in this text have been creatively applied. Last, a few final words bring this book to a close.

## Revisiting Projective Identification

By now you have likely realized that I am leery of the theory of projective identification as a way to understand the impact of a client's emotions on the psychotherapist. In this, I am not alone. Even some psychoanalysts eschew the concept, cautioning that it provides fertile ground for client blame and avoidance of therapist responsibility (Grotstein, 1981; Whipple, 1986). Looking to cognitive, emotional, and somatic empathy for the source of the phenomenon provides a more logical and liberating explanation. Paying attention to somatic empathy and all that it encompasses makes it possible to put yourself in charge of your own feelings, sensations, and behaviors—even when you are working with difficult clients.

Since its inception, many psychotherapists, including Grotstein (1981) and Schore (2002), have found the concept of projective identification to be confusing, an enigma at best. At the same time, others have embraced it as a foundational theory of their practice. In *Narcissism and Intimacy*, Marion Solomon voiced a commonly held interpretation of Klein's theory:

"The process involves psychologically transferring a piece of oneself into another and then inducing the other to behave in accordance with the projection" (1989, p. 88). Others, Schore (2003), Stark (1999), and Grinberg (1979) among them, have similar beliefs about the power of one person over another, including the patient's power over the therapist. Following that idea, a therapist might believe that her own critical outburst—or other inappropriate behavior—can be induced by her client's unconscious need. Unfortunately, many of today's psychoanalysts and psychotherapists believe that clients can, and do, control therapists' feelings and actions. That the phenomenon of projective identification occurs is not up for dispute. What is disputable, however, is the mechanism. From the bulk of literature on the topic, it seems that projective identification is perceived as an active process on the part of the client and a passive one on the part of the therapist. Both notions can, and should, be challenged.

When a therapist falls back on projective identification to understand his own discomfort with a client, he may endanger both of them. The client may be unfairly blamed, and the therapist may end up feeling a helpless victim. Adhering to such a belief can leave a psychotherapist all the more vulnerable to the consequences of compassion fatigue, vicarious trauma, and burnout.

Rooted in the understanding of empathy, including facial and postural mirroring (for a review, see Chapter 2), empathic imagery (Chapter 3), and identifying self-talk (Chapter 4), what has been believed to be projection for more than 70 years may now be seen as the therapist's empathetic response. Identifying the active mechanism of projective identification as something that occurs inside you puts you firmly in the driver's seat to control how much, how often, and how intensely you will resonate with your client's feelings. This makes it possible to prevent, or at least relieve, ill effects from resonance.

Contrary to many of his colleagues, Stolorow and associates (2002) found the theory of projective identification outmoded and outdated. They described projective identification as "one of the last, seemingly unassailable strongholds of Cartesianism in relational psychoanalysis" (p. 88). They went on to point out that therapists who subscribe to the theory of projective identification are mistakenly "inferring causation from correlation" (p. 91). They believed that two people (spouses, therapist and client, etc.) can have the same feeling (correlation) without one inducing it in the other (causation). That is, the fact of shared feelings does not prove that one caused the feelings in the other. As discussed in the section Somatic Empathy in Chapter 2, people are affected by the emotions of others all the time, usually inadvertently. Being affected by another's emotion is not the same as having an emotion induced or put into you.

If you are to mediate your own compassion fatigue, vicarious trauma, or burnout, you need to recognize that you are not helpless to resist induction of the emotional states of your clients. Such a belief undermines your power to choose. Therapists who believe they are their client's pawn put their own well-being at great risk. They are also at risk of harming the very people they endeavor to help, if only by blaming them for their discomfort. Of course, emotions can be communicated, sent, and received. That is the main theme throughout this book. But they cannot be induced. Certainly, your ability to resonate with or experience your client's feelings can be a valuable tool. However, if you perceive yourself as an involuntary recipient with no control over reception, then the therapeutic relationship and your own emotional health will suffer. Some clues to how to control unconscious mirroring—when it is believed to be projective identification—are provided by Martha Stark (1999) in *Modes of Therapeutic Action*. Stark believed her analytic patients "get me to" (p. 266) do all sorts of things that she would not otherwise do: experience feelings, act out behaviors, and so on. A few pages later, though, she acknowledged that the analyst can get herself out of the projection by "either a subtle (and often unconscious) shift or a more dramatic (and sometimes more conscious) *shift in her position*" (p. 276, emphasis added) or by taking a "step back" (p. 283) to recover impartiality. While Stark was referring to cognitive processes for regaining objectivity (shifting position and stepping back) such as dual awareness, it is even more effective to take her advice literally: When you find yourself being infected by a client's emotions, literally sit back, actually turn your chair, actively step away (step back), or shift your position to break the body-to-body resonance. For good measure, stepping back or shifting position both physically and mentally will give you a powerful way to distance yourself from the client's affective space (for a review of additional strategies, see Unmirroring in Chapter 2).

## To Each Her Own Chair

In her exceptional book, *In the Other Chair*, Yvonne Tauber (1998) illuminated the difficulties involved when Holocaust survivors and their children ("Second Generation") are psychotherapists for those in the same populations. While those are specialized pairings, many of the same hazards apply to all sorts of therapeutic relationships. Tauber reminded us how easy it is for psychotherapists to lose themselves in their clients, to merge—to sit in the client's chair, so to speak. Adopting an image of therapist and client, each in their own chair, can help to shed light on the dance of psychotherapy. When therapists are maintaining their professional distance, they are firmly planted in their own chairs. However, when they are succumbing to the impact from the feelings or states of their clients, it is as if they are no longer in their own chair. In those instances they have, in essence, moved over into the client's chair and are sitting there with them, experiencing what they are experiencing. From the client's chair, it is no longer possible to discriminate your own body and feelings, have a professional distance, or think clearly.

As demonstrated in the foregoing pages, this process can have deleterious consequences. To help you avoid, or at least greatly reduce, the risks of compassion fatigue, vicarious trauma, and burnout, you are advised to learn to stay in your own chair—that is, to feel your own body and your own emotions, and to limit the imagery and mirroring that would pull you into the client's chair, so to speak. A periodic quick visit to the client's chair can be useful and give much-needed insight. However, to be able to adequately help your clients, you must remain in your own chair most of the time.

I have learned through many years of supervising and training psychotherapists that the idea of reducing resonance with their clients can seem threatening for some. Putting the concept into a continuum has been helpful for understanding that the goal is to be aware of what level of contact you choose, navigating between symbiosis on the one hand and separation on the other; adjusting your personal empathy dial. Remember that you have many choices also in between. When you are together with a particular client, your range of contact should be changing periodically, with all points on the empathy dial possible depending on what is needed at the time and what is optimal for your own well-being.

It is up to each reader—either on your own or with assistance from colleagues or a consultant—to discover which combinations of principles and strategies, from this volume and other sources, will best help you to stay in your own chair. You will probably need to experiment with several skills to find your own optimal mix. As an example, one successful combination of theory and tools is illustrated in the following case. (It has been published elsewhere in slightly altered forms [Rothschild, 2002a, 2002b].) As you read this case, please remember that what works for Ruth is merely one possible mix of tools. Each of us needs to tailor our own individual strategy to take charge of managing our own particular risks for compassion fatigue, vicarious trauma, and burnout.

---

Ruth is a clinical social worker in a family service agency. After a few months on a new job she was beginning to feel exhausted and depressed. In fact, she was so depleted, she was afraid she would have to quit her job and go on disability. Though she knew it was difficult counseling victims of disaster, she did not know what else to do. This was her chosen profession, her life's ambition. Usually it provided her with an intense feeling of satisfaction. She liked to bask in the success of helping desperate people using her talent for resolving stress and trauma. But now she feared she was speeding toward that dreaded therapist risk: burnout. Happy to be able to help others who were less fortunate than herself, Ruth felt lucky. She wanted to give thanks with her service. However, she was frustrated to think that she might have to cease the work that was so meaningful to her rather than risk her physical and mental health.

I was hired by Ruth's workplace as a consultant and supervisor.

During a weekly meeting, she bravely revealed her predicament. The first thing I wanted to know was how long she had been feeling this way. To the best of her recollection, it was fairly recent, in the last few weeks. Her answer cued my next question: Were there any unusually difficult new cases during that time? Yes, there were, and she proceeded to tell me about one particularly demanding case. As Ruth spoke about her new client, she began to show distinct signs of heightened stress arousal. She became very pale and broke out in a cold sweat. I could see that her hands were shaking slightly. I stopped her report and drew attention to her body responses. She named sensations that corresponded to what I had observed: She was cold, wet, and shaky. Tears came to her eyes. When I asked what she was feeling, she began to cry. "What is happening to me?" she asked. "I used to be able to handle much more than this!"

While Ruth's reaction was intense, it was not unusual. Working with traumatized people is demanding and wearing and can be upsetting. Some cases are easier to handle than others, but the need for self-care and self-protection is always pertinent. In each case, there are several areas worth exploring. Below, these are first assessed. In the last section, strategies for intervening and helping Ruth's difficulties are described.

### Evaluating Risks for Vicarious Trauma
Three major areas of investigation are pertinent to Ruth's situation:

- How she processes the information given by the client for clues to the source of her upset.
- Assessing the interaction between Ruth and her client could be very useful. There might be something in the interaction itself that is having a negative impact on her.
- In this instance, it also seemed a good idea to look for any issues that may be personally provocative (countertransference). This will not always be the case, but it is worth looking into.

## PROCESSING CLIENT INFORMATION

I asked Ruth to tell me a little about this distressing case. As she described the details of her client's situation, I periodically stopped the narrative to ask Ruth what she was feeling, seeing, and hearing in her mind. She was able to answer easily. She was always accustomed to picturing a client's situation in her mind's eye, creating images of the client's life and struggles.

It became immediately clear that when Ruth pictured her client's situation, she was not an objective observer seeing the situation from the outside. Ruth tended to imagine herself in the client's perspective, in her shoes, and see the situation, as it were, through the client's eyes. From that angle, Ruth was also vulnerable to feeling a similar stress in her body and similar emotions. Though she was used to this method of gaining empathy with her clients, usually she was better able to separate the client's experience and feelings from her own. But in this case, Ruth's usual talent had failed her. To find out why and how, I needed to explore further.

## OBSERVING THE INTERACTION

"How," I asked, "do you sit with your client? What is your interaction like when you are in your office engaged in helping the client?"

Ruth usually placed the client's chair close to her or at the side of her desk so that they could almost literally put their heads together at times. Ruth tended to lean toward the client and was accustomed to mimicking facial expressions and gestures as a way of communicating empathy. For example, when the client had a pained expression, Ruth would copy it on her own face. She wanted her clients to see that she was moved by their plight.

## PERSONAL PROVOCATION

Finally, I asked Ruth to consider if anything in her client's situation reminded her of anything from her own personal history. That was a bit more difficult for Ruth to address. She prided herself on her ability to be objective with her clients and not let her private life interfere. She was embarrassed to even consider that she might have let personal feelings intrude into her work.

No, she had never experienced anything like her client's situation. Nothing. Nonetheless, I asked her to look more broadly, perhaps into the situation of someone close to her. Slowly a realization dawned on her. There were many parallels between her client's situation and something that had happened to an older cousin who had been Ruth's caretaker when she was a child. When the cousin got into trouble, Ruth had been too young to help her. The cousin had not received the assistance she had needed and had suffered grave consequences. Ruth had silently vowed to help others as she had not been able to help her cousin. In fact, Ruth realized, her fervor for her profession had roots in her cousin's misfortune.

### Reversing the Effects of Vicarious Trauma

In Ruth's case, the keys to her vicarious trauma and burnout emerged quite clearly. This is not always the case, but often at least one category of vulnerability will be visible. Over three supervision sessions, Ruth was helped to identify and rectify the source of her vicarious trauma. The details of the strategies Ruth found helpful in each area are outlined below.

## LIMITING IMAGERY

As discussed in the section Controlling Empathic Imagery at the end of Chapter 2, it is not necessary to picture a client's situation to understand it. In fact, sometimes—as in Ruth's case—producing traumatic pictures in the mind's eye can be very upsetting. Ruth needed to learn how to listen to her client, letting the words communicate the situation. I suggested that Ruth experiment with varying her way of being with her client. She could try sometimes to attend only to words and observing her client, and sometimes rely on her usual mode of creating images. She might also experiment with creating images from different angles: from the client's perspective, from an observer's perspective, an aerial view, and so forth. The idea was to give Ruth more control over how she received and processed information. I suggested she keep a record of which strategy she was using and to evaluate each according to her somatic and emotional responses after the client left. Such investigation should eventually lead Ruth to a style of empathy that would not debilitate her.

## PROXIMITY MAY MATTER

While necessary to the helping professions, what constitutes empathy is often misconstrued. Understanding someone's pain is not the same as feeling it. The former is needed for helping, but the latter can hinder it.

The interaction between Ruth and her client in the office exacerbated what the imagery had started. In such close physical proximity, mimicking gestures and expressions, Ruth came to feel nearly exactly what her client was feeling: depressed and desperate. The difficulty with this is common sense. It is not possible to help a desperate person if the therapist is likewise feeling desperate. One person in the room must be able to maintain objectivity to be able to identify and engage helpful action. A desperate client is not capable of this, so it is up to the therapist to establish enough emotional, and sometimes physical, separation to maintain the ability to help.

Again, experimentation was in order. Ruth was encouraged to practice mindfulness (see Chapter 1), particularly mindful self-awareness, paying attention to her body sensations and facial expressions. She discovered that she needed to practice facial expressions that would communicate concern without leaving her vulnerable to catching every emotion the client was feeling. Ruth came to the conclusion that she needed greater distance between the client and herself (see How Close Is Too Close near the end of Chapter 3). She moved the client's chair across the desk from her own, instead of at the side. The desk, Ruth felt, provided a natural boundary that protected her, to some degree, from feeling so much of her client's pain. She also set out to learn to identify when she was mimicking her client's facial expression (see Conscious Mirroring in Chapter 2). When she noticed this, she found that sitting back in her chair and taking a deep breath cut the flow of client emotion into her own body. Much to her surprise, though, it did not diminish her ability to understand and be sympathetic. Actually, she found her ability to help increase proportionately.

## HEALING OLD PAIN

For most psychotherapists, their own history impacts greatly on their choice of career. In general, we are a field of wounded healers. If this is also the case for you, take note that this puts you at a huge advantage, but it can also be a deficit if you try to delude yourself about your motivations or deny the effect of your own history on your work.

Finally, with the help of her own therapist, Ruth took a deeper look at the impact of her cousin's trauma. It was necessary for Ruth to separate the client's situation from her cousin's, to be able to see that nothing like her cousin's trouble threatened Ruth now. With the aid of supervision, Ruth could maintain intellectual awareness of the difference. Therapy helped her to achieve a deeper healing of this issue.

Compassion fatigue and vicarious trauma can be healed and even prevented when the mechanisms leading to them are identified and made conscious. Once vulnerabilities are assessed, strategies for increasing awareness and control can be instituted. Experimentation and evaluation are the keys to helping each therapist discover which interventions are most effective for staying in one's own chair.

# Final Words

> *Automatic empathy has all the [force] of running or tumbling downhill, controlled empathy is as effortful as climbing up a mountainside.*
>
> —Hodges and Wegner, "Automatic and Controlled Empathy"

We all know that empathy is the connective tissue of good therapy. It facilitates the development of trust in our clients and allows us to meet them with our feelings as well as our thoughts and skills. Empathy also hones our tools of insight and intuition, and complements our theoretical knowledge. But when the mechanisms of empathy are not in our awareness or under our control, we can find ourselves in real trouble.

In the pages that follow, I have strived to shed light on the neurological, psychological, and somatic mechanisms by which this gift, our capacity for empathy, can turn back on us with a vengeance. Without mastery of our own talents and tendencies toward empathy, it can mutate, twisting our compassion into compassion fatigue and our resonance into vicarious traumatization. It is my hope that the theory, insights, and skills offered here have helped you to better manage your empathy for the benefit of both yourself and your clients.

# Original Pilot Research

Over the past few years, along with colleagues Maggie Shiffrar, PhD, at Rutgers University in New Jersey and Emerald Jane Turner, MA, at London Transport in the UK, I have directed three pilot research projects. At this point, we have mostly raw data from rather small samples. However, descriptions of the projects and our preliminary findings are very pertinent to this book. Readers are cautioned to regard this material as completely preliminary. Nonetheless, it is hoped that you will find interest and value in its inclusion. Further, anyone wishing to conduct similar studies is welcome to contact me for consultation.

## Research Project I: Postural Mirroring and Somatic Empathy

One of these experiments was briefly described in Chapter 2. Here is more detail.

During a pilot study conducted in the early 2000s (Rothschild & Shiffrar, 2003, 2004) as part of a training course in Europe, I asked one of the group sponsors to silently model his posture after something reminiscent of an emotional situation from his life and to hold it steady for a few minutes. He struck a pose with one arm elevated behind him, the other reaching outward and down in front of him; his feet were about a foot and a half apart, placed one in front of the other; his torso bent slightly forward. No words or verbal information of any kind were communicated to the group members.

Half of the group was instructed to copy his posture, the other half just to observe it. Following the exercise, the group members filled out question-naires indicating the physical sensations, feelings, thoughts, and images they experienced, and to guess what the model may have been remembering. After the group members had a chance to note their personal responses and fill out their questionnaires, the sponsor was allowed to speak. He told us that he had remembered being a teenager, saving a younger sibling from drowning in a stream in the woods. The responses to the questionnaires from the mirroring half of the group were fascinating. No one had known what the situation was—none had somatic markers for anything similar. However, several in that half felt a powerful effort or struggle in their own bodies and a sense of urgency. Generally they reported feeling strong and focused. Fear was the predominant emotion. Some had visual images of being outdoors and of water or trees.

Considering that the remembered scenario was something totally out-side of the average person's experience, the results were quite astonishing. With the same group, another sponsor modeled a posture that would be quite familiar to almost anyone (i.e., most would have somatic markers for it): feeding her infant grandchild. The results were intriguing. Among both the mirroring and the observing halves, there was an extremely high cor-relation of sensations, emotions, and images. In addition, the majority eas-ily guessed that the situation had something to do with caring for a young child. Likely, these higher correlations could be predicted since just about every adult has somatic markers for caring for a baby.

The set of pilot studies, of which the one above is part, began a long time ago as the mirroring exercise that appears in Chapter 2. For many years I have informally used this exercise during 12-day professional train-ing programs (and actually still do). It is very useful in helping the profes-sional participants to understand somatic empathy. The results were always astounding but were never documented. When this book began to take shape, the idea to formally use that exercise to obtain hard data was born. I approached Maggie Shiffrar, a professor at Rutgers University who spe-cializes in the study of movement recognition. We had been corresponding about her work for a while. Together we drafted feedback forms. Several pilot studies were conducted using these forms, including one with a group of nearly 200. Those early attempts were disastrous, and we learned to simplify our forms and drastically reduce our sample size.

There were 16 participants in the European sample described above. The group was divided in half. For each of the two runs, half of the group precisely mimicked (mirrored) the posture and the other half merely observed it, not changing their own posture in any way. For the second run-through, we reversed the groups, letting the previous mirrors now be observers, and vice versa. In the end, each subject tried being both a mirror and an observer.

Even the observers accurately guessed the theme of the second model's posture. We suspect that is because caring for a young child is within just about everyone's experience. However, emotions and body sensations were not shared as strongly in the observer group as in the mirror group.

The experience with the first model was different. He was remembering something outside of usual experience. Observers were totally at a loss for any kind of matching. The empathy of the mirrors was much weaker than with the second model, but still there were significant resonances.

Our major problem with this series of studies was in refining the feedback instrument to rule out confounding factors.

# Research Project II: Applications of Mirroring and Unmirroring in Practice

The goal of this single trial (Rothschild et al., 2005) was to determine if adding both theory and tools for mirroring and unmirroring would decrease vulnerability to vicarious trauma and burnout in a group of professional psychotherapists. I directed the project and Emerald Jane Turner, a supervisor for an agency that primarily treats traumatized clients, conducted it. Maggie Shiffrar was our research consultant. (All three of us successfully completed the Rutgers University Human Subjects Compliance Program.) Turner was responsible for the supervision of 12 practitioners, 9 of whom agreed to participate in this study. We realized from the start that this was a very small sample—4 in the experimental group and 5 in the control group. Each group received the same biweekly individual supervision as always. The experimental group received, in addition, instruction in body awareness, postural mirroring, and unmirroring (as discussed in Chapter 2). We pretested, posttested at the end of the trial, and additionally posttested at 3 months using the Compassion Fatigue Test (Figley & Stamm, 1996), Maslach Burnout Inventory: Human Services Survey (Maslach & Jackson, 1986), and the World Assumptions Scale (Janoff-Bulmann, 1996).

Over the duration of the study, which lasted several months, two dropped from the control group and one from the experimental group. In the end, there were, unfortunately, just three in each group. The reasons for dropout point to some of the difficulties in conducting studies on vicarious trauma: One subject left the agency due to administrative restructuring; one had extended personal leave due to family illness; and the third was absent for an extended period of time due to surgery and convalescence. Also, during this time the agency moved and a new director was appointed— both events greatly affected all of the staff. Of those participating in the trial, during the trial period, two lost close family members and another was witness to a tragic incident. Turner reports that all of these factors made it difficult to keep supervision sessions focused on work with clients, let alone trying to teach new theory and tools. She suggested that testing the same hypothesis might be easier with a group of therapists in private practice. At least then the skewing due to intra-agency issues would be absent.

Despite the small number of participants, preliminary analysis of this project's data is encouraging: There was a 25% reduction in burnout scores in the experimental group.

## Research Project III: Pilot Help for the Helper Training Course

In October 2004, I conducted the first 4-day professional training utilizing the theory and skills of this book (Rothschild & Shiffrar, 2004). The course included lectures on the theory, practice in the skills and exercises, and individual consultation sessions for those who desired them (in much the same style as some of the transcripts in the text). I regret that I did not pretest the participants. However, a few months following the course, I polled them for their feedback. Using a typical 1–10 scale, I asked the group about levels of stress before (as well as they could recall) and following the course, and what kind of impact the course had had on their professional lives. Of course, the investigative format was much too loose to count as hard data. Nonetheless, the results are useful and have provided me both with encouragement and with ammunition to further refine the course. Basically, everyone found some aspect of the course useful for their professional lives. A majority found many aspects useful. Attendance was kept small to allow time for individual attention. In all, 14 professionals participated over the 4 days of the course. All but two of those attending had come to the course with stress levels of 5 or higher; half were at 7 and up. Two-thirds of the group had significant drops in stress over the first week following the course, and all but one maintained lower stress levels at the time of the poll. One participant had an initial increase in stress due to increased awareness of workplace problems, but the stress decreased when she was able to apply skills learned in the course. All but two found the course meaningful for improving their work situation and none thought it worsened their job stress.

Of course, it would be terrific to see any or all of these studies conducted on a larger scale. Any readers interested in following up on any of these are welcome to contact me (per info on the copyright page).

# Acknowledgments

## Acknowledgments to the Revised Edition, 2022

In addition to the acknowledgments from the First Edition, below, I would like to add:

Big thanks also to Jeanne Ladner, Vanessa Bear, Emma Radway-Bright, and Sally Landau for their keen eyes and warm hearts. Your support in making this a better book is appreciated more than you can know.

And even though I already said it before, I would like to again thank my amazing editor, Deborah Malmud, and awesome publisher, W. W. Norton, for the more than *two decades*, seven books, and the 8 Keys to Mental Health Series that we have produced together. I believe I am one of the luckiest authors in the world!

## Acknowledgments to the First Edition, 2006

Every book owes its existence to more than the credited author or authors. That is certainly the case with this volume; many have assisted with its gestation, labor, and birth. I would like to thank all who gave ideas, wisdom, criticism, and support. Hopefully, I will remember you all, but if one or two of you slip past me in a "senior moment," please forgive me and remind me for future printings.

First, I would like to recognize Marjorie Rand, PhD, for her contributions to the first draft of the first edition of this book, particularly the sections Countertransference, Projective Identification, Revisiting Projective Identification, and Empathy. Despite multiple revisions (including this new edition), many of her thoughts remain.

Innumerable professionals—supervisors, teachers, colleagues, students, and supervisees—have inspired the creation of this book. Your shared experiences have been instrumental in shaping these ideas and helping me to explain them cogently.

Many, many thanks go to colleagues who read earlier versions of this manuscript and dared to offer their brutally honest opinions: John May, PhD, Bonnita Wirth, PhD, Sima Rae Stanley, MSW, Vicki Salvin, MSW, Maggie Shiffrar, PhD, Phoebus Tongas, PhD, Alan Karbling, PhD, Yvonne Tauber, PhD, Ellert Nijenhuis, PhD, and Marion Solomon, PhD.

Much appreciation goes to Charles Figley, PhD, who coined the term compassion fatigue as the title of his 1995 book. He graciously gave permission to use his term in the subtitle of this volume.

Special thanks are extended to pioneer Elaine Hatfield, PhD. Her book, *Emotional Contagion*, inspired several of the ideas in this volume.

Last, I would like to give many, many accolades to everyone at the Professional Books imprint of W. W. Norton—in both the New York and London offices. Per usual, all have extended help and support generously, thoroughly spoiling me for any other publisher. And special thanks to my editor, Deborah Malmud: Your savvy, common sense, warmth, and good humor have helped me through some very rough times. This book would not have made it to press without you!

# References

Adolphs, R., Damasio, H., Tranel, D., Cooper, G., & Damasio, A. R. (2000). A role for somatosensory cortices in the visual recognition of emotion as revealed by three dimensional lesion mapping. *Journal of Neuroscience, 20*, 2683–2690.

American Psychiatric Association. (2013). *Diagnostic and statistical manual of mental disorders* (5th ed.). Washington, DC: Author.

Andreas, A., & Andreas, T. (1987). *Change your mind and keep the change: Advanced NLP submodalities interventions.* Moab, UT: Real People Press.

Arbib, M. A., Billard, A., & Iacoboni, M. (2000). Synthetic brain imaging: Grasping, mirror neurons and imitation. *Neural Networks, 13*(8–9), 975–997.

Ax, A. A. (1964). Goals and methods of psychophysiology. *Psychophysiology, 1*, 8–25.

Bandler, R. (1985). *Using your brain—for a change.* Moab, UT: Real People Press.

Bandura, A., Ross, D., & Ross, S. A. (1963). Imitation of film-mediated aggressive models. *Journal of Abnormal and Social Psychology, 66*(1), 3–11.

Benjamin, L. R., & Benjamin, R. (1994). A group for partners and parents of MPD clients: I. Process and format. *Dissociation: Progress in the Dissociative Disorders, 7*(1), 35–43.

Blairy, S., Herrera, P., & Hess, U. (1999). Mimicry and the judgment of emotional facial expressions. *Journal of Nonverbal Behavior, 23*(1), 5–41.

Bodynamic Institute. Bodynamic Institute Training Program, 1988–1992, Copenhagen, Denmark.

Brantbjerg, M. H. (2012). Hyporesponse: The hidden challenge in coping with stress. *International Body Psychotherapy Journal, 11*(2), 95–118. http://www.ibpj.org/issues/articles/Holm%20Brantbjerg%20-%20Hyporesponse.pdf

Brantbjerg, M. H. (2020). Widening the map of hypo-states: A methodology to modify muscular hypo-response and support regulation of autonomic nervous system arousal. *Body, Movement and Dance in Psychotherapy, 15*(1), 53–67. doi:10.1080/17432979.2019.1699604

Bremner, J. D., Southwick, S., Brett, E., Fontana, A., Rosenheck, R., & Charney,

D. S. (1992). Dissociation and posttraumatic stress disorder in Vietnam combat veterans. *American Journal of Psychiatry, 149,* 328–332.

Cannon, W. B. (1929). *Bodily changes in pain, anger, fear and rage, on account of recent researches into the function of emotional excitement* (2nd ed.). New York: Appleton.

Cartwright, J. (2017, June 23). Mystery Hill [Video]. https://www.jaycartwright.com/work/2017/10/10/mystery-hill

Chartrand, T. I., & Bargh, J. A. (1999). The chameleon effect: The perception-behavior link and social interaction. *Journal of Personality and Social Psychology, 76,* 893–910.

Chollet, F., DiPiero, V., Wise, R. J., Brooks, D. J., Dolan, R. J., & Frackowiak, R. S. (1991). The functional anatomy of motor recovery after stroke in humans: A study with positron emission tomography. *Annals of Neurology, 29,* 63–71.

Classen, C., Koopman, C., & Spiegel, D. (1993). Trauma and dissociation. *Bulletin of the Menninger Clinic, 57*(2), 178–194.

Coleman, R. M., Greenblatt, M., & Solomon, H. (1956). Physiological evidence of rapport during psychotherapeutic interviews. *Diseases of the Nervous System, 17,* 71–77.

Cozolino, L. (2002). *The neuroscience of psychotherapy: Building and rebuilding the human brain.* New York: Norton.

Damasio, A. R. (1994). *Descartes' error.* New York: Putnam's Sons.

Damasio, A. R. (1999). *The feeling of what happens: Body and emotion in the making of consciousness.* New York: Harcourt Brace.

Damasio, A. R. (2003). *Looking for Spinoza.* New York: Harcourt.

Darwin, C. (1965). *The expression of the emotions in man and animals.* Chicago: University of Chicago Press. (Original work published 1872)

Decety, J., & Chaminade, T. (2003). Neural correlates of feeling sympathy. *Neuropsychologia, 41,* 127–138.

DiMascio, A., Boyd, R. W., & Greenblatt, M. (1957). Physiological correlates of tension and antagonism during psychotherapy: A study of "interpersonal physiology." *Psychosomatic Medicine, 19,* 99–104.

DiMascio, A., Boyd, R. W., Greenblatt, M., & Solomon, H. C. (1955). The psychiatric interview: A sociophysiologic study. *Diseases of the Nervous System, 16,* 4–9.

Dimberg, U. (1982). Facial reactions to facial expressions. *Psychophysiology, 19,* 643–647.

Dimberg, U., Thunberg, M., & Elmehed, K. (2000). Unconscious facial reactions to emotional facial expressions. *Psychological Science, 11*(1), 86–89.

Duclos, S. E., Laird, J. D., Schneider, E., Sexter, M., Stern, L., & Van Lighten, O. (1989). Emotion-specific effects of facial expressions and postures on emotional experience. *Journal of Personality and Social Psychology, 57,* 100–108.

Ekman, P. (2003). *Emotions revealed: Recognizing faces and feelings to improve communication and emotional life.* New York: Times Books.

Ekman, P., Levenson, R. W., & Friesen, W. V. (1983). Autonomic nervous system activity distinguishes among emotions. *Science, 221*, 1208–1210.

Fadiga, L., Fogassi, L., Pavesi, G., & Rizzolatti, G. (1995). Motor facilitation during action observation: A magnetic stimulation study. *Journal of Neurophysiology, 73*(6), 2608–2611.

Figley, C. R. (1995). *Compassion fatigue: Coping with secondary traumatic stress disorder in those who treat the traumatized.* New York: Brunner/Mazel.

Figley, C. R., & Stamm, B. H. (1996). Psychometric view of compassion fatigue self test. In B. H. Stamm (Ed.), *Measurement of stress, trauma, and adaptation.* Lutherville, MD: Sidran.

Forester, C. A. (2001). Body awareness: An aspect of countertransference management that moderates vicarious traumatization. *Dissertation Abstracts International: Section B: Sciences and Engineering, 61*, 10-B.

Freud, A. (1937). *Ego and the mechanisms of defense* (rev. ed.). Oxford, UK: Hogarth.

Freud, S. (1922). *Group psychology and the analysis of the ego.* London: International Psychoanalytic Press.

Freud, S. (1953). The future prospects of psychoanalytic therapy. In J. Strachey (Ed. & Trans.), *The standard edition of the complete psychological works of Sigmund Freud* (Vol. 11, pp. 141–151). London: Hogarth. (Original work published 1910)

Freud, S. (1953). Observations on transference love. In J. Strachey (Ed. & Trans.), *The standard edition of the complete psychological works of Sigmund Freud* (Vol. 12, pp. 159–171). London: Hogarth. (Original work published 1915)

Gallese, V. (1999). From grasping to language: Mirror neurons and the origin of social communication. In S. Hameroff, A. Kazniak, & D. Chalmers (Eds.), *Towards a science of consciousness* (pp. 165–178). Cambridge, MA: MIT Press.

Gallese, V. (2001). The shared manifold hypothesis. *Journal of Consciousness Studies, 8*, 33–50.

Gallese, V., Fadiga, L., Fogassi, L., & Rizzolatti, G. (1996). Action recognition in the premotor cortex. *Brain, 119*, 593–609.

Gallese, V., Ferrari, P. F., & Umilta, M. A. (2002). The mirror matching system: A shared manifold for intersubjectivity. *Behavioral and Brain Sciences, 25*(1), 35–36.

Gallup, G. G., & Maser, J. D. (1977). Tonic immobility: Evolutionary underpinnings of human catalepsy and catatonia. In M. E. P. Seligman & J. D. Masser (Eds.), *Psychopathology: Experimental models* (pp. 334–357). San Francisco: W.H. Freeman.

Gill, M. M. (1983). The interpersonal paradigm and the degree of the therapist's involvement. *Contemporary Psychoanalysis, 19*, 200–237.

Gill, M. M., & Hoffman, I. Z. (1982). *The analysis of transference* (Vol. 2). New York: International Universities Press.

Gladstein, G. A. (1984). The historical roots of contemporary empathy research. *Journal of the History of the Behavioral Sciences, 20*, 38–59.

Grandin, T. (2005). *Animals in translation*. New York: Scribner.

Grinberg, L. (1979). Countertransference and projective counter-identification. *Contemporary Psychoanalysis, 15*, 226–247.

Grotstein, J. (1981). *Splitting and projective identification*. Northvale, NJ: Jason Aronson.

Harris, J. C. (2003). Social neuroscience, empathy, brain integration, and neurodevelopmental disorders. *Physiology and Behavior, 79*(3), 525–531.

Harrison, R. L. (2007). *Preventing vicarious traumatization of mental health therapists: Identifying protective practices* (Unpublished doctoral dissertation). University of British Columbia.

Hatfield, E., Cacioppo, J. T., & Rapson, R. L. (1992). Emotional contagion. *Review of Personality and Social Psychology, 14*, 151–177.

Hatfield, E., Cacioppo, J. T., & Rapson, R. L. (1994). *Emotional contagion: Studies in emotion and social interaction*. Cambridge, UK: Cambridge University Press.

Hedges, L. (1983). *Listening perspectives in psychotherapy*. Northvale, NJ: Jason Aronson.

Heide, F. J., & Borkovec, T. D. (1983). Relaxation-induced anxiety: Paradoxical anxiety enhancement due to relaxation training. *Journal of Consulting and Clinical Psychology, 51*(2), 171–182.

Hess, U., & Blairy, S. (2001). Facial mimicry and emotional contagion to dynamic emotional facial expressions and their influence on decoding accuracy. *International Journal of Psychophysiology, 40*, 129–141.

Hodges, S. D., & Wegner, D. M. (1997). Automatic and controlled empathy. In W. J. Ickes (Ed.), *Empathic accuracy* (pp. 311–340). New York: Guilford.

Hsee, C. K., Hatfield, E., Carlson, J. G., & Chemtob, C. (1990). The effect of power on susceptibility to emotional contagion. *Cognition and Emotion, 4*(4), 327–340.

James, W. (1884). What is an emotion? *Mind, 9*, 188–205.

Janet, P. (1887). L'Anesthésie systematisée et la dissociation des phénomenés psychologiques. *Revue Philosophique, 23*(1), 449–472.

Janoff-Bulman, R. (1996). Psychometric review of World Assumption Scale. In B. H. Stamm (Ed.), *Measurement of stress, trauma, and adaptation* (pp. 440–442). Lutherville, MD: Sidran.

Johnson, J. O. (2013). Autonomic nervous system physiology. In H. C. Hemmings & T. D. Egan (Eds.), *Pharmacology and physiology for anesthesia* (pp. 208–217). New York: Elsevier.

Kabat-Zinn, J. (2013). *Full catastrophe living: Using the wisdom of your body and mind to face stress, pain, and illness* (rev. & updated ed.). New York: Bantam.

Kendon, A. (1970). Movement coordination in social interaction: Some examples described. *Acta Psychologica, 32*, 1–25.

Klein, M. (1946). Notes on some schizoid mechanisms. In *The writings of Melanie Klein* (Vol. 3, pp. 1–24). London: Hogarth.

Kohut, H. (1959). Introspection, empathy and psychoanalysis: An examination of the relationship between modes of observation and theory. *Journal of the American Psychoanalytic Association, 7,* 459–483.

Kohut, H. (1971). *The analysis of the self: A systematic approach to the psychoanalytic treatment of narcissistic personality disorders.* New York: International Universities Press.

Kohut, H. (1978). *The search for the self* (Vols. I & II). New York: International Universities Press.

Kohut, H. (1981). *Reflections on empathy.* Lecture tape, University of California, Berkeley Extension Division, Continuing Education Seminars, Progress in Self Psychology, Berkeley, California.

LaFrance, M. (1976). Postural sharing as a nonverbal indicator. *Group and Organizational Studies, 1,* 328–333.

LaFrance, M. (1979). Nonverbal synchrony and rapport: Analysis by the cross lag panel technique. *Social Psychology Quarterly, 42,* 66–70.

Lakin, J. L., Jefferis, V. E., Cheng, C. M., & Chartrand, T. L. (2003). The chameleon effect as social glue: Evidence for the evolutionary significance of nonconscious mimicry. *Journal of Nonverbal Behavior, 27*(3), 145–161.

LeDoux, J. E. (1996). *The emotional brain.* New York: Touchstone.

Levenson, R. W. (1992). Autonomic nervous system differences among emotions. *Psychological Science, 3*(1), 23–27.

Levenson, R. W., Ekman, P., & Friesen, W. V. (1990). Voluntary facial action generates emotion-specific autonomic nervous system activity. *Psychophysiology, 27*(4), 363–384.

Levenson, R. W., Ekman, P., & Heider, K. (1992). Emotion and autonomic nervous system activity in the Minangkabau of West Sumatra. *Journal of Personality and Social Psychology, 62*(6), 972–988.

Levenson, R. W., & Ruef, A. M. (1997). Physiological aspects of emotional knowledge and rapport. In W. J. Ickes (Ed.), *Empathic accuracy* (pp. 44–72). New York: Guilford Press.

Levine, P. (2010). *In an unspoken voice.* Berkeley: North Atlantic.

Lipps, T. (1964). Empathy, inner imitation, and sense-feelings. In M. Rader (Ed.), *A modern book of esthetics: An anthology* (3rd ed.). New York: Holt, Rinehart, and Winston. (Reprinted from *Psychologie, 1,* 1903)

Little, M. (1957). "R"—the analyst's total response to his patient's needs. *International Journal of Psycho-Analysis, 38,* 240–254.

MacDougall, W. (1908). *An introduction to social psychology.* Boston: Luce.

MacLean, P. D. (1973). *A triune concept of the brain and behaviour.* Hincks Memorial Lecture. Oxford: University of Toronto Press.

Martin, Josh. (2010, June 15). How to make a work-life balance pie chart. Josh Martin Ink. https://joshmartinink.wordpress.com/2010/06/15/how-to-make-a-work-life-balance-pie-chart/

Maslach, C., & Jackson, S. E. (1986). *Maslach Burnout Inventory: Human services survey.* Palo Alto, CA: CPP.

Maxfield, L. (1997). *Advanced clinical interventions: A training manual for work with survivors of trauma, abuse, and violence.* Thunder Bay, ON: Author.

McCann, L., & Pearlman, L. A. (1990). Vicarious traumatization: A framework for understanding the psychological effects of working with victims. *Journal of Traumatic Stress, 3,* 131–149.

McClintock, M. K. (1971). Menstrual synchrony and suppression. *Nature, 229,* 244–245.

Meltzoff, A. N., & Moore, M. K. (1983). Newborn infants imitate adult facial gestures. *Child Development, 54,* 702–709.

Meltzoff, A. N., & Moore, M. K. (1989). Imitation in newborn infants: Exploring the range of gestures imitated and the underlying mechanisms. *Developmental Psychology, 25,* 954–962.

Mental Health Daily. (2015, March 15). *Relaxation-induced anxiety: Potential causes and solutions.* http://mentalhealthdaily.com/2015/03/15/relaxation-induced-anxiety-potential-causes-solutions/

Merriam-Webster. (n.d.). Empathy. In *Merriam-Webster.com dictionary.* Retrieved September 3, 2021, from https://www.merriam-webster.com/dictionary/empathy

Miller, K. I., Stiff, J. B., & Ellis, B. H. (1988). Communication and empathy as precursors to burnout among human service workers. *Communication Monographs, 55*(3), 250–265.

Morris, D. (1979). *Manwatching: A field guide to human behavior.* New York: Henry N. Abrahams.

Neff, K. (2011). *Self-compassion.* New York: William Morrow.

Neff, K. (2021). *Fierce self-compassion.* New York: Harper Wave.

Niedenthal, P. M., Barsalou, L., Winkielman, P., Krauth-Gruber, S., & Ric, F. (2005). Embodiment in attitudes, social perception, and emotion. *Personality and Social Psychology Review, 9*(3), 184–211.

Paccalin, C., & Jeannerod, M. (2000). Changes in breathing during observation of effortful actions. *Brain Research, 862,* 194–200.

Parsons, L. M., Fox, P. T., Downs, J. H., Glass, T., Hirsch, T. B., Martin, C. C., Jerabek, P. A., & Lancaster, J. L. (1995). Use of implicit motor imagery for visual shape discrimination as revealed by PET. *Nature, 375,* 54–58.

Pearlman, L. A., & Saakvitne, K. W. (1995). *Trauma and the therapist: Countertransference and vicarious traumatization in psychotherapy with incest survivors.* New York: Norton.

Perls, F. (1968). *Gestalt therapy verbatim.* Moab, UT: Real People Press.

Pines, A., & Maslach, C. (1978). Characteristics of staff burnout in mental health settings. *Hospital and Community Psychiatry, 29*(4), 233–237.

Platek, S. M., Critton, S. R., & Meyers, T. E. (2003). Contagious yawning: The role of self-awareness and mental state attribution. *Cognitive Brain Research, 17*(2), 223–227.

Poe, E. A. (1984). The purloined letter. In *Complete stories and poems of Edgar Allan Poe*. New York: Doubleday.

Porges, S. (1995). Orienting in a defensive world: Mammalian modifications of our evolutionary heritage. A polyvagal theory. *Psychophysiology, 32*, 301–318.

Porges, S. (2003). The polyvagal theory: Phylogenetic contributions to social behavior. *Physiology and Behavior, 79*, 503–513.

Porges, S. (2011). *The polyvagal theory*. New York: Norton.

Preston, S. D., & de Waal, F. B. M. (2002). Empathy: Its ultimate and proximate bases. *Behavioral and Brain Sciences, 25*(1), 1–72.

Ramachandran, V. S. (2000, May 31). Mirror neurons and imitation learning as the driving force behind "the great leap forward" in human evolution. *Edge 69*. https://www.edge.org/conversation/vilayanur_ramachandran-mirror-neurons-and -imitation-learning-as-the-driving-force

Reich, W. (1972). *Character analysis*. New York: Touchstone.

Reik, T. (1948). *Listening with the third ear*. New York: Grove Press.

Rizzolatti, G., & Arbib, M. A. (1998). Language within my grasp. *Trends in Neuroscience, 21*, 188–194.

Rizzolatti, G., Fadiga, L., Gallese, V., & Fogassi, L. (1996). Premotor cortex and the recognition of motor actions. *Cognitive Brain Research, 3*(2), 131–141.

Rogers, C. R. (1946). Significant aspects of client centered therapy. *American Psychologist, 1*, 415–422.

Rogers, C. R. (1951). *Client centered therapy*. Boston: Houghton-Mifflin.

Rosenheck, R., & Nathan, P. (1985). Secondary traumatization in children of Vietnam veterans. *Hospital and Community Psychiatry, 36*(5), 538–539.

Rothschild, B. (2000). *The body remembers: The psychophysiology of trauma and trauma treatment*. New York: Norton.

Rothschild, B. (2002a). Case studies: The dangers of empathy. *Psychotherapy Networker, 16*, 4.

Rothschild, B. (2002b). The mind and body of vicarious traumatization: Help for the therapist. *Psychotherapy in Australia, 8*, 2.

Rothschild, B. (2003). *The body remembers casebook: Unifying methods and models in the treatment of trauma and PTSD*. New York: Norton.

Rothschild, B. (2004a). Applying the brakes. *Psychotherapy Networker, 28*(1), 42–45, 66.

Rothschild, B. (2004b). Mirror, mirror. *Psychotherapy Networker, 28*(5), 46–50, 69.

Rothschild, B. (2006). *Help for the helper*. New York: Norton.

Rothschild, B. (2010). *8 Keys to safe trauma recovery*. New York: Norton.

Rothschild, B. (2017, 2021). *Revolutionizing trauma treatment*. New York: Norton.

Rothschild, B., & Shiffrar, M. (2003). Postural mirroring and somatic empathy [Unpublished raw data].

Rothschild, B., & Shiffrar, M. (2004). Pilot Help for the Helper training course [Unpublished raw data].

Rothschild, B., Shiffrar, M., & Turner, E. J. (2005). Applications of mirroring and unmirroring in a practice setting [Unpublished raw data].

Scheler, M. (1972). *The nature of sympathy.* Hamden, CT: Archon. (Original work published 1912)

Schoenewolf, G. (1990). Emotional contagion: Behavioral induction in individuals and group. *Modern Psychoanalysis, 15*(1), 49–61.

Schore, A. (1994). *Affect regulation and the origin of the self.* Hillsdale, NJ: Lawrence Erlbaum.

Schore, A. (2002). Clinical implications of a psychoneurobiological model of projective identification. In S. Alhanati (Ed.), *Primitive mental states: Psychobiological and psychoanalytic perspectives on early trauma and personality development* (pp. 1–65). Los Angeles: Other Press.

Schore, A. (2003). *Affect regulation and the repair of the self.* New York: Norton.

Shalev, A. Y., Peri, T., Canetti, L., & Schreiber, S. (1996). Predictors of PTSD in injured trauma survivors: A prospective study. *American Journal of Psychiatry, 153*(2), 219–225.

Shindul-Rothschild, J. (2001). *Terrorism and trauma: Psychiatric nursing implications.* Slide show presented to the Rhode Island State Nurses Association. http://www.risnarn .org/presentations/2001_pstd/

Siegel, D. J. (1999). *The developing mind.* New York: Guilford.

Siegel, E. V. (1984). *Dance-movement therapy: Mirror of my selves; the psychoanalytic approach.* New York: Human Sciences Press.

Slow Mo Lab. (2014, April 22). Bizarre balloon burst at 60,000fps - Slow Mo. https://www .youtube.com/watch?v=E_Xe486i-Q0

Solomon, M. F. (1989). *Narcissim and intimacy.* New York: Norton.

Solomon, Z., Waysman, M., & Levy, G. (1992). From front line to home front: A study of secondary traumatization. *Family Process, 31*(3), 289–302.

Stamm, B. H. (1995). *Secondary traumatic stress: Self-care issues for clinicians, researchers, and educators.* Lutherville, MD: Sidran.

Stanek, B., Hahn, R., & Mayer, H. (1973). Biometric findings on cardiac neurosis. III. Changes in ECG and heart rate in cardiophobic patients and their doctor during psychoanalytical initial interviews. *Psychotherapy and Psychosomatics, 22,* 289–299.

Stark, M. (1999). *Modes of therapeutic action: Enhancement of knowledge, provision of experience, and engagement in relationship.* Northvale, NJ: Jason Aronson.

Stern, D. N. (1992). Commentary on constructivism in clinical psychoanalysis. *Psychoanalytic Dialogues, 2,* 331–363.

Stern, D. N. (Speaker). (2002). Conference: Attachment: From early childhood through the lifespan (Cassette Recording No. 609–617). Los Angeles: Lifespan Learning Institute.

Stiff, J. B., Dillard, J. P., & Somera, L. (1988). Empathy, communication, and prosocial behavior. *Communication Monographs, 55*(2), 198–213.

Stolorow, R., & Atwood, G. (1992). *Contexts of being: The intersubjective foundations of psychological life.* Hillsdale, NJ: Analytic Press.

Stolorow, R., Atwood, G., & Orange, D. (2002). *Worlds of experience: Interweaving philosophical and clinical dimensions in psychoanalysis.* New York: Basic Books.

Strack, F., Martin, L., & Strepper, W. (1988). Inhibiting and facilitating conditions of the human smile: A nonobtrusive test of the facial feedback hypothesis. *Journal of Personality and Social Psychology, 54*(5), 768–777.

Sullivan, H. S. (1947). *Conceptions of modern psychiatry.* Washington, DC: White Foundation.

Sullivan, H. S. (1954). *The psychiatric interview.* New York: Norton.

Tabler, D. (2017, August 18). The house that makes broomsticks stand on end. Appalachian History.net. https://www.appalachianhistory.net/2017/08/house-that-makes-broomsticks-stand-on.html

Tauber, Y. (1998). *In the other chair.* Jerusalem: Gefen.

Terr, L. C. (1985). Psychic trauma in children and adolescents. *Psychiatric Clinics of North America, 8*(4), 815–835.

Thompson, I. A., Amatea, E. S., & Thompson, E. S. (2014). Personal and contextual predictors of mental health counselors' compassion fatigue and burnout. *Journal of Mental Health Counseling, 36*(1), 58–77.

Titchener, E. B. (1909). *Lectures on the experimental psychology of the thought processes.* New York: Macmillan.

Tomkins, S. S. (1963). *Affect, imagery, consciousness* (2 Vols.). New York: Springer.

van der Kolk, B. A., McFarlane, A. C., & Weisaeth, L. (Eds.). (1996). *Traumatic stress.* New York: Guilford.

Waysman, M., Mikulincer, M., & Solomon, Z. (1993). Secondary traumatization among wives of posttraumatic combat veterans: A family typology. *Journal of Family Psychology, 7*(1), 104–118.

Weller, L., & Weller, A. (1993). Human menstrual synchrony. *Neuroscience and Biobehavioral Reviews, 17*(4), 427–439.

Whipple, D. (1986). Discussion of the merits and problems with "The concept of projective identification" by Janet Finell. *Psychoanalytic Review, 73*(2), 121–128.

Wikipedia. (n.d.). *Piet Hein, scientist.* https://en.wikipedia.org/wiki/Piet_Hein_(scientist)

Wilson, J. P., & Lindy, J. D. (Eds.). (1994). *Countertransference in the treatment of PTSD.* New York: Guilford.

Wolf, N. S., Gales, M., & Shane, E. (2000). Mirror neurons, procedural learning, and the positive new experience: A developmental systems self psychology approach. *Jour-*

*nal of the American Academy of Psychoanalysis and Dynamic Psychiatry, 28*(3), 409–430.

Wolf, N. S., Gales, M. E., Shane, E., & Shane, M. (2001). The developmental trajectory from amodal perception to empathy and communication: The role of mirror neurons in this process. *Psychoanalytic Inquiry, 21*(1), 94–112.

Wolpe, J. (1969). *The practice of behavior therapy.* London: Pergamon.

Zajonc, R. B., Adelmann, P. K., Murphy, S. T., & Niedenthal, P. M. (1987). Convergence in the physical appearance of spouses. *Motivation and Emotion, 11*(4), 335–346.

# Index

# About the Author

**Babette Rothschild**, MSW, has been a practitioner since 1976 and a teacher and trainer since 1992. She is the author of six books, (translated into more than a dozen languages including Danish, German, French, Spanish, and Japanese) all published by W. W. Norton: *Revolutionizing Trauma Treatment* (2017, 2021); her classic bestseller, *The Body Remembers* (2000); *The Body Remembers CASEBOOK* (2003); *Help for the Helper* (2005, 2022); *8 Keys to Safe Trauma Recovery* (2010); and *Trauma Essentials* (2010). She is the series editor of Norton's 8 Keys to Mental Health series. After living and working for nine years in Copenhagen, Denmark, she returned to her native Los Angeles. There, she is writing her next books while she continues to lecture, train, and supervise professional psychotherapists worldwide. For more information, visit her website: www.trauma.cc